DO YOU KNOW . . .

Which hetero traditions can add romance to your life—
and which ones just add complications?

What to do when his definition of fidelity is
incompatible with yours?

How to *be* together without living together?

How to love the "nonscene" (partially closeted) man?

The ways men fake intimacy?

The "shadow lover"—
the Jungian opposite who may be just right for you?

What to do when the honeymoon is over
but the relationship is not?

"The List"—three sheets of paper that will help you
decide if "love will conquer all" or if it's time to break up
and look for a man who can really make you happy?

Whether your first date was a night at the opera or a
conversation at the gym, you can turn a good time into a
great long-term partnership. This invaluable guide, the first
gay reference to go beyond eroticism to the complex
emotional issues that can make or break a relationship,
teaches you everything you need to know to find and nurture
the love of a lifetime!

Also by Craig Nelson

Bad TV: The Very Best of the Very Worst

FINDING TRUE LOVE

IN A

MAN-EAT-MAN

WORLD

The Intelligent Guide to Gay Dating, Sex, Romance, and Eternal Love

·· ♂ ··

CRAIG NELSON

A Dell Trade Paperback

A DELL TRADE PAPERBACK

Published by
Dell Publishing
a division of
Bantam Doubleday Dell Publishing Group, Inc.
1540 Broadway
New York, New York 10036

Library of Congress Cataloging in Publication Data

Nelson, Craig (Craig D.)
    Finding true love in a man-eat-man world : the intelligent guide to gay dating, sex, romance, and eternal love / by Craig Nelson.
        p.   cm.
    Includes bibliographical references.
    ISBN 0-440-50689-1
    1. Gay men—United States—Social conditions.   2. Gay men—United States—Sexual behavior.   3. Etiquette for men—United States.   4. Dating (Social customs)—United States.   5. Gay male couples—United States—Social conditions.   6. Intimacy (Psychology)—United States.   I. Title.
HQ76.2.U5N45   1996   95-24742
305.38′9664—dc20   CIP

Printed in the United States of America

Published simultaneously in Canada

February 1996

10   9   8   7   6   5   4   3   2

BVG

for Mark

A huge thanks to Leslie Schnur, whose idea this was; I only hope I've come close to achieving her original dream.

"Life is like
 a New York City playground.
 You've got to jump over a lot of dog shit
 to get to the swings."

—Steven Infantino

♂ Contents

♂ Love in a Man-Eat-Man World

Are these stories familiar?

I'm very successful in my career, and in many ways have never been happier. But I can't figure out how on earth to meet someone special. It's something I never really wanted, or at least never cared so much about—I was always content dating a lot of guys and being single and independent. Now I'd really like to meet someone to share things with and I just don't know how. The guys I meet seem to all be damaged in some way, but honestly I don't even meet many of *them*. I just don't meet anyone, it seems. . . ."

"Bob and I broke up four years ago, and ever since then I've been looking for a new man. But no matter what I try—the bars, the dance clubs, even the bathhouses—nothing seems to happen. My friends tell me I'm cute and fun to be with, but every guy I meet turns out to be an asshole. They never call; they lie; they're just so fucked up. I don't know; I'm ready to just give up. Maybe there's something wrong with me. . . ."

Hundreds of thousands of gay men ask themselves these questions (or versions of them) every single day. In fact they don't just ask themselves, they ask their friends, their family, and they even write constantly to gay magazine "Dear Abbys" about why they're so unsuccessful in finding love.

While it's common to think of us queers as being continually on the prowl for sex (and admittedly, many guys are doing just that), a new day has dawned in most of our emotional lives. Ten years into a never-ending plague of AIDS, combined with a generation of baby boomers hitting their forties, have created a profound social shift: Never have so many wanted so quickly to settle down and get spoused—and never have so many had so much trouble doing exactly that.

If our collective attitudes and goals have changed, then why is it still so difficult to get the relationship everyone seems to want? You grew up thinking your life would eventually be like the Ricardos, or the Brady Bunch, or that incredibly loving and understanding *Family*, or even your own damn parents; then you came out of the closet, and all those assumptions turned upside down.

Romance between men is so completely different from that between a man and a woman that most of the guidelines we all learned as kids need to be thrown out the window. Very rarely do gay couples follow the heterosexual norm of meeting in high school or college, getting married, raising rug rats, and trying to keep the honeymoon going as long as possible. In fact most gay men don't even know a male couple who've been together longer than ten years, since long-term lovers usually vanish from the public gay life of bars and dance clubs after settling down. One long-term elderly couple I know deliberately avoid going out because they're so tired of other gay men seeing them as role models and constantly asking for "the secret"!

Why is gay coupling so difficult, and so complicated? In many ways our social life is young, awkward, and still in its young-adult stage. I like to think that it's twenty-five years after Stonewall, and public gay life is like any other twenty-five-year-old: just starting to really define oneself as an adult, insecure, filled with hopes and dreams, arrogant, experimenting with new ideas, naive, exhilarated with freedom, fickle, vain, and of course, obsessed with sex. It's a scene where some male couples are now starting to hold hands in public (at least in our bigger cities) while at the same time certain personal ads demand "disease-free, and you be too." It's the best we've ever had, and the worst that anyone can remember.

In this twenty-five-year-old milieu there are practically no rules, no guidelines, nothing set in stone for gay couples—we each have to make it up as we go along. While het lovers may know what to expect at various stages as their relationships grow, the rules of gay coupledom consist of everything that anyone has ever thought of trying . . . and *more*.

One pair of long-term lovers may be living much as a strictly married het couple would: being monogamous, combining finances, even going so far as to adopt children. Another pair may live in separate cities, each pursuing sex with other men—yet they are just as devoted and committed to each other. One of my friends has a new boyfriend who's still living with and taking care of his ex-lover, who has AIDS. They find it just as confusing as you do, but my friend and his new man are as strong a couple as any I know.

These nontraditional styles, however, bring up a host of emotional conflicts that tear at each lover's deeply held beliefs and undermine their commitment to each other. Without the social forces of legal marriage and children, breaking up is not so hard to do.

There is an endless supply of other factors that can cause deep problems for any gay couple. As boys we learned that being ruthlessly competitive in sports and business was the way to win; this same ruthless competition, however, frequently appears between two men trying to make a go of it, creating a no-win situation. We learned that being a man meant being strong, stoic and silent—yet it's unlikely that a marriage between two Clint Eastwoods would last for very long. We learned that being faithful was a key element in love and marriage—"My Husband Had an Affair!" is still a regular feature in all the women's mags—yet sex with strangers is such a core element of gay men's lives that strictly monogamous, long-term male couples are rare. Is it any wonder that keeping a male marriage going sometimes seems like the biggest job you can have?

Finding True Love in a Man-Eat-Man World is the first guide to gay romance that explains all the problems men face in trying to be part of a lifelong couple, and exactly what the solutions might be. From the psychological blocks that hold men back from finding and keeping a lover, to advice on going to a bar or sex club, where to find men and the kind of men you will find, sex tips for both the novice and the experienced lover, predictable problems you'll encounter when you finally find the man of your dreams, expert advice on how to keep your relationship going and your romance alive, and even how to break up and recover from the loss of a lover, *Finding True Love* covers the waterfront of male desire.

Why Me?

Right now you may be wondering, "Who does this queen think she is? Telling me about romance and finding the man of my dreams. Why, she's not even a Ph.D. therapist, for chrissakes!" You're absolutely right; I'm no therapist—and you should be thanking your lucky stars I'm not.

Think about it: The therapist who is normally the author of this kind of book is someone who spends all her professional life listening to people with such serious problems that they need to see a therapist. When she writes a "relationship" book, she writes about what she knows—her deeply disturbed clients—and if you buy one, you'll be reading about alcoholics who are addictively codependent with each other, gay spouse abuse, men who don't understand why it's a bad idea to compulsively have sex with all their friends, men whose long-term love affairs with their fathers keep them from finding a boyfriend, even how to come out to your in-laws (like this is the worst problem you'll ever face and like they haven't taken one look at you and figured out the whole story in two seconds). Finally, since they're based on deranged men and their nutty boyfriends, therapist relationship books are filled with oddball advice you don't need —like recommending that you should plan a special dinner, go over old memories together, exchange gifts, and feel free to cry—when you and your boyfriend are breaking up!

If you or your lover *are* seriously disturbed, please stop buying relationship books and get thee to a therapist. But if you're a reasonably normal man who wants some ideas and strategies for finding another man to have some fun with and maybe more, then this is the book for you.

First off, I'm the kind of guy everyone else comes to with all their love troubles, and I've saved countless would-be spouses from certain doom (including getting some to dump their deadbeat boyfriends and go out and meet someone decent for a change). So in this book you'll get to hear the details of all those soap operas and what happened in the end. Secondly, just for you I've researched *all* the other books and trashy magazine articles and obscure scientific publications on this topic, thrown out the dreck, and included all the good ideas in this single, bargain-priced tome. You'll never have to read another word on this subject again. Then I interviewed hundreds of men (all of whom have had their names and identities completely changed, so don't even try to guess who they are) to get their funniest, most revealing, most intimate stories and tips on guy getting and keeping. They're honest, they're touching, and some are really, really funny. Finally, I threw in my own tales of transcendent marital bliss and wacky sex adventures, just to play fair. So if you want to be a homo in love, what more could you want?

My one flaw? That I couldn't make this book be for both men and women. Besides the fact that I'm not competent to give romantic advice to lesbians, guides for gay men and women really must be two separate books. Here's why:

Bob Eubanks: What did you two do on your very special second date?
Lesbian couple: We started living together, of course.
Gay male couple: What do you mean by "second date"?

Chapter 1

♂ Are You Ready, Willing, and Able?

No one can make you feel inferior without your consent.

—ELEANOR ROOSEVELT

Making Mr. Right

The most important thing about finding love is being ready for it when it happens. Very few men really are ready, because there are so many stumbling blocks inside that they can't respond competently when the right guy comes along. By getting your act together and putting your own life in order, you'll be a man other guys take seriously over the long haul—as well as someone who can deal with problems when they inevitably appear.

Many of us spend plenty of time, effort, and money to turn ourselves into hot, attractive men. We work out at the gym as much as we can; we get haircuts and clothes that are as flattering as possible; we shave our bodies, use skin creams, and even go in for cosmetic surgery if we think we need it. Our homes are decorated; our sex accessories are admired; even our pets are fetching.

1

Lots of us in fact have basically the same idea in our heads: "If I could only lose fifteen pounds, everything would be great." "If I'd get another two inches on my chest, everything would be fine." "If this minoxidil really works, then I'll have it all together." We are trying as hard as we can to become hot guys—but what about becoming great boyfriends? How much long-term spouse potential does that dreamy guy at the gym really have? Steven, one of my friends from college, looked at the difference between hot guys and great partners, and decided that there were four kinds of men in the world:

- Pretty, but not nice

- Nice, but not pretty

- Not pretty, and not nice

- Nice, and pretty too

We are all looking for the love of a good man; to get one, maybe we need to spend time working on our insides as well as our outsides.

Remember the psychiatrist on *Saturday Night Live* who only said, over and over again, "Look at yourself. Just look at yourself!" It was funny that she made a career as a shrink from just this one idea; what's even funnier is that this one idea is completely true. By learning as much as you can about yourself, you'll be happier with your strengths, more accepting of your weaknesses—and a terrific companion for another guy. You'll know what you want out of life, so you'll know faster when a relationship isn't working. You'll know you have weaknesses like all human beings, and you'll be able to understand and accept weaknesses in others—including your boyfriend. You'll be happy with yourself, you'll be getting as much out of life as possible—in short you'll become Mr. Right.

The central issue for any human being is Who am I? It all started when you were an infant and your daddy said, "Where's baby?" and it finishes when you know, completely on your own, who you are, and you don't need Daddy around anymore to ask the question. You bonded, and then separated, from your parents, and how this happened can affect your role as a lover for the rest of your life. If during your infancy your parents were distant, you may forever fear closeness and possible abandonment from others; if they were invasive, you may forever fear closeness and possible suffocation from others. With all this going on, it's no wonder that many blocks to self-awareness and maturity can appear along the way.

Babies in perfect physical health who are not picked up and cuddled can give up living, waste away, become idiotic, lose consciousness, and die. Before this fact was known, institutions taking care of abandoned or orphaned children had an immensely high infant mortality rate. In 1915 the American Pediatric Society reported that at ten of these institutions, every child under the age of two had died. The report was so horrifying that a study was undertaken of twenty-four children. Half were left in orphanages with no care and half were taken care of by loving foster families. After twenty years all of the first group were either dead or in mental institutions; of the second, all had jobs, had finished high school, and were married (well, there had been one divorce).

We are born alone and we die alone and we are constantly confronted by the fact that solitude is the *ur*-element of human life. Trying to avoid this essential condition by determinedly fitting into a group, never leaving home, or depending blindly on the love of a good man is pointless. You have to, all on your own, establish an "I" and become a "me"—or what exactly is it, after all, that someone else might fall in love with? As Louis, one of my friends, put it, "*That's* what love is all about—reacting to what is unique in a human being."

The lifelong search of Who am I? can never be ignored; in fact every significant relationship you have will take you to a greater understanding of who you, as a human being, really are. While being in love makes us truly alive, having close intimacy with another man makes us, paradoxically, see ourselves with new clarity. But the only way to meet a wonderful man and have a great relationship is to develop yourself first—and isn't it odd that the most important aspect of romance and relationships can only be achieved on your own? Isn't it even odder that the more an individual you and your lover are, the closer you can be together?

We would like to think that, by finding the right guy and spending the rest of our lives with the perfect companion, our essential aloneness in the universe will be overcome. What happens, though, is the unexpected. Say you're with a guy and he's done something you think is inhuman, something so seriously against your principles, it makes you waver about staying with him. There you are, on your side of the bed, seething and mulling and feeling trapped and trying to decide what exactly your ultimate response will be, and there he is, on his end: The Enemy. The Creep. The Embodiment of Loathsomeness.

You will never again, for the rest of your life, feel as utterly alone as you do right now.

With that in mind the first question to consider is: Should I even be with another guy? In America singledom is grossly underrated and coupledom completely overrated; it seems like everyone has to have a damn spouse or else. If you're unhappy being by yourself, however, you're still going to be unhappy being with someone else; you're just trading one set of problems and difficulties for another, and it's not like he's going to give you a personality transfusion or something.

Single men are utterly free, and too many crazed husband-seekers forget all about this. When you're single,

- Your mood isn't dependent on someone else's indigestion

- No one else's ignorant opinion and bullheaded stubbornness has to be taken into account when you make living or job or apartment or sex plans

- You don't have to ask permission to do things in your own home

- You don't have to spend hours listening to a lot of whining, huffing, nagging, teary declamations and stone-cold dead silences over issues you don't care two cents about

- You don't have to negotiate what you're going to eat and when, and what you're going to do in bed and when, and what you're going to buy at the grocery store and when

- You never have to hear such lines as "I don't know if you *need* to have another piece of pie" (as if anyone ever *needs* another piece of pie)

- You don't have to waste lots of time and effort ignoring another human being's irritating habits and overwhelming personality disorders

If none of this sounds so bad, then maybe you are indeed ready to get hitched—so let's go back in time. When you've had relationships in the past that didn't work out, whether they lasted for years or even just a few dates, what happened? Don't claim it was always the other guy's fault (and don't say that every single time "it just didn't work out"). What did you do, what expectations did you have, what problems arose that you couldn't solve? If you really have no idea what happened, ask your friends to honestly tell you what *they* think. By looking closely at your own behavior in trying to spouse up in the past, you can unravel clues to what's keeping you from establishing a relationship now, and in the future.

Later on in this book you'll learn tips for writing a personal ad in case you want to try to meet guys that way. But if you were going to write a long, long ad that said who you really were (and wasn't based on sex talk and "warm, sharing, caring" clichés that could apply to anybody), what would it say? What, specifically, are the most attractive and interesting things about yourself? If your friends were setting you up with a blind date, how would they describe you?

If you join a gay computer bulletin board, singles organization, or dating service, you'll be asked to fill out a form describing yourself and your interests. The following questionnaire, when answered as honestly as possible, can help to give you some self-definition and insight about yourself. You may even want to have a friend check it over to see if your answers are on the money.

- Educational background:

- Face: handsome, okay, less-than-attractive?

- Body: muscles, okay, skinny, flabby?

- Hobbies and interests:

- Pets, owned or wanted:

- What is your job, and do you like it?

- Do you smoke, and do you mind if others smoke?

- Do you drink, and do you mind if others drink?

- Do you use drugs, and do you mind if others do?

- What are your favorite types of food?

- What do you like to do for fun?

- What kind of sports do you enjoy?

- What kind of books and movies do you like?

- What kind of vacations do you take?

- How and where do you meet people?

- A perfect date would be:

- How romantic are you?

- How many dates do you usually have before sex?

- What are your sexual tastes?

- What is your attitude on dating and HIV status?

- How out are you?

- In the past have you fallen into roles? Are you a daddy, a brother, or a son?

- If you had to pick a "type," what type would you be?

- In what ways are you passive? In what ways are you aggressive?

- In what ways are you flexible? In what ways are you rigid?

- What are the best and worst things about you physically?

- What are the best and worst things about you mentally?

- What are the best and worst things about you emotionally?

- The things I like most about my life right now are:

- My obituary/tombstone will say:

- The things I like least about my life right now are:

- If I could change myself in any way, I would:

You and Your Mirror

You should also take a realistic inventory of your looks—and by "realistic," I mean the exact opposite of what you think. Practically every gay man in America is overly critical about how attractive he is (something you can see immediately in the bathrooms of big gay clubs, which frequently look like holding pens for crazed Miss America contestants). Gay men can look at themselves in the mirror for hours and hours, finding flaw after flaw after flaw; it seems that if we don't look as good as the hottest new movie star, a Tom of Finland drawing, this year's porn sensation, or this weekend's bar godlet, we're *nothing*. Frequently if you ask a gay man to tell you about himself, he'll either exaggerate whatever he can or make a list of what he doesn't like about himself—neither case being exactly self-esteemarama.

Guys, get over it! If you've done the basics—good haircut, flattering clothes, eating right, and exercise—stop beating the shit out of yourself that you don't look like some insipid masturbatory fantasy. You're losing your hair—so what? Lots of men are losing their hair; if it's such a big deal, wear a hat. You're not the most handsome man on the planet? Well, that's life.

If you can't convince yourself just to cut it out with this endless flaw finding, there are two techniques you can try. The first is to realize that the mirror and the camera lie. Though there are some people who are truly photogenic (if, for example, you saw Madonna in real life, you wouldn't look twice at her), most of us don't reflect well. You can see it by standing near the mirror and comparing how your skin looks in real life with how it's reflected. Especially for fair-skinned men, the mirror's silver backing washes out the skin tone, making us look paler, less healthy, and less alive.

The other technique has to do with how you look at your face. Most people, in front of the mirror, put on an absolutely flat expression (like they're at a funeral) and maybe smile for a second or two. But in real life your face is constantly alive with thoughts and emotions, your eyes are twinkling, you're smiling and grinning and animated. Try out all those things and see which you like most; grin, half-smile, full smile? Head tilted down or up? Don't try to glue the expression on your face when you're out, but do remember that you have an attractive look you can flash at the right moment. One of my friends is convinced he's got the ugliest face in the world, but when he grins, his dimples pop out and he looks completely different from his "funeral in the mirror" expression. Until I pointed it out, he'd never seen himself look like that. You may have similar nutty ideas until you really look at yourself—"Just look at yourself!"

One issue, though, you should do something about. There are plenty of men everyone thinks of as being "hot" who are as ugly as toads. Why? Because they've got gorgeous bods. Whether you like it or not, right now we are living in a culture where bodies are IT, and instead of complaining that no one loves you because you're as fat as a whale, why not just work out? If the idiots you meet can make themselves look like Greek sculpture, you can too.

If you're really out of shape, see your doctor first, and consider hiring a good trainer so that you can learn the right form and get efficient results. The secret to a great workout is to try all the machines and the various kinds of weights and pick exercises that you enjoy; that way you'll keep wanting to go to the gym. My own favorite exercise, for example, is abs, since between workouts you get to lie down. It may be "body fascism," but it's easy, it's healthy, and it's a great way to meet guys—as we'll see later on.

If you just can't get in shape, however, you should still stop beating yourself up over it and just find someone who wants a lover like you. If you're all-out fat, for example, you must have heard of chubby-chasers and bear-lovers: hot, successful, perfect-in-every-way guys who can get turned on by big, fat, hairy, sweaty, stinky pig men. If there are attractive guys who get turned on by that, just think: There's got to be someone for you too. Yes, even you.

Wants Vs. Needs

> People often say that this or that person has not yet found himself. But the self is not something that one finds. It is something that one creates.
>
> —THOMAS SZASZ

The second part of the "know thyself" equation is figuring out, when it comes to another guy, what you need *vs.* what you want. When discussing what things in another man we find attractive, it's common for us to talk about our wants, but not our needs, and it's all too common for us to want our lovers to be everything we weren't—but wished we were—in high school.

We were out of shape and never picked to be on anyone's team, so now we want bodybuilder lovers. No girls ever wanted to go out with us in a million years, so now our romantic type is drop-dead-gorgeous model material. We were shy, closed off, friendless; so as adults we now want an outgoing, vivacious, popular boyfriend. We were made to feel effeminate, less than a man, so now we want guys with big dicks. Collectively in fact we have lousy taste in men—I, for example, never get laid so much as when I'm dressed like some cheap hustler. As Jeff Cohen, Bob Smith, and Danny McWilliams put it, "Our favorite kids' magazine was *Highlights for Children* because of Goofus and Gallant, those boys who were total opposites. Gallant did everything right; he was considerate, responsible, neat and respectful of adults. He reminded us of ourselves. Goofus did everything wrong; he was selfish, irresponsible, sloppy and rude. He was the one who gave us a little thrill."

Unfortunately none of this has anything to do with what we need from our long-term significant others (s.o.s): compatibility in making a life together. It's the same issue as the hot-man-versus-great-boyfriend problem above: if you have a job that involves lots of traveling, you may want a lover with a ten-inch dick, but you *need* someone who's okay with you being gone so often. If you're turned on by lots of muscles, but emotionally you need a man to spend lots of time, effort, and attention taking care of you, it may be extremely difficult to find those two qualities in one guy. It all comes down to: Would Goofus be a decent spouse for *anyone*?

Needs are meat, pasta, and broccoli: the qualities in a lover that your inner emotions require and that reality dictates. Wants are sauce (or chocolate). Think hard about this issue when you're starting to get serious about someone. It's something few of us take into account until it's too late, and things are falling apart. Here's a "needs" list to help figure out what's really crucial for you:

11

- Educational background:

- Time together: daily, weekly, occasionally

- Sex: as often as possible, daily, weekly, occasionally

- Romance: flowers and candy, regular guy, not romantic

- Romantic experience: gay divorcé, average, first-timer

- HIV: positive, negative, not important

- Real estate: living together, weekends together, living apart

- Couple attitude: desperately clinging, he needs me, normal, take it or leave it

- Face: gorgeous, average, not important

- Body: muscles, average, not important

- Brains: genius, average, not important

- Money: rich, average, not important

- Job: high-powered, nine to five, blue collar, not important

Betty Berzon, in her wonderful book *Permanent Partners*, has created a dream list of what she feels is crucial for a lover, and it really bears some thought (though there's no man alive who could do *all* these things well). Is the guy you're considering as lover material someone

- Who seems as if he will grow as an individual and not become overly dependent on me to make his life work?

- Who is in touch with his feelings, who can talk about them freely, who is comfortable expressing anger as well as affection?

12

▶ Who doesn't have to run away from conflict, who is willing and able to confront relationship problems and work on them?

▶ Who listens when I talk, who gives me the feeling that I am being heard and understood?

▶ Who can give as well as receive, who would be able to take care of me if I should have that need?

▶ Who can receive as well as give, who is able to ask for what he needs, so that a relationship would afford opportunity for both of us to give as well as receive?

If, after all this, you still find yourself and your needs a mystery, one answer may be to keep a very intimate journal. Every night before going to bed, write down the significant things that happened to you that day and how you felt about them. After a few months you can look back at your life, and it'll be like reading a novel; you'll see yourself as a character. Some find journal writing so illuminating that they make it a lifelong habit.

The other way to learn about your needs is to think back and remember what caused you pain in your past. If, when you remember, that pain comes back like a fist, you've hit a need. For example, I spent a number of years of my childhood by myself and, for the rest of my life, I will always feel deeply alone—and will always feel attracted to someone similar. If that someone, however, is distant, unavailable, and "not there," things aren't going to work out between us over the long haul because he isn't doing much for that need. It's not his fault and it's not my fault; it's just there, and it's something I need to know about.

Do you still remember how much your parents criticized you and ignored you? Maybe what you need is someone who accepts you and enjoys giving you lots of attention. Do you still remember all the times your sister belittled you? Maybe what you need is someone who admires your achievements. Did a guy cause you serious grief because he was so capricious and quixotic? Maybe what you need is someone who's emotionally constant and steady.

Gay Self-hatred

> Sometimes I feel discriminated against, but it does not make me angry. It merely astonishes me. How can anyone deny themselves the pleasure of my company?
>
> —Zora Neale Hurston

All Americans have one inalienable right not written in the Constitution: the right to think that sex is filthy, disgusting, and repugnant. Remember childhood? Jack off and your palms will grow hairs; touch a girl, she'll get instantly pregnant and it'll be all your fault. Many kids were even taught that just *thinking* about sex would get them sent straight to hell. Do you remember how shocked you were when you realized that your parents were fucking? How you thought they were sickening and disgusting and you swore you'd NEVER do such a terrible thing?

All gay Americans, however, get a double shotgun blast of guilt and shame over sex. When we were little boys, we grew up hearing all about fucking faggots and goddamn queers and limp-wristed queens and girly men who preyed on little boys. Practically all of us heard these epithets screamed at us by schoolmates or strangers or even our own families. Almost always, this abuse came from other boys and men, even from our own fathers, brothers, and uncles. In 1989 the U.S. Department of Health and Human Services studied teenagers

14

who killed themselves, and found that 30 percent of them turned out to be gay and lesbian—an awfully big leap over the estimated 10 percent of the general population who are gay.

Why do so many American straights—especially teen boys —hate gay men so much? George Weinberg, who introduced the word "homophobia" in his book *Society and the Healthy Homosexual,* believes it stems from five sources: religious training; fear of being gay oneself; envy that gay men have a freer and easier life than straight married men; fear of others who live outside of social norms; and being disturbed that gay people aren't part of the cycle of childbearing. The most recent idea from the sociologists proposes that serious gay hatred pops up when a society defines the difference between men and women very strictly, making men powerful and aggressive, while the women are weak and passive. In a culture like this gay men are considered girly-girls who've deliberately tossed aside their male privileges, while lesbians are thought of as power-crazed bitches who want to be men. Both upset the social order, muddy the waters, and are considered crazy, a subspecies.

Homophobes like to think that homosexuality is "an unnatural act"—probably because they haven't tried it. However, as Dr. Helen Fisher has pointed out,

Homosexuality is exceedingly common in nature. Female cats housed separately from males display all of the behavior patterns of homosexual arousal. Wild female gulls sometimes mate as lesbian couples. Male gorillas band together and exhibit homosexuality. Female pygmy chimpanzees have regular homosexual interactions. . . . In fact, homosexuality is so common in other species—and it occurs in such a variety of circumstances—that human homosexuality is striking not in its prevalence, but in its rarity.

Two-thirds of human societies today consider same-sex sex utterly normal and gay people completely acceptable. There's even a tribe in central Australia—the Aranda—where everyone's either gay or bisexual. Many cultures throughout the centuries, in fact, have found gay men's difference to be exotic and welcome; there are the cross-dressing shaman *berdaches* of the American Indians; the Sacred Band of Thebes in ancient Greece; the Army of Lovers in Papua New Guinea; the mythological *mahu* of Polynesia (one of whom created the hula dance), and religious *hijras* of India.

In America today, though, that same strangeness is cause for alarm, giving rise to fear, envy, and hatred. We do have very defined gender roles, and because of the size and geographic isolation of the United States, we tend to be xenophobic and afraid of people who "aren't like us." When the boy next door turns out to be the neighborhood faggot, many straights feel they've been deceived. The way we're shown in the press ends up not helping much either; instead of shots of social organizations for gay teens and AIDS charity services, the TV news is filled with roller-skating, tutu-wearing leather transsexuals and their nine-year-old boy lovers. Of course it makes sense when you're trying to produce an exciting TV show, but it certainly doesn't help would-be homophobes understand people like us. What's the biggest compliment we get from most straights? "But you don't *seem* gay; I never would've guessed." And how many personal ads from gay men do you see where "straight-looking" is mentioned?

Growing up gay and coming out of the closet involves accepting yourself, but it also means accepting that you have desires that many in straight society think are disgusting and evil. Before coming out, practically all gay men felt they were disgusting and evil, and were filled with shame. If we grew up learning that other men are a source of fear and hostility, is it any wonder that some of us have trouble with relationships?

Many gay men are living an "ugly duckling" fable with their lives. As kids or teenagers we were "different," not like regular guys, outsiders, perhaps effeminate, confused and uncertain about ourselves; some of us even knew we were gay at a very young age and thought it was disgusting and sinful. Straight teens ostracized us, fag-baited us, ridiculed us; we withdrew into ourselves, drank, ate, or drugged too much, or became outrageously different, anything to compensate. One of the great paradoxes in life is that the girlish "sissy" qualities many of us were condemned for as kids—being sensitive, not being particularly competitive, making compromises—are exactly what we need as adults when we fall in love. As we got over the hump, however, we got comfortable with ourselves, started working out, and became the hot, sexy, attractive men we are today—with many, however, still having at least a little of that ugly duckling deep inside.

How to Avoid Love

Of course you've heard the old saw that you can't love others unless you first love yourself. What's probably more true, however, is that you can't *receive* love from others until you are at least okay with yourself, an area where gay self-hatred and lousy self-esteem can bog up the works.

Some men actually spend their lives grieving for their lost heterosexuality, constantly fantasizing about "what might have been." Some spend years consumed by guilt, feeling worthless and unlovable, suppressing their sexuality, and frequently suppressing all their other emotions as well. Others had plenty of sex from the get-go but because of homophobia, they always denied any emotional attachments for other men, and they're still doing this as adults. Casual sex is, for them, a cinch . . . but relationships are impossible. Some guys have to pursue compulsive sexual conquests to prove themselves worthy, or flit from one lover to another, never finding the one whose devotion can overcome their own self-hatred—since no such love exists. One man said it this way: "The fact of the matter is that gay men have traditionally been told or conditioned to believe that they aren't worth anything and don't deserve anything. Many gay men react to this by fiercely throwing themselves into sex, the only arena in which they can find self-worth. The old, tired notion that we are who we are because of how and how often we have sex is what keeps the gay community from advancing beyond the angry little kid stage."

You've probably met plenty of guys over the years who did things that made you wonder, "Just what the hell is going on here?" Say you're going out with someone and everything's going really well, when suddenly he starts backing off and ends up vanishing for no reason that you can figure out. We all have a friend who says, over and over, how much he wants a boyfriend, but it seems that even though he dates lots of seemingly fine guys, nothing ever works out long-term, and always for the most ridiculous of reasons. The answer, in many cases, is internal homophobia and bad self-esteem— our secret antilove plague. See if any of the following stories don't sound familiar:

Mr. Miserable This kind of guy is always focusing on his weaknesses instead of his strengths, his disabilities instead of his abilities, his lacks instead of his haves. He thinks he doesn't deserve to be happy. Ever. When he does get to a point of happiness or fulfillment, instead of enjoying it he's immediately consumed with anxiety, terrified that life will destroy these good feelings with some horrible tragedy, which would be exactly what he (being worthless) deserves.

Sometimes this feeling is so strong that he undermines whatever good things and good men happen to him—because "it doesn't feel right."

Mr. Sabotage
A man feels lonely, goes looking for a lover, gets one, is happy and content. Then as things develop and the relationship turns serious, he starts coming up with excuses why the lover isn't "right," and he undermines things. He's glad to be free, gets lonely, and goes looking for someone new, starting the cycle all over again.

As a boyfriend, he may be completely in-your-face promiscuous with other men, or turn cruel to "test" his lover's devotion; he may make one self-critical comment after another waiting to be corrected; perhaps he becomes hysterically possessive and jealous. No matter what, you can never show him you love him enough; he's always building a new summit for you to climb. You'll say, "You're so hot!" and he says, "Right," and you say, "You're such a sweet guy," and he looks at you funny, and you say, "I love you," and he says, "Who are you trying to kid?"

The "I'm So Lonely" Whore
Inside, this kind of man thinks he's inadequate as a friend or husband; he doesn't deserve love or even companionship. He keeps distant from everyone else, never letting anyone get too close, which makes him feel incredibly lonely. He then tries Band-Aiding over the loneliness with quickie insta-sex, but never gets to the root of the real problem—and commonly ends up complaining that the only thing gay men want is quickie insta-sex.

Frequently this kind of guy is gorgeous, buffed, striking—someone you'd think has it all. Inside, however, there's another story. When a guy with okay self-esteem meets someone new, he thinks, "What do I think of them?" But when an "I'm so lonely" whore does the same thing, he thinks, "What do they think of me?" His inner worth is up for grabs, and he constantly has to look to others to confirm that he's good, worthwhile, attractive, lovable.

"I'm Ugly"　John is a middle-aged man with a regular, straight-guy kind of body. He is charming, witty, kind, financially independent, intelligent, handsome—terrific husband material. All of that vanishes from his mind, however, the minute he goes out to a bar or a club; he sees all the other guys with beautiful tits and abs, and only has one thought: "I'm Fat I'm Fat I'm Fat I'm Fat I'm Fat I'm Fat."

In reality John could afford to lose about fifteen pounds, but in our body-conscious age he becomes so obsessed and depressed about this one issue that he can't even bring himself to stay on a long-term diet or go to a gym. Ignoring his fine qualities and focusing on his one less-than-attractive feature is illogical, unrealistic, and doesn't do anybody any good —yet it's utterly common.

"I'm a Giver"　Everyone's gone home with someone to discover that they're utterly selfish, but sometimes you meet someone who is relentlessly unselfish, always looking for your satisfaction, but never seeming to care if he himself gets off. At first you may think, "Hey, this is great!" since you don't have to take what he wants into account and everything revolves around you. But if you get together a few times, you'll start seeing that the whole situation is completely lopsided; he's ignoring his own wants, and you'll feel like you can't satisfy him. He doesn't think enough of himself to enjoy (or believe he deserves) satisfaction in bed; he may act strangely about being touched, withdraw from you after coming, and even act like a martyr.

Mr. Silent Treatment Being emotional and wearing your heart on your sleeve isn't considered the most manly way to act in our society, so it's no wonder that many guys have trouble talking about how they feel. But if your man never tells you a damn thing, something more serious is going on. He thinks, "What I feel isn't important" or "I shouldn't have these feelings" or "If I really tell you how I feel, you won't like me anymore." In severe cases he may feel so unsure and inadequate about himself that he doesn't want to reveal his fears, doubts, passions—what he's really like.

Gay couples (especially lesbians) are notorious for over-processing, talking about every little thing that happened between them with "what did you mean when you said that after I had said what I was trying to say" . . . *ad nauseam.* Sometimes we talk to each other so much, we make the relationship a burden and even develop communication fatigue. As compensation, you may be perfectly happy not to have someone blabbing about their every little emotion all the time, and it could be that, with time and your help, he'll overcome some of his bad feelings about himself, and learn to trust you enough to talk . . . a little.

Fear is probably our biggest, most primal emotion, the response that protects all animals from danger and keeps them alive. But if you're afraid of letting someone see you, warts and all, or worried that if you really fall for a guy and he leaves you, you'll be destroyed, then fear is protecting you from love. Part of being single means being safe; you don't have to worry about anyone else's opinions, about being rejected, about someone finding out something about you he doesn't like. Being part of a couple means being completely exposed—something many guys aren't ready to do.

Miss Achilles Heel This is when you, a queen megabitch, know exactly what your friends and boyfriend, deep down inside, feel bad about in themselves—and you never let them forget it for one single minute. If your lover's unhappy about his bald spot, for instance, you'll be sure to say, and in public no less, "Harry, did our minoxidil run out this week? Seems like you're showing a little more than usual." The brittle, witty, ironic gay commentator is a long-standing stereotype (based on truth) in our culture, and there's nothing wrong with a good joke—but consider what may be the source. If you hate yourself, trying to feel superior by trashing other people doesn't work in the long run, and it can additionally undermine the close ties with friends and lovers that are part of the real solution to your inner homophobia.

The Velvet Ropes One common outlet of gay self-loathing is how frequently the gay community (or groups within it) love being exclusive and belittling to others who don't have this year's flannel shirt or mustache or body or haircut or Speedos or polo short or leather sneer. Rejected by straight society, gay cliques created their own "clubs," and nonmembers need not apply. The velvet ropes at the front doors of many bars are manned by guys looking to keep out the old, the fat, the poorly dressed, the unattractive, anybody "not like us." An outrageous example was when one of my hottest, sexiest friends showed up at the opening of a new leather bar and was refused entry—because his sneakers had *white* shoelaces. Straights wouldn't accept us, and those velvet ropes are carrying on an age-old tradition.

If you find yourself looking exactly like twenty of your friends and having a vicious comment for every occasion, maybe it's time for a vacation—and if you still have feelings in the back of your mind that you are a worthless, unlovable human being, you will have an extremely difficult time ever feeling loved. No matter how many times you hear someone tell you he cares about you, you can't believe it; no matter how much his actions prove his devotion and caring, it won't sink in. You may, however, find some comfort in the fact that you are not alone, since these feelings are unfortunately popular with many of us. Some couples with similar levels of gay self-loathing, in fact, compensate by being the most tradition-bound husband-and-wife on the face of the earth, mimicking June and Ward Cleaver down to the last detail.

Along with "knowing thyself," try to see if, in your past relationships, some leftover shame hasn't kept you from being the spouse you could be. If it seems to be an issue for you, the best way to cure gay self-loathing is by becoming more active in the gay community; deal with it by taking more of a part in gay life and culture—through clubs, political groups, and charity organizations—and you may get your pride up.

Love Leagues

Since we fuck the same sex, we're constantly able to compare ourselves with other men. Self-esteem junk, however, keeps us from seeing ourselves and one another whole. We forget about the package, the bundle of plusses and minuses that make up every human being, and instead we're always meeting someone younger, prettier, better built, richer, more interesting, smarter, more outgoing, and with a bigger dick. They may be an illiterate psycho, but that bigger dick is what we'll remember.

The answer is to see yourself and your position in the world as clearly and realistically as possible. Remember your finer points and, if necessary, work on your weaker ones. But don't let insecurity overwhelm your realistic sense of yourself; keep in the back of your mind all your excellent traits. And if your current lover, best friend, parents, or close relatives are always putting you down, criticizing you, trying to get you to change and treating you with condescension and disrespect, get away from them. Being with the wrong person or around people who don't love you for who you are can damage your self-image more than practically anything else.

In the mid-eighties I wrote a book with Andy Warhol called *America,* and in it was Andy's and my theory about packages and balance, which we called *love leagues:*

Being single is best, but everyone wants to fall in love. I guess it's because they hear it on the radio and they've got to have it. But it seems to never work out, unless you know all about your "love league."

This girl who really gets around and always has the best guys told me about "love leagues." Or maybe I read it in a magazine. But what you do is look at yourself in four ways: face, body, money, and power or prestige. Because these are the four things that make people fall in love. So you look at your own four things, and you give yourself ratings—terrific, medium, or nothing—but you have to be really honest and objective.

Let's say you decide you have an OK face, a great body, medium money and no power or prestige. That means you should go after other people who also have two mediums, a terrific and a nothing. It's not supposed to matter which categories the different things fall in as long as it's two mediums, one terrific, one nothing. You could get a husband with a medium body, medium money, a terrific face and no prestige, or one with a medium face, medium power, a zero body and lots of money—whatever you're interested in, as long as the person's in the same "love league." And it should work out OK.

But if you're two mediums, a terrific and a nothing, and you go after someone who's four terrifics, or someone who's four nothings, it'll just be trouble and it'll never happen. I don't know if all of this makes any sense, but I'm sure someone could turn it into a pretty good book and about twenty talk shows.

Also, how come personality isn't included in the "love leagues"? You used to always read that the best people were those with "personality plus." I guess nowadays it takes too long to get to know someone's personality, and you have to be able to decide fast whether someone's worth your time and trouble.

Empathy

When you have empathy, you're able to feel for yourself what other people are feeling, and during a fight you're more capable of understanding their point of view and seeing their side of an issue. A very empathic person, besides being able to get along extremely well with a wide range of personalities, has a great deal of power—he can practically read other people's minds. Obviously this is a great asset in meeting guys, keeping your relationship together when things go wrong, and really being there when your lover needs you.

A secret that empathic people know and regular guys don't is that in order to really know what's on someone's mind, you have to watch and listen to them on multiple tracks at the same time. You have to listen to what they say, but you also have to hear the tones in their voice, watch their facial expressions, and pay attention to their body language. When meeting men who seem standoffish, it's frequently not because they think you're Frankenstein but because they're shy, are afraid, and don't know what to do next. By thinking about these conflicting feelings and trying to be empathic, you can gauge their interest in you through eye contact, and you can tell if they're being shy through the stop-and-start tones in their voice and their withdrawn body language. You can also tell when it's time to move on if someone is not interested—something many unempathic people never seem to get.

You may want to develop your empathic powers to aid you when meeting strangers. A great way to practice is with a friend; the next time he tells you about some problem or difficulty, try to put your own opinions, feelings, and attitudes out of your mind entirely and focus completely on him:

- Is the tone in his voice smooth and comfortable, or does the flow constantly change, with gaps, shifts in speed, and rising and falling pitches?

- Is he sitting comfortably with his head and hands making natural movements; is he crouched back and withdrawn; is he overly demonstrative?

- Do his eyes and facial expressions match up with what he says, or is he flat and stoic, or overly animated?

- Is any of this in conflict with what he is telling you? Is he extremely upset and doesn't want to show it, or is it a small matter to him personally and he's trying to make the story more exciting and dramatic for you?

A common group-therapy experiment proves the unique power of intuition and empathy. Everyone in the group pairs off with someone who is a complete stranger. Without saying a word, each looks at the other, absorbing each other, trying to imagine what the other is really like. When ready, one tells the other his or her impressions; the subject corrects or modifies what the first is saying; then they switch roles—and practically everyone is astonished at the results. Many of them are extremely accurate in guessing a stranger's secrets, all through empathy.

By stilling your own thoughts and feelings and really listening and paying attention to other people, you can "drink them in" and really see what's going on. With enough practice you'll know how to become in tune with others as much as you can be and not let your own beliefs and attitudes get in the way of real communication. You'll know another human being with a whole new depth than ever before, and you'll become the kind of "good listener" that we all want in our friends and companions.

The Dream . . . the Gift . . . the Power of Self-Esteem

> *Love is patient and kind; love is not jealous or boastful; it is not arrogant or rude. Love does not insist on its own way; it is not irritable or resentful; it does not rejoice in wrong but rejoices in the right. Love bears all things, believes all things, hopes all things, endures all things.*
> —1 Corinthians 13:4–7

What are we all searching for? Someone who will love us for ourselves, just as we are; someone who will love us unconditionally, without any reservations or second thoughts. We want to be cherished, not for our body or our money or our stature or our youth, but for who we are inside. We don't want our lovers thinking, "I'd *really* be in love with him if he was in better shape," or "*Maybe* he'll start making real money in a few years and then everything will be fine." We want to be taken as we are now, whole. But just as charity begins at home, so does this kind of ultimate love. Stop thinking, "I'll be attractive once I lose fifteen pounds," or "I'll be happy when I'm in a relationship," and start thinking, "I may have flaws, but overall I'm a pretty great guy." Remember the package. It's trite, it's a cliché, and it's absolutely true: Only after you love yourself unconditionally can you love others with the same purity of heart and generosity of spirit.

Once you know and accept yourself, once you've understood how, overall, you're a fine fellow and a real catch, and once you've confronted any possible gay self-hatred you may still have, you will have learned the secret method of being happy and finding a great guy. Your self-respect is in your hands, and it is far more valuable than anyone else's opinion of you. If there's one big revelation in this book, here it is: Good self-esteem and a solid sense of yourself will take you farther in attracting a long-term lover than any other qualities you (or anyone else) may have.

Some guys think they'll be happy if they could only get the hottest man at the gym to become their lover. Others think they want to meet someone wealthy who can take care of them for the rest of their lives. Still others look for someone who's going to shrink them out, daddy them up, and solve their leftover childhood problems. None of these men are ever going to be happy chasing these goals, even if they find and catch their dream lovers. If you think a relationship is what you can get out of it and what someone else can give you, you've sealed your eternal doom. Instead, Mr. Right's idea is: What do I have to give? Once you're strong enough inside to be completely generous with yourself—the Gift— you'll attract boyfriends like flies to honey.

The secret to always being happy in love is to give it unconditionally, and expect absolutely nothing in return.

This sounds easy, but in fact it's probably impossible for human beings, if not living saints. How many times, in love, do we end up thinking, "How can he treat me like this after all I've done for him?" How many times, when our lover is unhappy about something, have we thought, "I've knocked myself out and this is the thanks I get." We offer our devotion, but we have to feel we're getting back in equal measure —or else.

You can only give what you have. The Gift is to offer yourself fully; to be generous, kind, forgiving, compromising, honest, and patient; to be strong and supportive. By getting your act together and making yourself strong as an individual, you'll be ready to give your all when the time comes.

Don't misunderstand; someone so full of himself that his head is the size of Paris doesn't have self-esteem; someone who's constantly belittling others and thinking he's perfect doesn't have it either. Good self-esteem means that you accept yourself as a human being, warts and all, and that this acceptance gives you a serenity and a comfort about your place, abilities, and talents in the world. This serenity and comfort is incredibly attractive, a magnet for luring someone to spend your life with—someone who's like you.

♂

Getting yourself in mental, emotional, and physical shape before you start even thinking of romance and marriage will take you far when an interesting man comes along. You'll be as attractive as you can be, and you'll attract others like you— people with a zest for living life to the fullest. Of course you won't be a perfect person in every way (no one is), but doing all you can to make yourself the kind of guy you'd like to meet . . . will make you meet exactly the kind of guy you like.

As Grace Jones sang, "I'm not perfect. But I'm perfect for you."

Chapter 2
· ·

♂ **Modern Love**

*The great love affairs of Lancelot and Guine-
vere, Heloise and Abelard, Romeo and Juliet live
for us as symbols of physical passion and spiritual devotion . . . implicit in the fact that the
lovers' commitment to each other represented a
defiant **no** flung in the face of their culture or
society, is the fact that such love was not re-
garded as a "normal" way of life or an accepted cultural ideal.*

—NATHANIEL BRANDEN

Many times when you're with a boy-
friend, you'll find yourself wondering, "Where does he get
this stuff?" When it comes to romance, what we think and
how we act are each person's individual creations. Watching
our parents and their marriage filled our childish heads with
ideas about love, and so did countless other tales, legends,
myths . . . and TV shows. Frequently gay men merged lots
of different material from boydom into one big romantic
wish, combining the obvious stories (like the classics above)
with other, not-so-obvious ideas.

Were you sparked as a youngster watching Mighty Mouse

save the lives of cheering rodents? How about seeing a wild brute of a man tamed into perfect husband material via charm, a good figure, purity of spirit, and the various editions of Beauty and the Beast? Were you dying to have an identical twin like Patty Duke; did you yearn for a bedroom down the hall from Greg Brady; or did your spirits soar watching such pals as Napoleon Solo & Ilya Kuryakin, CHiPs, Starsky & Hutch, Mel Gibson & Danny Glover, or Butch Cassidy & the Sundance Kid?

Inside our hearts we've each collected a history of stories and images that enthralled us, inspired us, and cohered into that complicated feeling we call desire. Inside our hearts each of us has created a Book of Love, anthologizing all the memorable figures and heart-starting yarns from all our various personal and cultural sources. Say you're a Trekker and you just love watching Kirk & Spock together; why do you cherish this so much? Perhaps the psychic split they represent—Mr. Action vs. Mr. Mull—is played out in your own inner life. Maybe you're the kind of guy who acts impulsively, and you'd really like a partner who's contemplative; or maybe you're eggheady, and you're dying for a Kirk-like muscular dentist in your private life.

When you first started recognizing your desires for other men, explicit gay stories may have been added to your heart's book with a big bang. What was it like being in Hebrew school and learning about the all-time archetypes of men who are best friends and lovers—David & Jonathan? While studying history in school, did you take a deep breath for the *real* "I would die for you" love of Achilles & Patroclus—or were you knocked out by the sagas of our first great gay warrior, Alexander the Great? Did you take an art appreciation course and see just why Emperor Hadrian was so crazy for his great love, Antinous? What about when you learned we even have our own gay constellation—Castor & Pollux?

Our Books of Love are never explicit; they are the secret, mythic longings that lie beneath the surface—deep waters coursing through our hearts' desires. Thinking about what kinds of stories first tickled your fancy will go a long way to help you understand what you're really looking for deep down inside with another guy, and maybe getting him to talk about his dreams of youth will help you understand his fantasy as well.

"The One"

One chapter in those Books of Love that practically all of us have, though, isn't so terrific. Many children's fairy tales, movies, TV shows, novels, even comic-book love stories tell you the same thing: Someday, if you keep looking hard enough, you'll find "The One" who will fall madly in love with you, take you away on an adventure of romance, and be the perfect person who will make your life utterly happy and complete.

Since you no longer believe in elves, witches, Santa Claus, and the Easter Bunny, why do you still believe in Prince Charming? Did you ever stop to think what happened *after* Snow White and her guy, Sleeping Beauty and her Prince, or Beauty and her Beast got married and had to live in the real world? ("You left FOUR INCHES of hair in the bathtub!")

Many guys (whether wholeheartedly or way in the back of their minds) still think this myth is the truth of romance, when nothing could be farther from the truth. It is typically a strong belief for gay men since, before coming out, they couldn't express their sexuality openly and so often daydreamed of imaginary, perfect lovers—men they're still looking for to this very day.

If you believe in "The One," you will never be able to have a decent relationship, since no one man can ever live up to your powerful romantic fantasies, and real life has little to do with never-ending honeymoons. You'll be constantly disappointed in your lovers for not making you instantly happy, and you won't be able to work on keeping things going with another man when conflict (something that seldom appears in our daydreams) rears its head. If you're dating someone and things look good but some little problem happens and he runs away, it's probably because he realizes that you're not "The One," and it's time to go off and keep looking. Sorry, there's not much you can do about it; but if *you're* the guy who keeps dropping someone over minor matters, maybe you have "The One" fantasy, and need to consider how it's just not jiving with reality.

The History of Love

Another major chapter in our Books of Love, another source of our hearts' inspiration, comes from past cultures and societies in history—how our predecessors viewed sex, romance, and marriage. These ideas have been passed down through the centuries—just like any butter-cookie recipe—and elements of each are probably roaming around your heart right this very moment.

One of the astonishing things that the history of love teaches us, for example, is that when the marriage vows "till death do us part" were created, very few people lived past the age of *thirty*. By the time a man died in his mid-twenties, he'd probably already been widowed twice. As Nathaniel Branden commented, " 'Forever' has a different meaning in such a context than it does today."

You've heard plenty of jokes about the ancient Greeks, but in fact it was those very Hellenes (and their boy-lovin' ways) who started, for Western civilization's sake, many of our ideas about love and lust. They believed that human beings began life as a merger of two people who were then split apart, only to spend the rest of their lives searching for each other—their better halves.

The Greeks also believed, as you may not know, that the pure, spiritual love that all human beings seek could only be found between two men—specifically between an older, married top and a teenage, single bottom. This was the only form of passion that they thought would improve and ennoble a man; even Aristotle, who didn't care much for gay sex, wrote, "Love and friendship are found most and in their best form between men." This passion was also one of the few that, in ancient times, caused lovesickness; as Morton Hunt described it, "The lover made passionate declarations, wrote ardent petitions of devotion, swore solemn oaths, performed foolish errands at the boy's command, and slept all night, cold and miserable, on his doorstep. He blushed when the boy's name was mentioned, bored his friends with incessant praise of the beloved, and became dumb and stupid in the beloved's presence."

In the Greek hierarchy of love, boys, courtesans, and prostitutes were the leaders; wives ran the household. In fact at one point marriage itself became so unpopular that Solon tried to pass a law making it compulsory for all citizens. If you love young, slim guys and want to help them learn the ways of the world, your personal Anthology of Love may be filled with lots of ancient Greek.

If you're a big fan of that cinematic masterpiece *The Women,* however, your yearning book may be mostly written via ancient Rome. There the game of love was actually considered a game; if one became infatuated and smitten, he was considered weak-willed and foolish. The Romans were all great precursors of the *Dangerous Liaisons* style of loving; the greatest joy was in carnal conquest, and the more difficult the quarry, the more exciting the hunt, the more passionate the game. We've all met guys whose love lives, just like the Romans, revolve around the catch of the day.

After sexual freedom went as far as it could go, the early Christians revolted, embracing the Greek split between flesh and spirit in a whole new way; the most spiritual, purest of unions, they felt, could only be sexless. Saint Augustine, bishop of Hippo, believed that since all life originates from the repulsive act of sex, all life is *ipso facto* tainted with sin from the very moment of conception. Considering women's anatomy, he noted, "We are born between feces and urine." As Jerome, the fifth century's leading thinker, put it, "A wise man ought to love his wife with judgment, not with passion. Let a man govern his voluptuous impulses, and not rush headlong into intercourse. . . . He who too ardently loves his own wife is an adulterer."

It took the Holy Mother Church seven hundred years to make priests celibate, but she did, ultimately, succeed. This love of chastity and hatred of the flesh grew so overwhelming in fact that any sex except for reproductive purposes was considered repugnant and even a heresy; the Christian forefathers became the very first culture in Western civ to make being gay a capital offense. If as an adult you think sex is nasty and dirty and really exciting, you may have those early Christian ideals firmly in place.

The end of the Dark Ages coincided with the beginning of a whole new concept of romance; an idea that, along with the Greek notion, is probably still one of our most widely held, cherished, and unshakable notions: Courtly Love. This paradigm can be described best with a story: You fall madly in love with someone who's impossible to get; you are forced to perform acts of immense courage, personal suffering, and grand achievement in pursuit of your love; these acts make you a great man, an upstanding citizen, and a more refined human being; your improved self finally makes your beloved swoon: Mission accomplished.

In our cultural history, Courtly Love was a revolution; it marks the first time, since the male affairs of ancient Greece, that falling in love would lead to self-improvement. It was also the first time since the Greeks that one became committed to another for love; that a man was supposed to think about his behavior and appearance in regard to capturing his beloved's heart; that fucking was supposed to take the other person's interests into consideration. Sadly no one thought these intense emotions, which for the first time inspired countless amateurs to compose songs and poetry, could be sustained in day-to-day life, and marriage continued to be a business and heir-creating arrangement. Today we commonly think of a split between the mad passion of those just fallen in love and the quiet, dreary partnership of the longtime couple. While there is in fact a sliver of truth in this idea, most of it is a myth we've all inherited from the sixteenth c.

When everyone got tired of being overwhelmed by their romantic feelings, the Age of Reason ushered back in the idea that love only made you foolish; the smart thing to do was to cover up the emotions as much as possible with the most rigid etiquette in history. As Horace Walpole put it, "The world is a comedy to those who think, a tragedy to those who feel." Puritans running Geneva, Switzerland, made elaborate hairdos a crime, and adultery punishable by death; Victorians thought all humans were, twenty-four hours a day, on the verge of being overwhelmed by their animal natures and needed constant vigilance to keep this horror from happening (so much so that male and female authors were separated in public libraries). All of this, of course, is part of our natures today; all written, sometimes in big bold letters and sometimes in barely legible italics, in our Books of Love.

Today's American attitudes about romance and marriage are as revolutionary, and as unseen before in history, as the era of Courtly Love. Never before in Western civ has so much of culture and entertainment—from songs to movies to books to television—focused on romance. Never before the America of the 1920s did youngsters meet potential spouses through our curious and completely modern ritual, the date. Never before was it considered inadequate to be single, or that everyone alive was on a personal mission: to find Mr. Right.

We Americans do indeed get divorced more than anyone before us, but that has more to do with the fervent search for a relationship of love and devotion (and women's modern fiscal abilities to live sans husbands) than it does with a failure of modern society. As Morton Hunt put it,

> In a manner scarcely found in earlier history, Western love in the mid-twentieth century was an effort to combine sexual gratification, affectionate and intimate companionship, and the procreative familial functions in a single relationship. Romantic attraction was considered . . . the only proper basis for choosing one's marital partner; . . . the sexual drives of both partners were supposed to be completely and permanently satisfied within marriage; . . . and tenderness, mystery, arousal and satisfaction were expected to survive in a milieu of household cares and childrearing problems. . . . All in all, according to anthropologists, it was one of the most difficult human relationships ever attempted; just as certainly, it was also one of the most appealing.

So if, right now, you're trying to have the kind of relationship we all want, you are, historically, a pioneer. Our forefathers would be looking at you and what you were attempting and they'd be sure to say, "What? Are you nuts?"

A New Idea About Life and Love

> Since the day I could cut the shape of a heart from a piece of red construction paper, I fell in love. I fell and fell until I hit bottom, the hard and rocky bottom of the pit of rejection. There I languished for an appropriate period of mourning, then picked myself up, dusted myself off, and rushed headlong to the flame again. No matter how often my heart was broken, I never stopped, virtually addicted to the state of infatuation, that breathless tumble through nothing-else-exists euphoria. My capacity for pain was equaled only by my capacity for bliss.
>
> —Marion Winik

Growing up, we all learned one romantic plot: During high school or college or just after, you'd meet Mr. Right, fall completely in love, and stay together for the rest of your lives. If this didn't happen, your marriage was a failure—either because of your faults or because he wasn't "The One." You'd then have to start all over again and get it right this time, either by being better as a husband or by doing a better job of spouse picking.

Since we all know that the divorce rate in America is 50 percent, since we all have divorced and single-parent friends and neighbors, and since we all know plenty of gay couples who break up, you'd think we could get this idea out of our heads. When asked why her relationships never lasted, anthropologist Margaret Mead replied, "I have been married three times, and not one of them was a failure." Perhaps Madge is right; maybe it's time for all of us to get a new plot.

In *Anatomy of Love,* Dr. Helen Fisher developed a new relationship theory from studying divorce rates around the world. It seems that instead of the notorious seven-year itch, humans in general have a four-year itch, which is, not coincidentally to Ms. Fisher's mind, the time it takes to conceive, bear a child, have that child develop past infancy, and be able to get around on its own. During the child-bearing years of teens and twenties, she believes, there is an ancient chemical urge to play the field; it's your DNA talking when you fall in and out of love and have multiple relationships. It's so common in fact for first-time, young couples to eventually divorce that a new term's been coined: "starter marriages." A young man whose first marriage lasted for four years (with the last three spent in couple therapy) told Deborah Schupack, "I was fairly in the dark about who I was. When you're young, you're just beginning to find out who you are as a person. You compound that with trying to find out who you are in relation to someone else, and it's like an algorithm. It complicates things several times over."

After around the age of thirty, worldwide divorce rates drop dramatically. What Dr. Fisher proposes is that, chemically speaking, our brains are wired to have a series of relationships when we're young and then finally to settle down when we get more mature. Instead of Mr. Right we meet a bunch of Mr. Rights, and it's age that makes the match long-lasting.

Our childhood dream? To meet someone and stay with him in romantic bliss for the rest of our lives. Our adult reality? To have a series of relationships, each of which ends for various reasons having to do with things happening between the two people instead of being any one person's fault. Remembering this simple fact may not make you happier about the times when things go wrong, but it will perhaps give you some perspective and hope.

To Spouse or Not to Spouse?

Americans marry to enhance their inner, largely secret selves.

—ANTHROPOLOGIST PAUL BOHANNAN

When discussing what keeps couples together over the long haul, practically every book, article, and survey (even the ones that match astrological charts) focuses on similarities. "Just have all these things in common," they preach, "and everything will work out fine." Sociological studies of what worked for straight, longtime married couples, for example, have come up with the following:

▶ Shared interests

▶ Sharing leisure activities

▶ Not coupling up at too young an age

▶ Mutual friends

▶ Being flexible

▶ Growing up in a loving home

▶ Knowing how to adjust to, bargain with, and fight with each other

In real life, though, I've discovered that this is only half true. The secret of successful long-term couples is that they can very delicately balance tight similarities and vast differences. The similarities make them a team, while the differences make for spice and excitement, and the combination of the two is much bigger than either alone could be. The differences that each part of a couple brings into their life together can be a source of tension, or one of enrichment.

Why is this "opposites attract" issue so significant for us? One idea has it that passion needs tension, the kind of tension that's readily available when two people have plenty of things not-in-common but are madly in love and try to merge together. Het couples have this in abundance, just from the fact that most men and women are so different from each other. Gay couples, though, have to make up for this lack, and the whole shebang becomes a tightrope act. Be too different from each other and you'll either turn distant or drive each other insane; be too similar, though, and your coupledom will turn lifeless and empty.

One pair I know has been married for twelve years, and I can't think of anyone better to illustrate this point. She's so airy, it's sometimes like watching "Flight of the Bumblebee" made flesh, while he's so earthy that she refers to him as "my mudman. Even after twelve years, we look at each other all the time and think, 'Who is this person?' If we were one iota more different, we'd never get along."

You've probably met a couple like my friends Richard and Daniel; the more you get to know them, the more you think, "What can they *possibly* see in each other?" Richard is acid-tongued while Daniel is a sweetie pie; Richard is hyper-aggressive while Daniel is Mr. Easygoing; Richard's always on the go while Daniel's always on vacation. They've been together for over twenty-five years, and their opposites provide another crucial thing for a happy couple: balance. Richard makes their world turn; Daniel makes it homey and loving.

The trick here is that, when you first meet someone, his differences from you will seem exciting and even exotic;

these qualities may even be what really draws you to him. Later on, try to remember how much you loved all these things in the first place when the differences make trouble; you always have to take the misunderstandings with the exotica.

You can also ask, "What pieces of myself really come to the fore from being around my lover?" Frequently the difference in you single and you married is the result of your differences with him, and frequently the change in your ideas and attitudes and personality from being with him are exactly the reason why you fell in love in the first place.

The Shadow Lover

The idea that "opposites attract" finds its greatest proponent in Carl Jung, who came up with an interesting concept— "the shadow self." Quickly explained, all of us are full human beings who've made choices; all of us have, buried within, the side of ourselves that we didn't choose. If you've decided to be a gym rat and work out as much as possible, there will always be a secret side of you that never wants to see the inside of a gym for the rest of your life. Or you've taken a job that's easy for you, that doesn't pay all that well but that gives you plenty of time for the other parts of your life. Inside, there's a piece of you that wishes you'd taken the opposite path, working at something that really challenges all your abilities and puts your ambition to the test. You're content with your life choices, but that doesn't mean that your other half, the "shadow self," has gone anywhere; according to Jung, it's still there, deep inside, lurking.

Many guys find themselves very attracted to men who've gone on "the road not taken," and frequently couples will be built on certain oppositions. If you're a big scene-and-circuit gay man but you're really only attracted to "regular guy" types . . . if you're quiet and reserved but you like men who are outgoing and vivacious . . . if you only get hot for muscles but aren't at all interested in having lots of your own, you are looking for your "shadow" lover. If you find him and you've also got shadows that he wants, it could be a match made in heaven (or at least at the baths). Your oppositions could also drive each other crazy.

If you're able to live with each other and not go insane, however, shadow lovers make great pairs. A muscle-homebody combo might make him more domestic and get you in better shape; with a shy-vivacious combo he perks you up while you calm him down; and the scene–regular guy match's benefits are legion (see below). In all these cases each guy gets to make a contribution to the couple that the other can't; each can have the benefits of what the other provides solo. Shadow lovers, in action, can be a powerful force.

The Art of Love

> It is clear that love is never simple, that it brings with it struggles of the past and hopes for the future, and that it is loaded with material that may be remotely—if at all—connected to the person who is the apparent object of love.
>
> —THOMAS MOORE

In the countless books and articles I've read to bring you all the information you need to know, there's one thing that's completely missing, and it is utterly crucial. No one mentions how there are, basically, three kinds of boyfriends (b.f.'s): the incompetent, the craftsman, and the artist. An incompetent is someone who's too self-absorbed, too goony, and too otherwise not ready to get it on seriously. A craftsman knows how to do everything it takes to keep things going between two guys, but there's no sense of magic, of romance, of being special.

An artist, on the other hand, is someone who knows the things discussed in chapter 1, someone who remembers what he learned from past mistakes in being part of a couple, someone who actively gets ideas about how to handle romance and living together from his friends, someone who sees the work that's involved and decides it's just the kind of job he likes. He puts time and effort into thinking about what gifts to get, what to do on dates, how to make sex fresh and exciting, what small surprises will please and excite his b.f. He writes love letters, thank-you notes, and does all the little things that mean so much; but he doesn't let petty things get in the way of staying together.

Later on you'll learn some basic "sex tips for guys" and "date tips for guys." Taking these ideas to heart will make you a craftsman; using them as inspiration to enhance your life, whether with a fuck buddy or with a long-term lover, will make you an artist. Think back on your past relationships and affairlets; what did other guys do that you still, to this day, remember? What can you do, right now, to let the man you love know it—and remember it? Just as you can't learn to play the violin overnight, learning to be an artist with other men takes time, effort, practice, and patience.

Especially after you and Señor Sueño have moved in together, this issue becomes more and more significant. It's common for couples, facing the mundane, day-to-day ups and downs of living together, to have the attitude that "if we're able successfully to attend to those mundane day-to-day items, everything else will work out just fine." In fact this is the smallest element of wedded bliss; you should be thinking, now more than ever, magic and art. Your husband came to you with deep inner needs for comfort and excitement, dreaming of a life with someone special, and you're spending all your time divvying up who does laundry and who does dishes?

Being a spouse means assuming a role of great, primordial stature. You can become the father he wished he had; the brother he always wanted; the best friend who is loyal, constant, and ready for new adventures; the student of whom he is justifiably proud; the sex partner who meets all his desires; the romantic lover who makes him swoon. When he was a child and something bad happened, his mother held him and made everything all right; now that's *your* job. As Thomas Moore comments, "It is the primary task of the marriage partners not to create a life together, but to evoke the *soul's* lover, to stir up this magical fantasy of marriage and sustain it, thus serving the particular all-important myth that lies deep in the lover's heart and that supplies a profound need for meaning, fulfillment and relatedness."

Your new role is larger than life, and it's up to you whether or not you will accept the challenge, rise to the occasion, and be the lover of his dreams.

·······························

Chapter 3

♂ How to Go to a Bar

The difference between sex and love is that sex relieves tension and love causes it.

—WOODY ALLEN

Going to a bar isn't for everyone; if you're not really ready, you'll probably be really sorry. Bars aren't the best places to meet guys (for the best places, see the next chapter), but they are how many men do meet, and going to them is a great way to practice your pickup skills. Most of what you need to know about going to bars will apply to any situation where you might want to meet someone. So get out there, practice your heart out, have fun, and remember the following basic tips:

▶ **Lower your expectations.** If you walk into a bar thinking, "Tonight I'm sure I'm going to meet someone great," you're just setting yourself up for disappointment. If you go thinking, "I'll drop in tonight and see what's going on," you'll be in a much better mood, you'll be less tense, and you'll dramatically improve your chances of meeting someone great.

▶ **Walk in, scout the landscape, and pick your territory.** Men genetically like possessing their surroundings, and there's nothing like a gay bar in which to practice your chemical urges. Whether it's barside or corner table, find yourself a locale that helps give you presence and makes you feel comfortable and at home. Besides all the psych benefits, staking your claim will mean that, if someone's interested, he'll know where to find you.

▶ **If you feel that you've developed enough self-esteem by now, you're 99 percent on the way to successful barhopping.** If not, fake it! Project your feelings into the crowd; send out the idea that you know, deep down inside, that you're one of the hottest guys in this place—and if someone gets to go home with you, it's their lucky night.

▶ **Do whatever makes you feel comfortable.** Even if you've got some new clothes that make you look great, if they make you feel awkward, it's just going to be trouble. You need to be able to look like you own the joint, and being relaxed is crucial.

▶ **Emphasize your good points and stop thinking about your less attractive ones.** If you've got a great body, let the world know it with revealing clothes; if not, wear black. Spend some time pulling yourself together before going out; show off the kind of person that you yourself would find striking and like to meet.

▶ **Wear your contacts or glasses.** Many men go out on the prowl without their glasses for vanity's sake, and end up blindly groping around. Steven, my friend from college who devised the "not pretty/not nice" scheme, would always do this, and the results were always the same:

He: "Just look at that hot guy over there!"

Me: "Where?"

He: "There! Standing in the corner in the denim coat."

Me: "You're out of your mind; he's a goon."

He: "No, he's really hot. I'm going right over there. . . ."

(one minute later)

He: "Well, you were right. . . . But look at that hot number over there!"

Me: "Where?"

▶ **Be distinctive.** As our role model Mae West once noted, "It's better to be looked over than overlooked." Don't go during your bar's peak hours when it's a giant mob scene with everyone meandering around like a herd of cattle and you can't be noticed; go early, late, or on off days. Don't dress exactly like everyone else, since then you can't be seen and you can't give an interested guy an angle of approach; he can't compliment you on something if everyone else is wearing it too. Stand in the light, and try to look like you're having a good time. In the not-perky atmosphere of most bars, this last point alone may make you so distinctive, you become the center of attention.

▶ **If you haven't learned how to enjoy flirting by now, here's your chance.** Make plenty of eye contact with those you find attractive; give them a grin. Check out the rest of the place and, if you feel you're still interested, look them over again. *Be bold.*

▶ **If you're the shyest man in the history of gaydom, learn how to appear "open to new experiences"—receptive, available, pleasurable.** At least learn how to return looks with that certain something.

▶ **Avoid the dreaded embarrassment-of-riches syndrome.** A key obstacle to bar pickups is that there can be so many attractive men in one room that you just can't make up your mind. What if you spend time pursuing someone, chat him up, it doesn't work out, and you miss someone else who would have been perfect? The "so many men, so little time" attitude, celebrated in song and T-shirt slogans, is an epidemic at our bars, making us simultaneously frantic and paralyzed. Watch out.

▶ **Circulate, but not so much that you can't be landed, and always return to your territory.** Pay attention; if someone looks, try looking back instead of thinking, "Oh, it was just a coincidence that he looked me right in the eyes for a few minutes."

▶ **If you see something that makes your heart or whatever give a bounce, go for it.** Be bold, try some empathy, and don't be afraid of rejection. Sooner or later we all get rejected; so what? If someone says no, don't push; there's more fish in the sea than you can ever possibly catch.

How to Go to a Sex Club

There's nothing like a jaunt to your local sex club to relieve the hectic tensions of a busy week. Some men prefer them, since when you pick someone up at a bar or wherever, there's often a surprise for you later when he's naked in your apartment. But something our mothers never taught us was the stringent etiquette followed at such establishments:

▶ **Every sex operation has its own idiosyncrasies, so remember your Scout motto and Be Prepared.** Know the peak nights and hours; the undress code; and most important (to keep from getting eighty-sixed), the in-house rules on safe sex.

▶ **When you first walk in, ease into it by getting to know the layout and the preferences of the locals.** Then, when in Rome . . .

▶ **Believe it or not, every rule from "How to Go to a Bar" applies here as well.** Lower your expectations. Establish your territory. Be bold, outgoing, and friendly to the point of naked aggression (in its most literal sense). Focus. Wear your contacts.

▶ **Once again, quell any fears of rejection by remembering that it's no big deal if an object of desire turns you down; there's plenty more fish in the sea (or in this case, the basement).**

▶ **When you go to a sex club, you are paying to have sex, and if you don't, you might as well be throwing money out the window.** Many men seem to forget this fact; they walk into a place, are overwhelmed by feelings of self-doubt or that no one there is good enough for them (same thing), and so do nothing. Besides wasting their own time and money, they aren't contributing to the healthy "anything goes" atmosphere that everyone else is there for. So if you think you're not going to be able to mix 'n' mingle, stay home; we don't want you lurking around anyway.

▶ **While the common practice is to have sex, and then say, as sincerely as possible, "Thanks, that was great," and toddle off, if you have an especially remarkable moment with someone, don't be afraid to talk to him later and exchange phone numbers.** I've met some wonderful guys at sex clubs and orgies, and you might, too, but not if you're too afraid to do anything about it.

▶ **Don't be so quick to say no.** Some less-than-utterly-attractive men have learned how to compensate for their deficiencies with technical mastery. They may be able to teach you a thing or two.

▶ **Unless you enjoy catching lots of colds and recurrent herpes, don't be so quick to kiss everyone you meet on the lips.** Stick to the cheek, the neck, and so on.

▶ **If you meet someone and have a wonderful, memorable time, leave right away.** Usually we'll try to top ourselves by staying and trying harder, and this almost never works. Don't push your luck; leave with a smile on your lips.

▶ **If you see guys having unsafe sex in public, hand them a rubber.**

The Pickup

The moment is at hand: "I've seen someone I'm interested in, but how can I tell if he's interested in me?" The answer is patience. Since everyone in the world feels uncomfortable giving and getting intimate looks from complete strangers, there's some eye dancing that always goes on first. We all have to go through these motions, so just take your time and wait it out.

You look at him with interest, desire, or at least pure, solid lust. He looks back, also interested, noticing your face, body, crotch, ass, but always, back to the eyes. Your looks bounce back and forth, each mirroring the other, each filled with growing interest, tension, and the questions of "Maybe you? Maybe tonight? Maybe something great?"

Mating dances between would-be couples are remarkably similar around the world. Here's a dance, described in Helen Fisher's *Anatomy of Love*, that took place in Kenya:

> The affair began one evening when a female baboon, Thalia, turned and caught a young male, Alex, staring at her. They were about fifteen feet apart. He glanced away immediately. So she stared at him—until he turned to look at her. Then she intently fiddled with her toes. On it went. Each time she stared at him, he looked away; each time he stared at her, she groomed her feet.
>
> Finally Alex caught Thalia gazing at him. . . . Immediately he flattened his ears against his head, narrowed his eyelids, and began to smack his lips, the height of friendliness in baboon society. Thalia froze. Then, for a long moment, she looked him in the eye. Only after this extended

eye contact had occurred did Alex approach her, at which point Thalia began to groom him—the beginning of a friendship and sexual liaison that was still going strong six years later.

One of my friends noted, "It sounds exactly like any gay bar—except for the six-years-later part." Just like it was for the baboons, your moving from looking to actually talking is the all-time most difficult moment in making a connection and picking someone up. Here are some pointers:

▶ **Always use a question or a compliment, since it means the other guy will have to respond and you can gauge his interest.** If you start off with something devastatingly wit-filled, it puts guys on the spot; they're supposed to respond in kind, but haven't been practicing for days like you obviously did. Keep it simple, stupid.

▶ **Even if you're surrounded by men in leather drag practicing their pouts and sneers, put some friendliness in your voice; you need to be able to appear simultaneously sexy and harmless.** Too gruff, and it puts him on the spot.

▶ **If you're completely stuck on opening lines, there's a new one that I thought was great:**

You: "See anyone you're interested in here?"
He: "I don't know; is there anyone you're interested in?"
You: "Yeah, I'm interested in *you.*"

And here are some others you can try:

"Having a good time?"
"Well, you're pretty cute, aren't you?"

"Nice to see a lotta hot guys here tonight . . . including you."

"Great tits! What gym do you go to?"

"How about those Mets?"

"I look at you and I can tell you've heard every stupid pickup line in the book . . . so one more won't hurt you."*

"Didn't we have sex a long time ago?"

"Hi, my name's Craig" (this to-the-point strategy was picked by our survey as being their number one favorite).

▶ **Find out his name, and use it regularly.**

▶ **Get him to talk about himself, but don't make it look like an interrogation.**

▶ **Move in.** Give good eye contact. Try a light touch here and there.

▶ **If things are still a little uncomfortable, you can try using body-language mirroring to smooth things over and build a sense of rapport.** When he takes a drink, you take one; when he leans back, you lean back; when he turns his head to look around, you do too. It may seem contrived, but accentuating your rhythm as a duo will make him more comfortable.

Rejection? Get Over It

> *Spare yourself some grief: Recognize that you are not the universal solvent, no matter how attractive you may be. No one is.*
>
> —CHARLES SILVERSTEIN AND FELICE PICANO

Gay men around the world have one thing in common: the fear of rejection. Even the handsomest man alive can be

---

* Courtesy of the sitcom *Taxi*.

nervous about approaching a stranger. Right now you're probably whining, "I'm shy! I can't just go up to a man I think is attractive and tell him I'm interested." Well, why not? What's the worst thing that could happen? As Celeste West has so beautifully put it, "In the sweet arts, you live like an epicurean only if you can afford to lose like a stoic."

If you get turned down, there could be any number of reasons: He's not in the mood; he's had a terrible day; he doesn't feel up to meeting someone new; he's there with a friend/boyfriend and can't get together; he's intimidated; he's already got plans for the evening; he just finished having sex and is just out for a nightcap—the list is really endless. A rejection has far more to do with him than it does with you; after all, he doesn't know you from Adam.

Practically all *personal* rejection, on the other hand, comes from the fact that everyone has a particular type that really gets their blood moving, and even if you're the world's biggest movie star, when you don't fit the type, you're not happenin' for him, baby. If you see the man of your dreams, but he's only interested in black (or Italian or bodybuilding or hairless blond) men, but you're not black (or Italian or a bodybuilder or a hairless blond), you're going to get rejected. It's not your fault and it's not his fault, and there's nothing either of you can do about it.

One of my all-time favorite stories about "types" and rejection is the night I met someone and we hit it off immediately; it was gangbuster sex and affection and romance for hours and hours and hours. Afterward, as we were lying together in postcoital bliss, he turned to me and said, "You're Dutch, aren't you?" and I said, "No, I'm Scandinavian," and he said, in terror, "You're not Dutch? You're not Dutch!" jumped out of the bed, threw on his clothes, and ran out of the apartment as fast as his legs could carry him. Guess his type was Dutch, and nothing else. (Secret tip: When asked about your heritage, just say, "Yes, I'm Dutch; how did you know?")

Much about love, attraction, and especially rejection is completely irrational. There's a beautiful man living nearby, and so of course I had to find out his name; it turned out to be Kip. I could never fall for anyone named Kip; it's the name of a small Chinese dog, or one of Barbie's friends, and so to me, he's not so gorgeous anymore.

Another story: When I was in my twenties, I had a lover who was in his early forties. He liked younger guys and I liked older guys; he'd point out a kid and say, "Isn't he cute?" and I'd say "Ick"; I'd point out a man and say, "Isn't he hot?" and he'd say "Feh." If one of the boys he liked came after me, I'd turn him down, and if one of the men came after him, he'd pass; but the other in each case would've said, "Yes!" Susan Page says it this way: "The person who rejects you is making a statement about himself; not about you."

There actually are men who enjoy going to bars or walking through gay neighborhoods, seeing how many guys they can attract, and then turning down every single one of them and going home utterly satisfied. They only enjoy proving their attractiveness to themselves, and they get a kick out of telling everyone else that they're not good enough. So if you get rejected by a guy like this, is it your fault?

Once you've decided to just throw in the towel, become bold, and stop worrying about being rejected, you'll be completely amazed at the results. Unless you're batting way outside of your love league, most men will at the very least be flattered, and you'll be finding yourself going on date after date after date—just because you've developed a little nerve. Being bold but friendly is more important in meeting guys than practically anything else you can do; it's the one quality that starts the engines, and something few guys do regularly. For some mysterious reason practically all gay men prefer being approached instead of doing the approaching. Doing this, though, is putting your future in someone else's hands.

Many smart guys have said that thinking you're going to be rejected is actually worse than the rejection itself. So if you stop with the anticipation and just throw yourself into the ring, you're 90 percent of the way home. Secondly, unless the object of your desire is brain-dead, he's going to find it charming that you're a little shy and nervous when you're trying to pick him up—no one in his right mind seriously expects you to act like Cary Grant or Luke Perry when you're coming onto him. So you're not a great beauty; great beauties are scary. If you're a regular man wanting to meet other regular men, they're going to be more comfortable with you than with Jeff Stryker.

If you're one of the many, many guys who are completely paralyzed by their fear of rejection, there are three great techniques to try. The first is the easiest. You see someone you're interested in, but you get scared. Before moving in, imagine that if you went up to him and said hello, he'd scream at the top of his lungs, throw his drink in your face, and run out the door. After this scenario, any turn-down will seem like no big deal.

The second technique is to try talking to a stranger whom you don't feel all that strongly about; not someone who repulses you (which will only give him the wrong ideas), but someone you think is okay, but no walking god. Since you aren't dying to meet and go home with him, you may be comfortable enough to be able to say, "Hi, my name's ———," or something equally lite, which is all it really takes to get a conversation going. Who knows? It's the okay guys who make the best husbands anyway.

The third suggestion is to make it your goal to talk to at least three strangers the next time you go out. You don't have to try going home with any of them; you aren't out to win any prize beyond being able to speak. If the mission's accomplished, give yourself a reward; the bigger reward, though, comes when this technique turns you into an easy talker at any bar or club.

A funny thing: Men who feel inadequate about their looks and constantly fear rejection don't realize that incredible hunks have their own unique problem: Everyone is afraid to approach them. Drop-dead-gorgeous men frequently get ignored at bars and clubs since everyone considers them out of their league, and frequently they end up going home alone. If you're a very hot guy, it'll be your responsibility to get things off the ground, and once you get hitched, you'll have to be constantly reassuring your lover of your devotion while he watches you fend off your many other admirers.

It's work, but you're up to it.

Going out specifically to meet someone fills practically all of us with dread. Instead of the fun evening we were so looking forward to, we end up spending most of our time out feeling nervous and inadequate. Remember this ridiculous irony when you next hit the streets, and try to develop a "take it or leave it" attitude. Instead of the usual nagging thought "If I don't go home with someone tonight, I'm a human zero," try "I'm going out to have fun, and if something clicks, I'll have even more fun." Forget about the goal, enjoy the process—and you'll increase your chances a hundredfold to boot.

Chapter 4

....

♂ # Where to Meet Men

Kissing is a means of getting two people so close together they can't see anything wrong with each other.

—RÉNE YASENEK

You now feel as ready as you're going to get anytime soon, and it's time to hit the streets and go on the hunt that'll create your future. First stop is the hottest bar in town, but when you get there, everyone gives you hostile, appraising glances that make you think you're not good enough for them. You try the newest dance club, but even though everyone's covered in sweat and dancing half naked, the music's so loud and everyone's so cliqued up that it's impossible. Then you try a sex club, where you have one intense carnal encounter after another, each ending with the other guy saying, "Thanks!" and walking away. Nothing is working; you feel even lonelier than ever, and so you rush back to the gym to work those biceps. "Maybe I'm just not good-looking enough."

Though it is possible to meet guys in bars and sex clubs, it's not easy. Dance clubs are the hardest, since smart dancers always go with their friends, dates, or lovers; bars are tougher than they should be since everyone is working so hard trying to get picked up that no one has any fun; and most sex-club goers are there to get off, not walk hand in hand under the moonlight (though of course, practically every single guy there would secretly like to end the morning that way). You may be going to the most obvious places to meet guys, but it's exactly these obvious places where the guys are hardest to meet.

Let's look at your fourth destination—the gym. First of all, you should be going to a gym with a good atmosphere and members who aren't unlike yourself. If you're fifty and in okay shape, but your gym is filled with megabuffed twenty-year-olds, you're not going to be as comfortable as you could be and have a great workout (unless of course you're a daddy/son kinda guy and there are plenty of complementary daddy/son members). But if you are going to the right gym for you, you've found one of the perfect places to meet someone (and, best of all, you can see ahead of time just what you're getting).

Remember: Practically everyone is shy around strangers, so if you see an object of desire, try a little boldness. You instantly have a topic of conversation: If you're a novice, ask for help; if you're experienced and see him doing something wrong, offer advice. Offer to spot (something always filled with a terrific erotic undercurrent). You can then move on to talking about how long he's been working out; what he thinks of the gym, the various machines and workout techniques; what gyms he belonged to before; what his preferences are in bed (well, maybe that's moving a little too fast). If you belong to a gay gym, you can always try the steam (a.k.a. "low self-esteem") room, but that's designed for quickies; try the conversational approach, just for novelty's sake.

60

♂

Your local gay community center is a great source of leads. Besides the obvious social events, the center can tell you about local organizations that may pique your fancy. You can look into classes you might want to take, meetings you might want to attend, and businesses you might want to patronize— all being where the boys are. Gay church and synagogue organizations, if you're spiritually minded, will automatically have members who match your inclinations.

If you have some special interest, you should definitely consider joining a gay group where you can follow your heart or brain and maybe meet some guys along the way. If politics is your bent, there's gay Democrat and Republican organizations to join, as well as activist groups such as Act-Up and Queer Nation (along with AA, commonly the biggest pickup spots in town). If you're HIV-positive, you might especially consider ACT-UP or Body Positive if you've been having trouble with HIV apartheid (more on this later). When some people feel a spiritual emptiness, they get back on track through charity and volunteerism, with organizations like Gay Men's Health Crisis and God's Love We Deliver. Do a good deed for someone less fortunate than yourself, and meet others who have similar values.

Practically any interest you may have can be answered by an organization in your area, from the Gay Community Services Center to the Gay Softball League, a businessman's organization like the Greater Boston Business Council, Gay Wrestlers Anonymous, Gay Journalists, New York Jacks, or Senior Action in a Gay Environment—there's a whole listing of organizations in the appendix at the end of this book. And if you can't find a group you want to join, why not start your own? All it takes is some classifieds in the local gay press and flyers at the bars and community center.

A great, outrageous idea I heard of just lately was a guy who answered "Gay Roommate Wanted" ads in the paper—even though he was perfectly happy where he was living! He'd meet guys (who were almost guaranteed to be single), get to see their place, and ask them all about their lives, their habits, their interests. He'd wait a day or two, call and say he'd decided to pass on taking the share, but what about getting together for coffee? By meeting guys in a more or less non-cruisey situation, they could have a talk without all the regular tension going on, and he would get to see what someone was really like right away.

Are you constantly telling all your friends how badly you want to meet someone and why can't they fix you up? If not, why not? Tell them; in fact tell them over and over again if you want. You can frequently meet great men through your friends; the trick is to make them think twice. Some guys actually have standing rewards (one I heard of was for a thousand dollars) for any friend who introduces them to the man they eventually move in with, and I think it's a great idea. But if you're not the type to pay off your chums, the least you can do is to forget your pride and ask outright. When one of them says, "There's this real cute new guy at the office," remember to say, "Do you think he'd be interested in me?"

♂

One of the most popular new ways to meet guys is via phone sex. You can dial up a professional sex talker, talk to other guys, listen and respond to recorded personal ads, place your own ads and see what kind of callbacks you get, and of course either have a mutual phone J.O. session or arrange to meet. One man I know swears by them; he says that if you keep talking until someone responds in just the right way, much of the time you've hooked a live one. It's become the easiest way for many guys to meet one another who don't care for our other, more obvious, venues.

There are any number of things to think about when using these services. One is cost; phone-sex service fees can range anywhere from 10¢ to $2.98 a minute. Some men become addicted to it, and are shocked to discover just what this new hobby costs when their bills arrive at the end of the month. Listen carefully when you first dial in, and make sure you understand how the fees are computed beyond what the ad with the megahunk promised.

Another issue is: do you want only sextalk, or do you want to get together in person? If it's J.O. talk, you can feel free to tell anyone anything you want that you think'll get him off. Let your imagination roam; "Be all that you can be!" Say your body's just like Arnold Schwarzenegger's while your head's like Alec Baldwin's and your tool's like Jeff Stryker's (if you think anyone'll believe it). Be a sailor on leave, a recent grad from the Police Academy, a big leather daddy monster; play whatever role you always wanted (but never could be) in real life. Remember, everything is in your voice, so if you want to be good at it, tell every little detail, and when you're coming, up your amplitude by at least 8 dBs.

If you want to meet in person, however, try to be reasonably honest (within the parameters of "phone-sex honesty" of course). Grossly overexaggerating your positive qualities will only bring the wrong men to your door and set them up to be completely disappointed, no matter how wonderful your personality may be. As Charles Silverstein and Felice Picano have said, "If you're standing in the rain at three A.M. ringing someone's doorbell, and you've described yourself over the phone as looking like Tom Cruise, although you more accurately resemble Henry Kissinger, don't expect to get in." Unfortunately most guys do fib like mad when it comes to phone sex (usually subtracting from their age while adding to their muscle and cock sizes), so you might be wise to lower your expectations when getting together in the material world.

When your contact leaves the digital and enters the physical, *caveat emptor*. Unless you're really good at saying "Nah, I don't think so" when some stranger's at your front door trying to get in, plan to meet at some neutral location so that you can suss him out ahead of time, and if anything feels fishy, bail out. There have been reports of professional thieves working the phones, some trying to get you into a conversation (and an invitation to your place) then and there, while others write down every phone number they hear on the lines, call later, and try to arrange a rendezvous.

There's also a privacy question you should know about. One of my acquaintances, a juicy young blond, met his current longtime hunkaroony beau through the phone lines (yes, it does happen). The night before they were going to move in together, he had a panic attack, dialed the phone-sex line, and made plans to get together with someone else later that night. What he didn't know until months later was that Mr. New Boyfriend had also dialed in, and was listening to the whole thing.

♂

If you live in a city with a decent-sized gay population, chances are there's an art gallery showing either gay art or at the very least doing business in a gay neighborhood. Get on the mailing list and go to their openings. Gallery openings are great places to meet new people, since they're usually just before dinnertime (giving you something to suggest doing if you bump into someone interesting). The art is a natural way to have a conversation; they usually serve wine and cheese, and they're *free*.

♂

If you've got a computer and a modem, there's a whole new way to meet guys: through computer bulletin boards. It's a lot like phone sex, but this time your computer telephones a huge central computer, where other computers are calling as well. CompuServe, America Online and GEnie all have gay subsections where you can talk/type live to other men, leave messages, browse user profiles, bring home sexy pictures, and set up blind dates. Having to wade through huge national listings of thousands of guys and possibly getting very involved with someone who lives on the other side of the country makes these tough, however, so probably a better idea is to look for a local service; there should be ads or listings of them in the gay press. After all, you've got enough problems to overcome besides adding geography to the list.

On gay bulletin boards, you fill out a profile describing yourself and your interests and then read others' question-naires to see where there might be a match. You can pick a "handle," or nickname, which conveys your attitude as well; *Single Dad* is obviously one kind of date, while *Bottoms Up* is another. You may be able to send them your picture, look at others' photos, or even watch digital, animated porn. If you're not interested in meeting anyone in person, for what-ever reason, you can just be a "lurker," and talk/type to your heart's content. If you're using the board for computer sex, don't be embarrassed that it takes a little practice to keep a hot talk going with one hand while beating the bishop with the other; you don't want to need a new keyboard every other week.

One caveat: just like on the phone, many BBS users take the opportunity to fib a little bit on their profiles, so when going on a blind date with someone you've only read about, lowered expectations are a good idea.

One technique that many men have used successfully is the personals. It's always better to take out an ad than to answer one, since then you're in control and you can decide how to respond. Even if you decide not to place it, writing an ad and getting yourself to look at your better qualities and what you really want in a b.f. is worth about ten weeks of therapy. Answering ads is additionally difficult since you need to know how to speak the very special language that is the personals. Here's an introduction:

What the ad says:	*What it means:*
B&D	Bondage and Domination
BB; muscular	Has arms and legs
FA/P	French Active (likes to suck)/ Passive (likes to get sucked)
Athletic	Able to walk
GA/P	Greek Active (likes to fuck)/ Passive (likes to get fucked)
Masculine	Not a pre-op transsexual
C&BT	Cock and ball torture
8″	Has visible penis
SS	Safe sex
Rugged	Face covered in scars
VA	Verbal abuse
Chubby	Ex–Sumo wrestler
Husky	Ex–Sumo wrestler
WS	Watersports
Looks not important	Quasimodo
Not bad-looking	Quasimodo
Financially secure	Quasimodo who will treat at McDonald's
Student	Looking for Quasimodo who will treat at McDonald's
UC	Uncut
Willing to relocate	Has no visible means of support
FF	Fisting
Artistic	Will read you his poems till dawn
JO	Jerking off
Likes to cuddle	Has Velcro for fingers
Lonely	Has Velcro for fingers

Dom	Dominant
Romantic	Owns extensive Barry Manilow collection
Sub	Submissive
Relationship possible	No, it's not

Just as the language of personals is inflated, so is much else about them misleading—you should remember to be as cautious with them as with any blind date. You may exchange photos, agree to meet in person, and then discover the photos weren't remotely accurate. One friend of mine carried on with an advertiser in another state, through writing and phone calls, for six months; he and his personals contact really turned each other on, and the picture he got was truly inspiring. In a fit of lust, he flew from New York to North Carolina to meet this seeming dream-come-true, only to discover that the picture was about fifteen years younger and a hundred pounds thinner than the man excitedly meeting him at the airport. Don't let it happen to you; try to find some mutual ground to meet on for your first face-to-face date, no matter how sure you feel about him.

Another serious personals issue is in writing to convicts. Your heart may be touched by their ads, which can be very moving:

"All alone . . . looking for a lasting friendship, possible relationship. Full of love, caring and understanding. Will answer all."

"Determined, honest, caring and hard worker seeks serious mate who wants a future and lifetime relationship together. Please be serious."

"I want to meet someone different and real. I seek someone
in touch with who he is and who knows what he wants from
a relationship. No game players, please."

The best material I've ever read on gay convict love was
written by Bob of Chicago and published in *Black and White
Men Together*:

The first thing anyone contemplating correspondence
should do is ask himself, "What am I trying to get out of
this?" . . . It may be a humanitarian impulse. . . . We
may secretly want to help the imprisoned fight the system.
. . . We may just be hoping for a sexual fantasy trip. . . .
We might relish the fact that we can easily become important to someone simply by writing once a week. . . . After
you review your motivations, check out what you think you
will be willing to offer. . . . Don't be any more rigid with
this friendship than with others, and no more foolish.

Unfortunately the number of innocent gay men looking
for love in all the wrong places who get scammed by cons is
really amazing. The typical ruse involves your cashing checks
or money orders or doing some other kind of banking for
your dreamboat jailbird, while he pulls a bilk operation you
never saw coming. Once again, *caveat emptor*.

You've decided, after all this, to take the plunge anyway.
When writing your ad, avoid saying the same things that
everyone else writes; think of it as a poem. The point is to
make clear your positive traits and your interests, to convey
these in a way that makes your ad pop out from all the rest,
and to do all this with as few words as possible. Avoid the
common nasty style of "No fats, femmes, fruitcakes"; instead
be upbeat: "In good shape and prefer you be too." You want
to evoke feelings and yearnings and uniqueness; you want

your ad to be remembered, to compel guys to contact you. Spend some time putting it together; have a friend look it over and make comments; get it perfect and don't waste your money. Here are some memorable phrases from others' ads, which might help you know what and what not to write:

"Great psyche, great chest."

"Your briefs get mine!"

"Enjoys reading, the outdoors, and making a heart smile."

"Do you get a thrill out of blowing up a balloon as big as possible? Do you get a kick out of bursting balloons? If so, contact me!"

"Why be lonely when I am just a letter away?"

When responding to your potential dates, always use handwriting; remember all the tips on compliments; send photos that say something about yourself beyond sex (such as posing on the beach, or with your German shepherd). Tell him what about his letter made you want to respond, and see if you can arrange a meeting in a relaxing public place (be careful out there). Write in the style that you get written to, and don't feel it's the defining moment; frolics can easily turn serious, and what begins as the hoped-for lifelong search can end as good friends. Finally, cut some slack; maybe you always loved blonds, but if a redhead looks good in every other respect, just give it a try for chrissakes.

Going on a trip with a bunch of like-minded men can dramatically enlarge your dance card. You'll be away from your day-to-day woes, and you'll be less tense, more relaxed, and more comfortable on vacation—making you all the more attractive. There are now a large number of gay travel agencies, almost all of whom set up tours specifically for men only, mixed gay men and lesbians, or single gay men only. You might also want to remember this idea when you're part of a couple and needing an injection of fun.

You can cruise New England (NYC, Newport, Nantucket, Martha's Vineyard, Provincetown, Boston) on RSVP's Seaspirit (800-328-RSVP); or explore Turkey, the Aegean, or the Galápagos Islands with Hanns Ebensten (305-294-8174); explore the natural wonders of the Southwest with Gay Spirit Journeys (505-984-9910); go on safari through Africa with Different Drummer Tours (800-645-1275); ski in New Zealand with James Dean Vacations (800-497-1524); cover the waterfront of Thailand with Tours to Paradise (213-962-9169); or even attend a gay weekend at Walt Disney World (407-857-1777). Other outstanding gay travel agencies include:

Club Le Bon	800-836-8687
Doin' It Right	800-666-DOIN
Gay Airline Club	213-650-5112
Islander's Club	212-206-6900
Men on Vacation	800-959-4636
Now, Voyager	800-255-6951
Olympus Vacations	800-9-OLYMPUS
Toto Tours	312-274-TOTO

You're constantly saying how lonely you are. You're attractive, successful, a decent person. Why don't you have a guy? But on Monday, Tuesday, and Thursday nights you're working at the office till nine P.M., and then falling asleep in front of the TV; on Wednesday you and Sally always go to the movies together; Fridays is dinner with your brother and sister-in-law and their new baby; weekends are spent out of town with your best friend and his longtime lover.

Being constantly busy can make us feel less lonely, but it doesn't do anything to fix that boyfriend problem. Meeting guys is work; if you're Mr. Workaholic, think of guy getting as a part-time job or as your most important hobby. If you're never available and you never try, you're leaving your love life completely at the mercy of coincidence, and you may be so filled with thoughts of work and social pressures that when that cutie in line at the DMV looks you over, you won't even notice. Want someone special? Make sure there's room for him, and make sure you are actively doing what you can to make it happen.

The other mistake many men make is to get into their own life so much that they stop being part of public life. If you love reading, don't sit home reading with the TV on; browse through the bookstores (especially gay ones), try the libraries, read on a park bench. If you're into physical stuff, don't just use the gym; join a softball, basketball, or swim team. If you're a writer, get a laptop (or a legal pad) and write in a coffeeshop or public spot where Mr. Right can ask, "What are you writing about?" Think of the leisure things you're doing at home, and see if you can't bring them more out into the open.

The easiest way to meet men, however, is just to wake yourself up. Here's the big secret to getting a boyfriend: *It doesn't matter what you do, as long as you do something.* Get out of the house, enjoy what you like to do, but do it where gay men congregate. Are you someone who loves to walk the streets in the evening and on weekends? Do it in a gay neighborhood; pay attention the next time you walk, and you might meet someone special. The same holds true for the Laundromat, the grocery store, taking out the dog, strolling through the park, even museums. Just as at the gym, don't put yourself on autocruise; just pay attention, be bold, and try to gauge the other guy's interest.

When you're out and around and you get a glance from someone interesting, here's what should happen next: Keep walking, count to two and a half, and look back. If he's interested and knows what he's doing, he'll do exactly the same thing. Smile bemusedly, and walk over. If you're the very shy type who never knows what to say to get a conversation going, you can just try what works best at bars: "Hi, my name's Craig," and ask what's on his agenda. You can also remember what happened at the gym: Ask for advice, or give some. On the street you can ask for directions or information about the neighborhood; in the grocery store you can ask where an item is or how to tell when something's ripe. Look alive to see if there's interest; if the cat's still got your tongue, try a light compliment; at some point he may rescue you and get the conversation going on its own steam. If it doesn't happen, don't let disappointment overwhelm; at least you tried and practiced, and you'll have more self-confidence and be readier for the next time.

Finally, always bear in mind the number one rule of dating: *Volume, volume, volume.* Most of the men who whine, "Why don't I have a boyfriend?" don't know this rule. If you're single and you don't like it, get out there and meet guys any way you can; become a dating maniac. Try to have something going two nights a week at the very least; find that congenial bar, sex club, and gym; join at least two social clubs; hit the phone and BBS lines; harass your friends; hit the gay neighborhood's streets; go to industry gatherings and meet 'n' greet; just knock yourself out. As the sayings go: "You've got to kiss a lot of frogs before you find a prince" and "Life is like a New York City playground; you've got to jump over a lot of dog shit to get to the swings." Don't just meet guys; meet as many as you can stand; that's the only way you'll find one who's right for you.

Chapter 5

....

♂ Sex Tips for Guys

I don't know why lesbians hate men.
They don't have to fuck 'em.

—ROSEANNE

Everyone likes sex, but only gay men pursue it with their signature brand of relentless gusto. That avatar of het screwing, Hugh Hefner, estimated he'd had sex with about a thousand different women over a thirty-year period; for a great many gay men, that's *nothing*. It seems we can transform any locale with a little privacy into an instant Trystville, with all of us genetically knowing the parks, beaches, trails, truckstops, piers, abandoned buildings, and even pay toilets where love can bloom (i.e., you can get off).

Why? Well, why not? David Crawford has an interesting theory: "It's no secret why so many gay men seek sex with the urgency they do: with the history many of us had of being branded eggheads or aesthetes, the prospect of being apprehended as pure, dumb meat has an irresistible allure. It's as close as some of us can imagine to being loved 'unconditionally'—not for our clever accomplishments but simply for the mute *flesh* we are."

For whatever reason, sex is a constant presence in our

culture, whether it's a bar with go-go boys and a "dark" room, gay mags where practically all the ads (even orthodontic services and rectal surgery) include a nude or two, gyms with notorious steam rooms, Jacuzzis and saunas, or just the nonstop cruising at practically every social event. It's wonderful that sex is so free and easy for us; what's tough is when this freedom gets infected by our common American attitude that fucking and love are opposites. We go out to get boytoys and hot men and slave bottoms and monster stud dicks; our mouths gape at that one's chest and this one's butt and that one's package; we spend a wonderful night with another man and the next day call him a trick. All this seems so utterly divorced from what we really want: the love of a terrific guy.

In 1994 the *Advocate* published the results of a sex and love survey of ten thousand gay men, and it was filled with surprises. In ranking what they love to do the most with another man in bed, the clear leaders were hugging, caressing, snuggling, and deep kissing. In ranking what they wanted to change in their sex life, most wanted more sex, but the second most popular choice was having sex be more intimate. Forty-four percent of the respondents are in relationships, 33 percent are living with someone, and of the single men, 87 percent say they wish they were in a relationship. Of those with a partner, 87 percent have made a long-term commitment and 40 percent have exchanged rings or had a commitment ceremony; 52 percent are monogamous; 26 percent have been together for ten or more years, and 65 percent rate their sex life as good or great. Where do you fall?

With all the practice we get, you'd think, by now, that at least every gay man in the world would be an expert in carnal technique . . . and you'd be utterly wrong. Just as most straight men are lousy in bed, so most gay men don't know what the hell they're doing either. They just do a lot of it . . . badly. Since Masters and Johnson revealed that half of all marriages are a "sexual disaster area," however, at least we're not alone.

If you're the common, run-of-the-mill rotten-in-the-sack kind of guy, this collection of basic info that follows is must reading. But even if you're a legendary Casanova, you might find some new ideas here:

The Basics

There are some things in life that you'd think everyone in the world would automatically figure out for themselves. Guess again. Here are the very basic rules of sex that anyone with half a head should know:

- **Get stocked.** Always have rubbers, lube, towels, soap, shampoo, toilet paper, toothbrush, toothpaste, an extra robe, coffee, milk, tea, juice, bread, and jam at home. If you have to stop 'n' shop on the way to your place together, do it. Inviting guests over without basic human accoutrements is *très de trop*.
- **Tidy up.** There's little that's as big a turnoff as when you go into someone's bathroom and the first thing you think is that you're bound to contract some rare fungal infection. Or, you're sitting in bed, naked, with a hard-on, waiting forever; he can't find the lube. Or he says, "Help yourself to anything you want in the kitchen," but you're afraid to go into the kitchen.

  So be a proper homosexual and clean up your act.
- **If you can't create pleasant, low lighting in your living and bedrooms, buy some new lamps.** Even the most golden, buffed Adonis can't heat it up with lighting best suited for open-heart surgery. If you don't know what the term "rheostat" means, get Dad to help redo the place.
- **Turn the volume on the answering machine down to zero.** I can't believe the number of times I've been with someone moving toward bliss when the phone rings and we spend

twenty minutes trying to keep our interests up while listening to Princess Pouty mouth off on her latest romantic disaster. Is there anything that destroys the mood for sex faster than a telephone? Well, maybe the cops.

- **Have an assortment of *quality* condoms available.** Bottom guys are famous for their good taste, so why do they always buy the world's worst rubbers? "Oh, three for twenty-five cents; these look good!" One of my ex-dates used to put out a bowl of the kind poor people get for free; you might as well use Saran Wrap and a rubber band. Since the wrong rubber can go far in ruining sex, this isn't an idle threat: If you don't know from condoms, learn which are the good ones— and maybe next time you won't be complaining when your paramour has trouble staying hard.

- **Balance out being romantic with being a whore.** Some guys are so kissy huggy smoochy lovey they barely get to coming; others are total icy fuck machines and nothing more. Combining and balancing the two will make you anyone's object of desire. Even raw, anonymous backroom sex can have some tenderness, some sweetness, some warmth; even the longest-term lovers can sometimes treat each other like the trashy sluts they were born to be. Be sweet, be loving, and be an insatiable whore; be tender, be kind, and be a rough street trick. Vibrate back and forth between these extremes, and he'll melt into your arms.

- **This is supposed to be fun, goddammit!** You have some trouble with his shirt buttons; there's a knock at the door; you know he likes it rough, but you're not sure *how* rough. There will always be times during sex (and when it's a first-time, maybe many times) where you're not the smooth, suave, professional porn star you think he wants you to be. Well, this may be impossible to believe, but a little awkwardness, a little shyness, a little display of being human is very attractive and, with the right attitude, very sexy.

▶ **HIV, AIDS, and so on.** Not only is AIDS a hideous, life-threatening disease, but what exactly you're supposed to do about it is in dispute. Most health departments in the United States consider ejaculating during oral sex to be risky (the theory being transmission via bleeding gingivitis), while the Canadian and San Francisco health departments consider it safe (the theory being that every gay man in the world would already be dead if oral sex were a likely transmission route). Stay informed; here's the generally accepted information at the time of this writing:

Believed Utterly Safe

Doing nothing whatsoever that exchanges fluids; keeping semen or blood from coming into contact with the mouth, the anus, or any open cuts.

Jacking off

Frottage (rubbing against each other)

Massage

Dry kissing

Unshared sex toys

Fisting with a latex glove

Using a condom with nonoxynol-9 spermicide for oral or anal sex, and then pulling out before coming anyway

Believed Probably Safe

Wet kissing

Oral sex without ejaculating in the mouth

Anal intercourse with a latex condom and a water-soluble lubricant

Water sports with no swallowing

Believed Unsafe

Anal or vaginal sex without a rubber

Swallowing semen

Fisting without a glove

Sharing sex toys

Sharing needles

Sharing razors

Rimming

In the 1994 *Advocate* sex survey, 45 percent of the guys said they love to get rimmed, but only 29 percent said they love to rim. Here's why: While not shown to be a common transmission route for AIDS, oral-anal sex is a great way to get amebiasis, giardiasis, shigellosis, hepatitis, mononucleosis, and parasites, which you may wish to avoid.

How to Have Oral Sex

One of my convictions is that, in order to be able to call yourself a gay man, you have to know how to give someone a blow job. Unfortunately if this rule were to be exercised, nine-tenths of America's gay population would vanish. Why is the world so full of incompetent cocksuckers?

The next time someone sucks you off and it's the greatest, please, for the sake of the commonweal, pay attention. Are their teeth scraping back and forth, back and forth? Do they nibble at the head like a rabid guppy? Do they accidentally come across what really turns you on, then ignore it for the rest of the evening? Do they put your cock in their mouths and bob up and down but you don't get any sensation? Do they rub your dick across their unshaved, stubbly cheeks and chapped lips until it burns? I don't think so—and *you* better cut this stuff out as well, missy:

- **If you're not in the mood, don't even try.** Cocksuckers who are bored, disinterested, repulsed, mechanical, or "all work and no play" are no good for anyone. If you're not into it, it'll be obvious to him; don't force it.
- **Lube up.** Get plenty of saliva going; it'll make things easier for you and more fun for him.
- **Teeth are for grinding, tearing, and mashing food into edible pieces.** They shouldn't come anywhere near a cock. Use your lips and the inside of your cheeks to keep them well away.
- **Five o'clock shadow has the consistency of sandpaper.** So if you aren't clean-shaven, watch your stubble.
- **Try a variety of things until you discover specifically what your guy likes.** Everyone has a different "sweet spot" that gets them going. For some it's the tip; for others it's the underside; for some it's deep-throating. Tempo is also impor-

tant here; some like fast and shallow, others slow and deep. Practically everyone likes it when you take a swig of beer, soda, or even warm coffee before starting up. When you find exactly what he likes by experimenting, you'll know it.

▶ **Don't stick to just doing that one thing.** The entire groin is alive with pleasure points, and by hitting them just right, you'll make quite an impression. The inner thighs, the muscle under the balls, the balls themselves, and the cock shaft and head should all be kissed, licked, and sucked. Learn a good routine, but don't be robotic about it.

▶ **There's a reason it's called "sucking."** Don't just open your mouth as wide as possible and plunge. You should relax on the downstroke and suck on the upstroke; thinking of pulling him into you.

▶ **Don't gag (unless you like it).** Blow your nose first so that you can breathe. Lift your chin to make your neck as straight as possible. Alternate deep and shallow rhythm; every so often, use your hands and take a breather. If you're especially gaggy, have oral sex in the A.M.'s, when the reflex is at its weakest.

▶ **Remember your high school geometry.** If his cock curves, the angle of attack is especially crucial; you may have to deep-throat using a "69" position in order for his and your angles to match up.

▶ **Idle hands are . . . just no fun.** You can be stroking his balls, tugging at his nipples, rubbing his thighs and stomach, or massaging his butthole and prostate.

How to Have Anal Sex

Before you were born, there was a big joke going around the Uranians (as gay men were called at the time): "If God had intended men to get fucked, he would've put a little hole where their butts are." Thankfully he did, and thankfully he made it one of the most profound sex organs ever. When properly clean (Summer's Eve, anyone?), properly lubricated, and properly relaxed, your ass will love being touched, caressed, toyed with, stretched, and probed, and your prostate gland, that clitoresque bump just inside, will crave being pumped, rubbed, and massaged.

If you've never been fucked, you're in for a real treat. First learn what a responsive, stimulating sex organ your butthole really is. Give yourself an enema, and then, with mild soap and water, slowly wash, inside and out. Make sure you're completely cleaned out, but don't force it; washing your ass can be a fun thing in and of itself if you relax and take it easy, for the first few times at least.

Rub and play with your body—your tits, balls, cock, whatever feels good. Lube up your finger real good, and start playing with your butthole. Try different positions to find which one's the most comfortable for you; some guys like lying on their back; others like being curled up on their side; still others prefer standing up with their back arched. You're going to be learning how to relax enough so that your butthole opens up all by itself, so comfort, especially at these early stages, is really important.

Probe and explore your sphincter muscles with your finger, and after a while you'll feel yourself starting to open up. Take your time; what's the rush? Rub just the outside at first, then give yourself a few fingerfucks; if you're relaxed, you'll be amazed at how easy this is and how good it feels. Take a short break if you need to, and try two fingers, then three. Buy yourself a buttplug that's about the size of two fingers and a dildo that's about the size of four; with your fingers and new toys, give your prostate a gentle massage. Find the spot, the speed, and the angle that feels the best; everyone's is different, and the wrong angle and action can be less than fulfilling and sometimes can hurt. When your wonderful lover fucks you, the position you're in and the way he does it should match up with what you've discovered.

Breaking yourself in with another man is a significant step; some guys love to pop cherry and are great at it; others range from somewhat to all-out incompetent. If you've got a lover or fuck buddy who really gets you hot, talk to him about it; he should have a playful, experimental, calm, and soothing style—as well as be the kind of guy who can instantly stir your loins. The right man will hold you and kiss you and suck you while playing with your butt; he'll take it slow and easy; he'll know to get you turned on and excited, just to the point of coming, before starting up; to begin with one, two, and then three fingers before putting in his cock; to put in his cock and wait for you to get used to it before pumping; and to pull out and stop whenever you feel the need. He'll know to use gobs and buckets of lube (and of course a rubber); to watch your face to see if you're getting uncomfortable; to be responsive when you think it's time for a break. He'll make you feel adventurous instead of awkward, and cherish being with you for this significant moment in your life. If you don't think you've got a guy who can do this just right, then wait for the right one to come along; your first time should be with a great, patient, understanding, and extremely sexy man.

The whole point here is to take it easy and let yourself relax; there will probably be some mild physical discomfort at first, but if you wait for penetration until you're loosey-goosey, there shouldn't be any real, tearing pain. If it is a problem, tell him to pull out, relax, and start again; almost always the pain will magically disappear; your butt's getting used to this. At certain times you'll probably think you need to take a dump, but after a while you'll learn which feeling is part of getting fucked and which feeling is indeed needing to take a dump.

One relaxation technique that many guys use is to take deep, slow breaths, concentrating on each in-and-out of the lungs, even imagining exhaling through the ass to focus the relaxation there. Everyone has a different favorite, hottest, most comfortable position to get fucked in; for the first time you might want to do it with him lying down and you sitting on top; it's a little awkward, but then you can be in control of all the action. Don't ignore the rest of sex and just lie there focusing on this one thing; play with him just like you always have before.

Many anal virgins are worried that they can be seriously injured. If you use plenty of lube and wait to relax, this is extremely rare. There can be mild tears in the skin, which will heal up quickly all by themselves; if after sex, however, you have a searing pain when you take a dump, you might have gotten a fissure, which does mean a trip to the doctor, but is about as serious as a hemorrhoid. Serious injury can result from going nuts with toys and fisting, especially if you use a vibrator (or unique food item) which doesn't have a proper hand grip and can slip inside. Not only can a punctured colon lead to a very serious, life-threatening case of peritonitis, but having to go to the hospital to get something fished out of your butt can be somewhat embarrassing (though believe me, the guys in E.R. have seen it all before).

After you've become adept with the basics, you can then learn the secret of a great fuck: the Squeeze Play. Get used to his fucking rhythm, then, when you feel his cock all the way in and about to pull back, clamp down; when it's almost out and about to plunge in, release. Squeeze; release; squeeze; release; pull him into you just like you learned in the oral-sex techniques above. Guys who've mastered the Squeeze Play never have to worry about getting laid ever again; in fact, they are thought of as living legends, with hundreds of hunky tops clamoring for their favors.

Fuck Buddies

The bed is like a metaphysical arena in which we play out the basic drama of our existence. . . . Bed can be a place where we play out our fear of intimacy. . . . Bed can be the place where two children hold hands against the mysterious terrors of the adult world. . . . Bed can also be the place where an individual's love affair with life explodes and overflows in a torrent of joy and excitement. Bed can be a place in which two lovers, in the act of worshipping each other, overflow the boundaries of flesh and spirit and make manifest the deepest values of their existence.

—NATHANIEL BRANDEN

A fuck buddy (f.b., instead of b.f.) is someone who, after a few dates, doesn't hold out much lover promise but is sexually compatible enough and personably agreeable enough, so why not keep seeing each other for sex? Although f.b.'s can eventually become friends or lovers, that's extremely rare; they commonly remain more than acquaintances but less than dates. Many feel that, save for a lover, they are the perfect relationship: good sex, with no expectations, no emotional quandaries, no pressure. Practically all of us have had our string of fuck buddies, but they are probably the least-explored arena of gay life.

There is no real counterpart to f.b.'s in the traditional het world, and there are no commonly held rules about what you're supposed to do with them. Too many times fuck buddies don't treat each other especially well: Each is a sex object for the other and not much else; each feels free to dump the other without regret; at some point the fact that there is no future here degrades the pleasure enough just to call the whole thing off. Frequently of course one side is hoping for more while the other likes things the way they stand, or one is still in "dating" mode while the other is just passing time. There are many fuck-buddy permutations, but even if both sides see eye-to-eye on their relative positions in each other's life, the whole thing is vague, uncertain, and unstable, with each waiting for something better to come along.

There's no reason why, with your next f.b., you can't be more than kind even though he's less than kin. This time try to see if you can't get more of a friendship going, if you can't stay in touch and include him in your life after things naturally come to an end. Just because we all have a tradition of treating our fuck buddies dismissively and not taking them seriously doesn't mean we can't upend that convention (just as we've done with so many others) and start something better, something new.

Seduction: Tone, Mood, Imagination, Variety

Couples often ask how they can keep sex alive and interesting after many years together. If we stop and think about it, this is a rather strange question. Who has ever heard a musician ask how to stay interested in music, or a poet complain about being bored by poetry?

—John Welwood

Most guys throwing a party for a few friends would spend hours on planning and preparation—but never go through any similar effort for a date. Especially if you have some feelings of inadequacy (and who doesn't?), compensating by putting some thought into seduction—setting the tone, creating a mood, and using your imagination—will carry you far. Even a pinhead knows how to pull something together for the first few dates: Dance music for hard-pumping sex, earthy chanteuses for soft, romantic sex; drinks and salty snacks for pre-sex and sugar foods for post-; candles and rheostats to help in making both parties feel comfortable in getting naked and getting it on. But it's when you've been seeing someone on a regular basis that seduction really comes into play.

One of humankind's closest genetic relatives, the pygmy chimps of Zaire, know this only too well. They like sex in the missionary position, but they also like switching over with the receptive partner on top, they love sex while lap-sitting, very much enjoy doggy-style, sometimes have both standing up, and really love fucking while hanging from tree limbs. If pygmy chimps can be this imaginative, why can't you?

If you're going steady with another man, you can have one of two attitudes about your sex together. The most common attitude is you know what you both like and you just do it, over and over by rote, like reciting math tables in the second grade: I cook—he cleans—cuddling with VCR porn—oral foreplay—to bed—missionary position—cigarette. While this may make for a perfectly nice evening, the other attitude you can have just as easily is that, since you've gotten to know each other so well, why not be completely bold about trying something new? As much as they love comfort, consistency, and knowing what to expect, all men, just as much, crave excitement, novelty, and delight, and nowhere can you see these opposing feelings stronger than in bed.

If you're nervous about this, the next time you're on the phone with him and making plans to get together, blurt it out: "You know what I'd really like to do? You walk in and

I've left the door unlocked and I'm already naked in bed and . . ." You can see how he responds, and if he doesn't like some mildly spicy fantasy, it's his problem—and maybe you should consider opening your eyes to some new adventures. Of course you don't want to upset someone with too much of a surprise, but if you give it some thought and it's someone you know, you'll do just the right thing.

You can get sex ideas from your memories of past dates and lovers, from masturbation fantasies you've always wanted to try but never have, and even from watching porn (one caveat: beach sex, with all that sand, is never as good as it looks). You can also try the following basic and simple techniques, ready in less than an hour:

Talk That Talk   If you're not verbal in bed, you're a fool. The right compliments and suggestions will inspire your lover to new heights of screwing and new feelings of sexual comfort. Tell him what a great lay he is, how much you like what he's doing, what great sex you have together, and what you want him to do next. One night beg; another demand; and another, be completely silent and use only your eyes and hands and sounds to accomplish exactly the same thing.

Talking during foreplay can be the most seductive thing you could ever do, especially if the two of you have a carnal history: "Remember the time when we _____, and then you _____, and then I _____? That was so hot!" You can also describe, in explicit detail, what you'd like to do for the evening, creating a script and seeing if his interest is aroused.

Reverse Time   If you're always doing dinner—cuddling —sex—sleeping, try a flip. There's one of my all-time favorites, making out—sex/dinner—cuddling—sleeping; believe me, when you're in a postlovemaking state of bliss and relaxation (and you're starving), food's never tasted so good. In this scenario, however, going to a nice restaurant is better than dragging your naked butt off to the kitchen.

Of course there's also appetizer—foreplay—main course —sex—dessert (especially good for oral enthusiasts), and making out—sex—dinner—cuddling—nap—dancing—sex —sleeping, for you energetic youngsters.

Toning Up
If you tend to have the same mood and tone every time you have sex, upend it tonight. Leave some rubbers and lube near your entryway, and the minute he walks in the door, say, "Hello," strip him, and get to it. Work it so that he opens the door and there you are naked on the couch, on your hands and knees, lubed and hard and ready. If you're always doing soft sex, try something rough and anonymous for a change; if you fall into strict top/bottom modes, start off with some role reversal. Try rough, trick sex; fun "boys will be boys" sex; or deeply serious "I'm so much in love with you" tones, if they're not a usual part of your repertoire.

Take one element of your lovemaking, turn it upside down, and you're in business.

Tease
If you're usually Mr. Available, don't be. Play with his expectations by leaning forward to kiss and then stopping, reaching out to do all the things you usually do but then doing something else; prep him for what he expects, and upend it. Toy with him, cat-and-mouse, until he's ready.

Coitus Interrupts
The next time you see your lover working industriously at his desk, get under there and blow him. The next time he spends a big effort on making you dinner, lube him up and fuck him. When he runs off to shower before sex, jump in there and kill two birds with one

stone. Use surprise to your advantage; if he complains, you can always just say, "Shut up and bend over."

Location, Location, Location   Try to seduce him onto every single piece of furniture you own (and don't forget the shower). It's also good to have sex at both of your offices; if you don't have enough privacy there, the boss's office or storage rooms are always good in a pinch. In the boss's, though, be careful for stains on those ubiquitous white Haitian cotton sofas.

Bad Boys   It's Act 3 of *Parsifal* and you've been sitting in that mezzanine seat for how long? Six hours? Listening to the same *motivs* over and over. You turn to your desired and whisper, "Come with me, I have to talk to you about something right now." You lead him out into the lobby and say, "Not here. This way." You lead him right into a bathroom stall, announce "I just can't *control* myself," and have sex then and there. The rest of the opera will be completely memorable and, since it's Wagner, you didn't miss a thing.

You can use this technique at a bar or dance club, but usually the prissier the place—the opera, the theater, a fancy restaurant, out with your parents—the more shocking and fun the surprise.

Ask Him, Goddammit!   Every so often, ask your man, "What haven't we done in bed yet that you've always wanted to do?" If he doesn't come up with anything on his own, tell him to remember to say so the next time he thinks of something, and bring up a few scenarios yourself to see if they rouse his interest.

The Porno Script   If either you or he feels uncomfortable saying what you really want to do in bed, try each writing a hot piece of porn: "I come home from work and all the lights are off and the house seems empty. I call your name, but there's no answer; I get a little worried, wondering where you are. I go back into the bedroom and find you standing there, naked, ready, your eyes telling me just what to do." You can make it as explicit and specific as you want. Then trade off and read your stories to each other; ask questions if you don't understand your role. Pick a script, set a date, and "Lights, camera, action!"

Position Available   One time I was dating a man in his mid-forties (who'd been with plenty of other guys) and we were having sex with him sitting in my lap. He said, "I've never done this before! This is wonderful!" and I was so astonished that at first I could only think, "He must be lying." At that age he'd never before assumed one of the most charming bed positions available?

If you haven't met someone who understands the art of the gymnast, or if you haven't at least browsed through the *Kama Sutra* to learn about "lap dancing," "over the mountain and through the woods," "gift wrap," "still waters run deep," "the industrious mole," and "the hopping frog" . . . what are you waiting for?

S&M

> *Trahit sua quemque voluptas.**
>
> —Virgil

S&M refers to a very wide range of sexual interest and behavior, from a fetish for leather goods and men who like to have

---

* *Chacun à son goût.*

their nipples pulled a little harder than normal, to out-and-out slave-and-master relationships, which include immobilizing bondage and contests of pain. Maybe you're one of the many men who are interested and excited by (though completely inexperienced in) S&M but who are terrified of going to leather clubs, thinking you'll be bound, gagged and whipped the minute you step through the door (in your dreams). Though this never happens, leather clubs *are* really frightening, since where else would you see four-hundred-pound hirsute men encased in three thousand dollars' worth of cowhide and fifty pounds of chains sauntering about? In fact the most common occurrence at an S&M club is that you meet someone and he whispers, "Rip my tits off! Bite them in half! Just tear me from limb to limb!" Then, when you barely touch him, he says, "ARE YOU TRYING TO KILL ME?!"

Though the majority of leatherbar denizens are only in it for the costumes, the ritual, and the theater, real S&Mers frequently develop very tight bonds with their lovers. Each has found another who matches the specific kink that they've always wanted to explore, and the secret romance of S&M is the great amount of trust between lovers that develops in bed. You must have great faith in another human being to let him tie you up till you're immobile and allow him to do whatever he wants; when it comes to pain, he has to be completely empathic to your desires to know how much is just right and how much is too much. Great S&M sex allows two men to explore, as far as they can, the hard-core animal elements of their personalities, and it can create a bond that's richer than that between vanilla lovers.

Or, of course, S&M can also just be an excuse to frequent army-navy boutiques while keeping the American cattle industry going during a period when consumers are eating less beef and more chicken and fish.

Sex offers a direct, sensory confirmation that happiness is possible. . . . A crucial element in this experience is the perception of our efficacy as a source of pleasure to the person we love. . . . We feel, in effect, "Because I am what I am, I am able to cause him to feel the things he is feeling." Thus, we see our own soul, and its value, in the emotions on the face of our partner.

—NATHANIEL BRANDEN

Chapter 6

♂ Date Tips for Guys

Experience is a hard teacher; she gives the test first, and the lesson afterward.

—Anonymous

It's the morning after. You met someone wonderful and the evening was legendary; you're both wiped out from so much terrific sex; you're both dizzy with euphoria from being with a guy who hits all your buttons (and only lets you sleep for three hours). Isn't it great? And isn't it terrible that the instant this bliss wears off, a new and not-so-fun idea pops right up: Will I see him again? You're aching to get together again but you don't really know what he thinks; you're filled with hope and wracked with nerves, all at the same time.

Have you ever thought that between gay men, the traditional boy-girl rules of mating don't apply, and you're confused about what you're supposed to do next? Welcome to the club. With straights it's always the guy's responsibility to call, and both parties know what's expected; but even the most sophisticated gay men can get emotionally stumped by things being unclear from time to time.

On top of that, most hets get to practice dating and mating

throughout their teen years, while most gay guys are still in the closet, dating only women, and only out of obligation and shame. So let's say you come out in your late teens or early twenties; basically you're just starting, then, to date others with whom you might really want to fall in love and get hitched. No wonder you feel awkward and goony. If you or your potential flame are just coming to grips with being gay, you or he may be swinging back and forth, wanting a man but then holding back, never committing because you just aren't there yet.

It's a pile of fish, as one man pointed out:

I often think about how straight people get the benefit of experience in socialization through "ordinary" means usually denied to gay people, and they benefit from it at an earlier age. We never (most of us anyway) got to date in junior high (or, not the person we really wanted to date), never got to go through the interpersonal developmental stuff among a circle of young friends with whom we could compare notes on experiences as well as people we'd met. I often wonder if some of the supposed trouble we have (I say "supposed" because I'm not sure all of our interpersonal difficulties are that much different from straights) are only delayed rather than inherently that different. I wonder if we don't get to go through some of the same situations—that is, puppy love, "false starts" on serious relationships, dating blues, crushes, all that—but it's just that it shows up later because we often only begin to interact romantically later, after a process of coming out and finding our community.

The Hearts of Men

Besides the delays in dating education, there's another secret problem we have. From looking at all the books, magazine articles, TV, and radio talk shows focusing on love and desire, you'd get the idea that women are the emotional ones and men are tough brutes who only want to fuck. This myth is repeated so often that it's become completely accepted in the United States, but wake up: The truth is that it's the men who are the emotional ones. Remember what's happened to you in the past with other guys, and you'll see it's completely true.

If we men are so tough, then why, when we're sick, do we all turn into such out-and-out babies? If emotions are such nothings to us guys, then why do we have such a hard time talking about them? If being part of a couple is so insignificant for us, then why are so many men totally devastated when it's over? Men's emotions are so overwhelming that we are constantly waiting for the other guy to make the first move at every single occasion (just look at any bar), and we're immediately gripped by fear if we're seeing someone and things aren't going absolutely perfectly. Women constantly say how *they* always have to be the leaders when it comes to romance, how they have to make undying declarations of eternal love just to get their guy to start thinking long-term stuff.

When you think about it, it's no surprise. Deep in our hearts, we men are all a bunch of chickens, and you can see it just about everywhere you look. Kevin is the kind of guy who works out every single day, going to one of New York City's most popular gay gyms, and he had this to say:

Did you read (I think it's called) *The Secret Life of Dogs?* There was this one dog in it, Misha, who never had anything to do with dogs smaller than him or bigger than him; he'd only have anything to do with dogs about his own size. Misha never was going after sex (maybe he was neutered); it was all about status.

Well, I think that's what happened at my gym. Everyone there is now looking for status, not sex like they used to. It's almost become like, if you have sex with someone who you're going to see all the time since you both work out there, it's incest or something. Everyone now says, "I'm only here to work out."

When you go all the time, you see lots of funny things, like guys who you know really want each other but neither makes a move. Finally one of them gets really frustrated, or mad that things aren't happening, and gets a little nasty with the other guy, and then that one's pissed too. So from then on there they are, still turned on by each other but now both thinking at the same time that the other guy's an asshole!

Why Wait?

If I think I may want to see someone again, I always try to get his number, wait a day or two, take a deep breath, and make that call. Of course it's not the greatest moment of my life when he claims not to remember who I am (or has a less-than-great memory of our meeting), but sometimes it happens, and sometimes something terrific happens next. Not taking the responsibility means putting a part of your future into someone else's hands, and since sooner or later when you're married you'll be doing too much of that anyway, try being in the driver's seat for now. If you wait for the call, if you wait for the "let's spend the weekend together" invites, if you wait for the "let's talk moving-in, sweet darling, I can't live without you" conversation, you may be waiting a lifetime.

Another thing to remember on this issue is that no matter how cool, butch, suave, macho, or devil-may-care this new date may be, he's going through exactly the same second thoughts, worries, concerns, and analyses that you are—unless he's autistic. Frequently in fact the cooler and smoother the man, the more intensely felt are his worries and needs for a lover. If you're comfortable enough with your own emotions, you can feel free to let them out, but if not, wouldn't you try that ever-popular Marlboro Man persona? You may be seeing a hard-hat tough guy or a growly-voiced bodybuilder or a hotshot corporate honcho and think, "They're so butch, they'll take the lead and make all the man moves." But in fact it's exactly these kinds of guys who are usually the biggest chickens when it comes to romance, and you'll probably end up doing most of the work.

Moving a pair of guys from one stage to the next—from making eye contact to meeting each other, an evening together, date two, seeing each other regularly, spending weekends together, spending weeknights together, serious real estate talk—always takes effort. One of you has to have the nerve; the other, if he's not ready to move yet, has to know how to say, "Not right now, but maybe soon." Each change is delicate, because in each one the couple has to negotiate and make up their own rules in deciding what's right for them.

Slam! Bam! Thank you, Sam!

For many, many years one thing that really distinguished us from hets was that if we met someone terrific and didn't jump into bed with them immediately, it was considered odd. I always thought that way; we had the freedom, so why not? But after interviewing many guys, I've had second thoughts. For many men there are a huge number of reasons to consider dating like high-schoolers at least a few times before jumping in the sack.

Colin has his emotions ruled by great sex; if he meets

someone and the guy's pleasant enough and two hours later they're both covered in sweat from nonstop fucking, Colin is *in love*. He wants to see as much of this man as he possibly can, and he frequently gets into these sort of sex-addict things that last about a month; then either he finds out the guy's "not who he thought he was" or the guy gets burned out by the immediate, intense relationship Colin's thrown at him . . . and it's all over.

Joel can't really respond to someone sexually on the first date; he gets into bed and lies there like a big dead eel, letting the other guy do whatever but barely responding. Later after he gets to know someone, he'll be as passionate and carnal as any Sicilian teenager, but most of the men he meets on one-nighters never get to find that out. Since his onetime lovers never had any necrophiliac tendencies in the first place, Joel rarely gets a second chance. If either of these men dated a few times, got to know someone, and then went to bed, their romantic lives might stabilize, and the sex would be even better than ever.

Switching from "slam, bam, thank you, Sam!" to dating isn't easy, but you're up to it. Ask him out to dinner at some relaxed, casual place; put your best foot forward, but do what you can to put him at ease; tell him the stories of your life that allow for a little closeness without making it look like you're proposing marriage. And try to have a good time doing all this, for a change.

Most of us are lonely; most of us would really like to be with another man over the long term; most of us would like to have the home and family life we may not be getting from our blood relatives because we're gay. Dating, which should be light, fun, easy, and pleasant, becomes charged, tense, and nerve-wracking because of this undertow. If you're a bundle of nerves just going to a movie with someone new, try to lighten up, for chrissakes! Click your heels and think, "It's only a date. It's only a date." The more relaxed you are, the more yourself you are, and the more attractive you'll be. Stop thinking this Chinese dinner is a crucial life moment and at any second you're going to fuck it up.

Taking a light approach when it comes to meeting guys is really the best way to go. When I told my mom that I was single again for the first time in twelve years and wasn't it fantastic, she said, "Are you getting a new hairdo?" It was the perfect attitude. Everyone today is so serious and traumatized over being single; just for a change, try a new-hairdo point of view.

You could also try making a date as easy as possible. Go where there are few distractions—no drop-dead go-go boys, ear-splitting noise, or big-screen TVs—and food that's easy to eat. As Judith Newman advised, "This is not the time to be hoisting those oversize sandwiches at the Carnegie Deli, leaving your date with the impression you were raised by wolves." The crowd noise should be perky but ignorable; tables should be intimate but not bedroomy, and lighting should be flattering but, again per Ms. Newman, "Don't go where candles are the primary source of light: you'll end up resembling Marlon Brando in 'Apocalypse Now.' You want to look mysterious, not frightening."

Reining Queens

So let's say you've done it . . . and now you're seeing someone steady, and things are looking pretty good. If your engines are racing, try to remember another crucial love law: *patience*. Learn to tell yourself, "Whoa, boy!" every so often; it will almost always make things smoother. Too often we jump to conclusions when a roadblock appears on the path to domestic bliss. With patience you can jump the blocks and be on your merry way.

Examples: You're love at first sight, while your new guy's slow to make up his mind; you're ready to go *chuppa* shopping, while he's still playing the field; you're thinking closet space, while he's never lived with anyone before in his life and isn't sure he wants to start now. If things are going well between you, be patient; don't be so fast to call the whole thing off just because he's not ready to move to the next level, and don't get annoyed if the shoe's on the other foot and you think he's being pushy and demanding. Make your desires known, but if he's not ready, get him to say how he feels and reassure yourself. Don't jump to conclusions.

Why are we all so quick to think the worst? In L.A. there's a local gay version of the TV show *Studs* called *Tricks*. One of the show's producers discovered that if the guys' first date did not go all-out gangbusters and fireworks but was merely okay, both of them thought exactly the same thing: that the other one didn't like him.

So why don't you stop being so quick to judge and so quick to think the worst—and give the guy a break? Rein it, queen. The obvious reason why: First-date catastrophes leading to wonderful long-term relationships are so common, they should get their own sitcom. One couple I know met when mutual friends of theirs set them up on a blind date—as a *spoof,* since these friends thought they were such utter opposites that it'd be funny to see what happened. It was funny, and they've been together for five years. Joel finally met Sal, a wonderful man, and they've been together for two years now, but their first time in the sack Joel was so nervous, he did his "dead thing in bed" routine, almost turning off Sal for good. When Bob and Robert (a couple you'll hear more about later) had their first date after meeting, Robert went to Bob's apartment in a scary part of town; Bob acted so nervous (he'd broken up with a lover of twelve years and was completely out of it being single) that Robert thought he was psychotic and actually feared for his life!

Let's say you've been seeing someone for a while and you're ready to up the emotional ante, but you're not sure how to proceed. Start with small comments about your feelings ("I really enjoy being with you, you know"), and never forget one of the absolutely true clichés about romance:

Little Things Mean a Lot

Believe it or not, all the old-fashioned dating ideas from your childhood should come into play at this moment. There's no one alive, for example, who doesn't get a thrill from opening the door to someone they find attractive holding a bouquet of flowers (candy is iffy; see "You and Your Mirror," page 8), and there's no one alive who doesn't enjoy a candlelit dinner with wonderful food, great wine, and someone he enjoys. Don't overwhelm them with romance; just try some moves now and then, served lightly.

In college I met someone completely attractive but didn't know what he thought about me. One day as we were talking, I mentioned the name of one of my favorite artists. That night a book of his drawings was left at my door. It wasn't an expensive book, but the thought behind it struck with a bolt —I swooned and fell for him right then and there.

If your guy loves dance music, how much effort does it take to show up at your next date with the hot new CD? One time I was seeing a man who was just getting over a cold; when we got together, I made him screwdrivers with fresh-squeezed orange juice. This small grace impressed him deeply (who would've thought?), but it's exactly this kind of thoughtfulness that makes relationships move to a deeper level.

Nothin' Spells Lovin' Like Something from the Oven

What is the most common denominator in worldwide court-ship? You get food and I get laid. Dating with meals must satisfy some primal urge; during illicit trysts between Amazonians, the guy usually brings his sweetie a fish; mean-while, in Arizona, the male roadrunner usually brings his woman a lizard. The most extreme case is the black-tipped hang fly, who catches something tasty—an aphid, a daddy longlegs—and has sex with his little gal while she eats it.

Bringing food to your lovechild, in whatever manner, shows you're the kind of man who's able to provide the necessities of life, just like our primeval forefathers. While of course it's lots of fun to take or be taken out to a knock-your-socks-off five-star big-bucks restaurant extravaganza, any meal can be romantic if you and your sweetie are in the right mood. Cuddling with pizza and beer can be one of the most memorable times in your life together. Food you can eat with your fingers (also known as food you can feed each other with your fingers) can be especially erotic and roman-tic. Figs, anyone?

When you're ready to move on to the next stage in your dating, cooking your lovebug a meal is way up there on the "urge to merge" charts. There's no man alive who isn't thrilled to see the guy of his desires coming at him with a big plate of something smelling wonderful. Even if you're no kitchen magician, the effort you put into providing a little domestic bliss will warm the cockles of his heart. If you're truly incompetent, you can at least try a little breakfast now and then (or cheat and find out what deluxe restaurants in your neighborhood will do home deliveries).

One of my exes is a great cook, and when we were to-gether, my friends eagerly looked forward to Christmas Eve and Easter and his eye-popping feasts. Seeing him make everyone so content and delighted, not just with the food but with the feeling of home, comfort, and family that such a meal creates, drove me further into his arms . . . and of course I also got to eat.

Comfort and Delight

Just as later we'll see how balance is a key to many things—balancing similarities and differences in a couple, balancing being together and being apart to strengthen our identities together and as individuals—good long-term daters and lovers learn how to balance comfort (making someone feel that you are steady, solid, there for them) and delight (doing what surprises, excites, and makes things new again). Some have trouble knowing how to make others feel relaxed; others don't work hard enough to create delight (you know exactly who you are). Knowing and practicing these techniques will make your life together more enjoyable, more passionate, more fully lived as a couple.

For Comfort:

▶ See him on a regular basis so that you both come to expect that you'll be together at certain times.

▶ Don't be stingy with compliments. You find him attractive? Say why.

▶ Find out what he likes to eat and drink (and so forth), and stock up. Learn what beverage he likes in the evenings, what special meal he likes for breakfast, and how he takes his coffee—and remember these things.

▶ Make sure he knows where things are in your bathroom and

kitchen so that he can shower, brush his teeth, get something to drink, and in general feel a *mi casa es su casa* kinda thing.

▶ Learn how he likes his back rubbed. If he's tired or has a cold, offer to rub his back, neck, and/or feet.

▶ During the winter warm his towel in the dryer while he's showering so that it's nice and toasty when he steps out.

▶ Have a robe or something nice he can wear for lounging around later that night or the next morning.

▶ Read aloud to each other in bed. Spend an entire day in bed.

▶ Tell him often enough about your steady (or growing) feelings.

▶ Cuddle, both with and without sex.

▶ Let him have the remote control.

▶ If you're going to be more than a few minutes late, call.

▶ If you have to be apart for a while, tell him the truth: You missed him.

For Delight:

▶ Show up with small gifts. Flowers, cookies, dried fruit, wine, his favorite liquor, his favorite rubbers, stylish underwear, or the right-sized dildo are always appreciated. But try showing up with different things, not the same damn daisies, which will soon be taken for granted. And every so often hide them so that he'll find them later.

▶ Send mail. It's great to come home from a bad day and find "bill, bill, junk, junk, ad, a letter from Rick?" It can be anything —passionate love letter, cartoon from the paper, interesting horoscope, funny magazine article. Just mail it.

▶ If your dates tend to be pricey, try something free; if most are cheap, splurge.

▶ Be eco-minded and shower together.

▶ Buy tickets to something you know he wants to see, but tell him only to mark his calendar and make it a surprise.

▶ Hide love notes where you know he'll find them later.

▶ If you're having ravenous sex dates, bring over video rentals and popcorn. If you're having video rental and popcorn, try a ravenous sex date.

▶ Use the special weekend package deals to stay in a fine hotel.

▶ Switch date plans, with surprise theater tickets or surprise restaurant reservations (but not if they require a sudden change of clothes).

▶ If you're meeting in a public place, give him a hug (and if you're nervous about PDAs—public displays of affection—make it a manly, football-player hug).

▶ Know his clothing sizes so that you can buy him things on the spur of the moment.

▶ No matter how long you've been together, keep dating.

▶ Godiva: 1-800-447-9393.

▶ Western Union: 1-800-325-6000.

▶ If you're starting to spend a lot of time staying home (and everyone goes through this period), come up with some adventure dates: horseback riding, boating, bicycling, miniature golf, a quick drive out of town to someplace odd.

▶ Take the date of something remarkable that happened between you and turn it into an anniversary.

▶ Add variety to your fucking with the "seduction" ideas in chapter 5.

Morning Sickness

So you've been seeing someone and of course you always want him to see you at your very best. You're working out more at the gym, spending more time thinking about what you're going to wear, getting your hair cut more often, thinking about what would make him happy, ignoring the little things he does that bother you, knocking yourself out to be great in bed. Then you start sleeping together—and the awful truth comes out when you wake up.

Mornings are a real test; it's when we're the least in control, the least rational, and the most our true selves. It's also when our facial muscles slacken and we look our absolute worst. Spending the night and sleeping together is meaningful on the path to romance because it means waking up together the next day, making you at this point more than mere dates. If you wake up comatose and want things quiet while pulling yourself together, while he pops out of bed in a full manic rage, fully organized, cooking major breakfasts and singing dance-hit medleys, you may balance out perfectly—or you may need to be able to afford major real estate, with room to get away from each other. Starting the day together nicely is crucial; if you can't do it, major trauma looms ahead.

At some point one of you is bound to insist that you undergo another one of Dating's Big Hurdles: "I've got a place to stay for free in San Francisco; wanna go?" Blowing town together is a major test of your potential couplehood; you can see how well you do together facing great pleasure . . . and great stress. Does it make you insane when you like to get to the airport ninety minutes early and he likes to see if they'll hold the plane? Does he lose his mind when you're both lost in the middle of nowhere because you read the map wrong? If a hotel causes trouble on your reservation because it's two men, will one of you stand up and take charge, or does it lead to a big squabble over who's out and who's in the closet?

Traveling as a pair can throw into startling 3-D how you deal with each other. Does he go along with whatever you want to keep the peace until finally there's a last straw and he blows up real good? Are you so intent on running the show that you both end up feeling like you're in a pretriathlon training session? Or are you both so ultra accommodating that you end up having Chip 'n' Dale conversations ("After you." "No, after you." "No, I insist, after *you*.") and you end up getting nowhere and doing nothing? On a trip you'll be finding out many things about each other, and very quickly.

All this of course is minor, compared with the ultimate challenge:

"Mom, Dad, I Want You to Meet My Special Friend!"

Wouldn't it be great if everyone in our families were just like all those loving, sharing, caring, understanding, and devoted Tom Hanks relatives in *Philadelphia*? Instead, when you bring Antonio Banderas home to dad, you know just what he's thinking: "Which one of you is the woman?" Some parents may even think that your boyfriend made you gay and that if he weren't in the picture, you'd be married and siring grand-children, just like they always wanted.

One of the major reasons finding the right guy is so important for so many of us is the lack of strong ties we may have with our blood relatives due to our being gay. The following is a true conversation:

"Hey, Mom, how're you doing?"

"I'm fine, dear. How about you?"

"Oh, you know, things aren't going so well with Robert; my job's sort of tough right now . . . I could be better, I guess."

"Oh . . . do you remember Susan Castrello?"

"From high school? Sure. What about her?"

"Well, she's dead. So count your blessings!"

We commonly transfer the family needs we're not getting from parents and siblings onto our lovers, and together make a new family all for ourselves. Wouldn't it be fantastic if our new domestic life and our original family could be merged into one big, strong combo—and isn't it really a shame how seldom this happens?

Even if you're fully out to your parents, there are many things about gay life they may not understand, and perhaps before meeting your boyfriend they were able to put your being gay comfortably out of their minds. With him in the picture, though, it really is an issue for them to think about; they may be relieved you've found someone and aren't out stalking the high schools, but the physical presence of that someone also allows them to imagine "things." So if you and Antonio walk in expecting the family to jump for joy like they did when big sis announced her wedding plans, lower those expectations.

Most straight people your parents' age don't really know anything more about gay men than what they figured out from watching Paul Lynde and Charles Nelson Reilly on *Hollywood Squares*. Besides "which one's the woman," they'll look at the two of you and wonder, "Is this going to last longer than a week? If so, are they going to have a wedding? Are they going to adopt children? And how am I supposed to react to all this?"

If you're having problems with your family, you might try to remember that this is new territory for them, and they may not be consciously antagonistic or "difficult" toward your new spouse, it's just that they don't know what the hell to do. Try to behave as you would with any confused person: Be firm but kind, and be patient. If your man's consistently getting left out of invitations to family events, explain all over again the seriousness of your relationship and how the two of you want him to be treated.

For example, many parents freak when they come to the home you share with your lover for the first time and see: *The Bed*. They can't help but imagine all the things about gay men they find less than appetizing (especially when they get a look at the chains hanging from the ceiling). It may be a better idea to let them get to know him outside of your home the first couple of times. If you know they're uncomfortable when you visit them, it may also not be the very worst idea to be okay about sleeping in separate bedrooms. Try some social activities together beyond the usual sitting, eating, and talking. If your b.f.'s a terrific bowler, for example, give him the chance to show off and be something besides "the boyfriend" while having fun with the entire family. If the bedrooms issue is too confrontational, there's always a hotel; then you'll have privacy and they can stop compulsively thinking about the whole damn problem.

As time goes on and as they become more and more comfortable with the idea, you can graduate slowly, piece by piece, to being more and more out with your family. One question that all couples have to deal with is PDAs (public displays of affection): You're torn because on the one hand you don't want to throw the issue in the face of your trying-but-troubled relatives, and on the other, shouldn't they realize you're a couple just like your brother and sister-in-law? While they sit with their arms around each other, every so often kissing and snuggling, you and Antonio are on the other couch like two genital-free Ken dolls—which can only make your relationship seem even odder to your relatives. If this conundrum is bothering you, maybe you should suss out your closest relative: What would everyone else feel if you two were more public? The reaction might be more accepting than you think.

If things are extremely difficult, there's an organization with pamphlets, regional meetings, and other resources: Parents and Friends of Lesbians & Gays (P-FLAG), P.O. Box 27605, Washington, D.C. 20038; 1-800-432-6459.

Heritage Is Destiny

Knowing your guy's genetic background and learning about his cultural characteristics is a huge clue to understanding what makes him tick, especially when what he does baffles you. My own life, for example, has been filled with Slavs. Two of my closest friends are American-born Slavs, a long-time lover and a man I recently fell in love with are both demi-Slavs, and a man I was with for six years was a total Slav. I never need to go to Eastern Europe; enough is enough.

On the surface you would never match up someone like myself who is, politely speaking, *manic,* with a bunch of Slavs —people who are awash in emotions and who bring new meaning to the word "dour." Remember when the Ukrainian orphan teen who won the gold medal in figure skating at the 1994 winter Olympics finished her routine and looked to the audience, supplicating, her eyes brimming with tears? This is what my life has been like since time began.

One of these guys, just sitting and relaxing looks at any minute like he's going to throw himself out the window. I would constantly ask, "What's wrong? Are you okay?" and he'd get really annoyed: *"Nothing!* I'M FINE!" Another wakes up every morning with this mission in life: To find something, anything, to be hideously upset and depressed about. A third is half-German, half-Slavic, and you can watch the two cultures warring it out like a psychological version of *Wrestlemania:* The Slav dystopia undermining the German industry, and the German coolness stifling the Slav warmth. Yes, some of these things are stereotypes, but yes, they do exist in the real world.

So if you can educate yourself about your lover's background, many things he does will become comprehensible, and if you understand the theory about great couples being a mix of similar and different elements, you can see why I'm so involved with this bunch. If I was with someone like me (part of a two-prong manic couple), or if these guys were with someone like themselves (doubling up on depressives), all of us would be driving each other and everyone we know completely insane. While the Slavs and I find each other incomprehensible enigmas, we also balance each other out extremely well; sometimes I have to warm them up and sometimes they have to cool me down.

Rules of the Game

There are going to be certain things stated over and over again in this book that probably should just be gotten out of the way right now: The ten commandments of love, the twelve steps of romance, the key things you need to know for living with men for the rest of your life. You may get tired of hearing them, but you'll never be sorry if you keep them in mind, both now and in the future:

▶ **Know (and love) thyself.** Figure out your strengths, weaknesses, crucial needs, and preferred wants—and give them the priority they deserve. Know your better qualities without losing the desire for self-improvement, but stop beating yourself up over your weaknesses and just accept them for what they are. Know what you really need from another guy and what are just those things that'd be nice but aren't crucial. Your self-respect is entirely in your care at all times and is infinitely more valuable than anyone else's respect for you.

▶ **Think about tomorrow, Scarlett.** Stop what you're doing every so often and really consider: Is this how I want to live, is this who I want to be, in five years? In ten years? Every so often pull back and plan your future. Set your priorities. Stop being afraid of change.

▶ **"He doesn't understand me."** So what? Do you understand *yourself* all the time? No, you really don't. You don't even understand yourself in those very ways you believe others ought to understand you. Nobody ever totally understands anybody else, ever, and this goes double for their own selves. Learn to enjoy this mystery instead of feeling lost, alone, and misunderstood, since we're *all* lost, alone, and misunderstood.

▶ **Be kind.** Instant attraction, love at first sight, perfect for each other, terrific chemistry, whatever you want to call it—it's mostly a leftover from our simian pasts. David Buss, a Michigan psychologist, studied more than ten thousand people in thirty-seven countries and made this discovery: "Men are more likely to just look at the physical features . . . clear skin, smooth skin, full lips, absence of gray hair. Females are more interested in resources . . . dependability, emotional stability, intelligence . . . ambition, industriousness. . . . A real turnoff to women is if the guy doesn't have any goals, or if the guy's lazy."

But what men and women ranked foremost for what they want in a mate is—are you ready?—*kindness*. Perhaps some of us gay men follow the male path, and desire beautiful lovers; some of us follow more of the female trends, looking for successful spouses, and some of us want a mix of both—but it seems all of us, for the long term, want someone who is kind.

As we all know, being a bitchy queen is tons of fun, but when it comes to your sweet love bucket, try a little tenderness —if only for novelty's sake.

▶ **Accrue patience.** Especially if you're thinking of spending the rest of your life with someone, what's the damn rush? He's not doing certain things you want; he's not ready to react in the way you want; he doesn't seem up to the challenge; there's some problem you keep coming up to over and over again. Give him some time; what've you got to lose?

Know how to make a relationship move slowly so that things will last.

▶ **Being wrong, in and of itself, is no big deal.**

▶ **Don't be stingy.** If you're the type who's always scaring guys off because you're completely overpowering and suffocating with your romance, this rule isn't for you. Most men, however, are wary of complimenting their lover on how good he looks, how powerfully he affects them, how great and satisfying he is in bed. They think being stingy is strategic—"If I keep him thinking that I'm iffy, he'll stay on his best behavior"—or that their s.o. gets tired of hearing the same thing over and over again. Most men also like economy; they think, unless they specifically tell you otherwise, that it should be obvious they're happy with you in bed, that they're satisfied with the relationship, that everything's fine.

Not telling him your honest good feelings isn't strategic, it's selfish and shortsighted; how you're feeling isn't obvious; and *no one* ever gets tired of hearing sincere praise. When you truthfully think he looks great, has done something wonderful, is the greatest fuck you've ever had, or that you love him so much, give him praise and give him thanks and tell him what you think. If he keeps being and doing all these things, keep giving praise and thanks and telling him what you think. Especially when it comes to sex, where practically everyone feels inadequate and worries whether or not they're making their lover happy, say how great it was that night and the next morning and as often as you can.

▶ **Don't be so quick to take things personally.** Taking it personally and then getting hurt is probably the most common mistake anyone in love makes; most of the time his bad or distracted mood has nothing to do with you.

▶ **Stop "Looking Out for Number One."** The corollary to not taking things personally is to think of yourselves together as a given as much as possible and to remember your commitment to being a couple. When things are difficult, when he isn't being the world's most perfect beau, when you're not feeling your best, try avoiding the automatic response of "Maybe I should be looking for someone new." Instead of always thinking "me" start thinking "us."

▶ **Give 200 percent of yourself, and remember that your other half thinks he's doing the same.**

▶ **Love your spouse but respect your man.** Balance time together with time apart. Letting him be an individual with his own life, hobbies, and friends without you will only make things stronger when he's with you.

▶ **Use hetero love traditions to your benefit, but don't be bound by their rules.** Why can't men bring each other flowers? Why can't we have marriage or union ceremonies? Why don't we pick the crucial moment of coming together—meeting, first big date, or moving in—and regularly celebrate our anniversaries? Keep the traditions you want, modify them as needed, throw out the ones you don't care for, and stop thinking, "We're reinventing coupledom from scratch."

▶ **Let each relationship last its natural term, whether long or short, appreciating it for what it is instead of what you wanted it to be.**

▶ **Remember to be little boys together.** Every man, no matter how forceful, mature, strong, masculine, straitlaced, rational, analytic, and powerful he may be has a little-boy side to his personality. For John Bradshaw, it's your "inner child" that still holds all the good and bad memories of your youth; for the ancient Greeks it's the Dionysian side of life that celebrates play, excess, chaos, and dreams. If your man's Butcher-than-Thou or an Egghead, he probably thinks this is the side of himself that's weak, irrational, immature, doubting, wacky, confused, polymorphous—and he'd be absolutely right.

Of course there are many "rational" reasons why we couple up with someone in particular: he's good-looking; he's smart; he has financial independence; he's great in bed. But what really magnetizes and holds us together as couples is all our little-boy reactions: "I don't feel lonely when I'm with him," "he comforts me when I'm upset," "we have so much fun together," "he makes me laugh," "he's so sweet, so kind, so gentle, so tender."

Too many men downplay or ignore this side of life. Some grew up with parents who constantly said, "Grow up!" Some are "serious" people doing "serious" work. Some are depressed, or cynical, or in a rut, and fooling around seems foolish to them. There are workaholics, who don't have any time to play, and hyperrationalists, who date solely to meet potential spouses (instead of having any fun) and once they get one, spend hours "working" on the relationship (instead of having any fun).

What commonly happens is that if you don't satisfy that little-boy side on your own, he'll do it for you. Compulsive random acts of meaningless sex; constantly drinking and drugging to the wee hours and to the point of self-destruction; uncontrollable, rebellious acts against your boss; being flighty and whimsical with your friends and dates—all playfulness gone wrong. If you're seeing someone and things start getting tired, dreary, rutty, bland, and diminished, that also means it's time to start being little boys together.

Ride bikes. Play Frisbee in the park with the dog. Wrestle naked. Bring home a toy. Watch a big, stupid Hollywood movie. Join a gay chorus group together. Go bowling. Get in the car, get out of town, and fuck *al fresco*.

Remember to play.

Chapter 7

· ·

♂ # Man Trouble

Old age has brought me the realization that it is impossible to fully and completely know another human being. Thank God.

—GORE VIDAL

Boyfriends come in all shapes, sizes, and colors, each with different interests, skills, tastes . . . and problems that will drive you completely insane. Of course no one alive has perfectly mastered the mental and emotional lover issues discussed in chapter 1 (including you your own self). So when meeting and getting to know a guy, you'll have to decide whether his unique form of love trouble is worth it—while he's having to decide the exact same thing about you.

There are men who are so off, they can't help but stop any potential good thing dead in its tracks. You can shower affection, love, and devotion on someone with zero self-esteem, and instead of being happy about it, they'll think you're a mental case to be crazy about anyone who's as pathetic as they are. If you're dating a guy who's completely unempathic, you'll know it immediately, since he can never figure you out emotionally and, if you want to be on the same wavelength, you're the one who has to do all the work. Some guys demand always to be in control, while others demand just as strongly that you always be in control, and like all these other love troubles, if it's not for you, there's little you can do about it.

When you're struggling to date someone who isn't really ready for a relationship, you may feel like the end of part 1 of *Angels in America,* when an angel crashes through the ceiling of a man's bedroom. The man, who's not ready, sees you, the angel, and he thinks, "Look at this incredible thing in my bedroom!" But he also thinks, "You made a big mess!" One guy I was dating for some time turned to me one evening in bed and said, "I wish I had someone to take care of me." I said, "I'd like to try to take care of you," and he screamed, "I KNOW! I KNOW!" burst into tears, ran away, and was never heard from again. Guess he wasn't ready.

Some gay men have turned the T-shirt slogan, dance-club hit, and favored birthday-cake decoration "So many men . . . so little time" into a philosophical tenet worthy of Socrates. It keeps them flitting like butterflies, never really ready to settle down. If your idea of public gay life is to live in an endless, eternal high school prom, decent boyfriends will not draw near.

You may fall so madly for someone that his personal difficulties fade into nothing; you may even think his less-than-stellar qualities are completely attractive. After all, would Karen Black be the great star we so fondly remember today if she wasn't cross-eyed? But don't think you can change someone, or that with time, all of their Achilles heels will vanish and they'll turn into your dream Mr. Right. All human beings grow and mature, but falling in love with someone for what they *could* be is like wishing on a star. . . . You can only have a relationship with a man the way he is, warts, flaws, and all, and ditto for you.

In 1992 Philip Shaver and Cindy Hazan published the results of a fascinating study, "Adult Romantic Attraction: Theory and Evidence," which found three ways a mother could interact with her baby—and three ways in which adults could interact with their lovers. Though this sounds too Freudian to be credible, the results are so interesting, you might want to know about it.

What Shaver and Hazan did was apply earlier child psychologists' findings to adults. Those kid shrinks had arranged for mothers to leave their very young children alone, in a clinic room, for a couple of minutes and then come back. The returning mothers who were warm, cuddling, and happy to see their children had excited infants who would toddle right over. The women who were cool and distant had babies who were equally cool and nonreacting. The third kind of moms, those who acted erratically, had angry babies who would strike out when they were picked up.

Shaver and Hazan found just the same three types with adults. They believe that of the men you will meet, about 55 percent will be more or less okay about being part of a couple. About 25 percent will be distant, afraid to let others see them, warts and all, not liking it when someone gets too close. About 20 percent are usually afraid that they'll be abandoned, fearful that they're about to get dumped at any minute, and never really feel loved enough. You'll probably want to think, if you fall in love with guys in these latter two categories, that they need professional help and they're bad people and they don't know how to love, or even that they're sick sick sick—when it just turns out to be your mother-in-law's fault. Unfortunately there's probably not much that can be done about it, so you'll have to decide: This is their wart; is it worth it?

Scott Wirth, a Jungian analyst in San Francisco, came up with the following list of typical warts he's come across in therapy with gay men, troubles you may commonly run across in the men you meet:

- A stylized female persona, "the diva, the bitch, the smothering mother, the sexual toy"

- An inflated and grandiose sense of the self

- Intimate relationship problems involving the loss of desire and the separation of desire from emotional closeness

- Overidealizing; compulsive rebellion against authority figures; superficiality or flightiness

- Sexual compulsion

- Social isolation and loneliness

- Grief from AIDS

- Gay ghettoization

- Chemical dependencies, eating disorders

- Inability as an adult to stop being in a child role with others

- Spiritual malaise

- Getting stuck in various gay roles and stereotypes

- Fetishization of body parts

- Hatred of men (having only female friends) or hatred of women (having only male friends)

- Heterophobia, being hostile to marriage and nuclear family life

- Homophobic self-hatred

- Fixation on youth and beauty and a fear of aging

- Overstudied false masculine posing and posturing

Overwhelming, huh? Well, that's just for starters. And you thought *you* had troubles. . . .

The Terminally Single

They're out there, and you've met them already—guys so desperate to find a lover, they turn off anyone who dares draw near. You see them in bars and baths and dance clubs and gyms, looking like plaintive, big-eyed Keane orphans. You try going out with one (since he pursues you like you've never been pursued before), but he's constantly anxious, on guard, tense, and always seems disappointed. On date three he tells you he's madly in love and why don't we just move in together right now? He calls you constantly, and if you don't return the call immediately, if you don't have an answer for every time you're not home and anytime you aren't immediately responsive, he throws a temper tantrum, then apologizes, then says he loves you more than anyone he's ever met . . . but he's always suspicious and nagging. For him life without a lover is an empty vacuum of nothingness.

Terminally Single guys are always looking at needs and holes in their life and thinking, "If I had a lover, this would be fixed." They think of themselves as being halves, and when they meet Mr. Right (their other half), the two will join into a whole. Real relationships between real men, however, are two wholes that join to make something even greater than the sum of its parts, not between guys who think they're half a man.

Many people have said how surprised they were to meet the love of their lives in the most unlikely surroundings, when they weren't even thinking of meeting anyone. But is this really so surprising? When you are desperate to find a husband, the desperation comes off you like an odor; your neediness makes you not the most pleasant person to be around, and you end up repelling exactly the guy you were hoping to get. But when you're satisfied with your life and not even thinking about finding romance, you're natural, casual, completely yourself—exactly the characteristics that will attract friends, sex partners, and possible long-term companions.

The Overenthusiastic Child The minute they turn twenty-one, some men are convinced that they're in imminent danger of becoming old maids, and just like the Terminally Single, they desperately search everywhere for love. After the third date you'll be inundated with phone calls, letters, and gifts; you'll feel like you're drowning in puppies. If you need constant attention, this may be just the guy you're looking for; unfortunately in the same way that he decided in minutes that you're the perfect man for him, he can just as instantly decide you're *not,* and vanish.

The Whiplash Lover This is the man who's always looking over your shoulder for someone better, and thinks, "Someday I'm going to meet a bodybuilding brain surgeon ex-Calvin Klein model millionaire who lives in a mansion conveniently located to midtown and who'll fall madly, devotedly in love with me for my personality." This is a guy who's basically O.D.'ing on "The One" fantasies, and no man alive will ever be "One" enough for him. If you enjoy being publicly humiliated, the Whiplash Lover will fill your life with joy.

The Sex Fiend While there are plenty of guys who turn sports fucking into their lifelong career, the *Fiend* is constantly using anonymous sex to give himself the feelings of self-worth he's not getting anywhere else. The sex hunt for him isn't fun and pleasurable; it's a contest, and a way of avoiding life's pain. He feels empty and lonely, or sad and frustrated; goes out and makes a connection; has a moment of triumph and conquest; then goes home and feels empty, lonely, sad, and frustrated all over again.

Lots of gay men enjoy insta-sex. But is it fun and pleasurable and a way to meet new guys, or is it desperate and uncontrollable and always leaves you feeling undernourished and wanting more—is it junk sex? If his attitude is the latter, and if you're not interested in monogamy and have always wanted to date a roller coaster, perfect.

The Gym Bunny

Not merely someone who spends a lot of time in a gym, this Bunny thinks there's no need for him to do anything else with his life, since everyone is already chasing him for his magnificent buns and pecs. If you can develop a meaningful, lasting relationship with a set of good abs, go for it.

The Butcher-than-Thou

If your romantic ideal is Clint Eastwood or Steven Seagal (while drag queens and swishy behavior make you nauseated), you'll probably end up being with a lot of men whose gay self-hatred is alive and well and living in Tom of Finland drawings. Isn't it just terrific that the key role model for our looks and style these days is a collection of sex cartoons? Dating a Butcher-than-Thou means sharing many intimate moments (such as contests to see which of you can drop your voice three octaves while looking mean and nasty). Spending so much energy trying to top each other in masculinity means, however, that you'll always get a good night's sleep.

The Biological Fetishist

Hot man seeks cornflower blue-eyed, strawberry blond-haired, big-dicked, lightly freckled, goateed muscleman who's a 29–31-year-old nonsmoking financially secure professional living downtown who likes skiing, Rollerblading, championship diving, and light bondage (top). Serious only, please.

Just as rejection has mostly to do with someone's type, there are those with such extreme hysterias over what they prefer, it's a wonder they ever meet anyone. John Tierney calls it "the Flaw-O-Matic," and lists some of the reasons his afflicted single friends used to explain why their last affairlet had gone south:

▶ "She mispronounced 'Goethe.'"

▶ "How could I take him seriously after seeing 'The Road Less Traveled' on his bookshelf?"

▶ "Sure, he's a partner, but it's not a big firm. And he wears these short black socks."

So if you want to spend your life being nagged at over things you can't do anything about and living with someone who finds you endlessly disappointing, this is the right guy for you.

The Middle-aged Kid   When you first meet this kind of man, you'll be completely charmed because he's so fresh and appealing. He's a guy guy (see below) who likes to wrestle, pal around, hang out, and talk about other cute guys on the street. You'll love being with him and being boys together; but then you discover that you get to be boys together *all the time.* He gossips constantly about the friends you have in common; he's always worried about his hair and clothes; he's always swooning over the new kid at the gym; it's like living in an eternal high school. But if your high school memories are better than mine, maybe he's your Mr. Right.

The Closet Case Going out with someone who's still completely in the closet means the only time you feel you have a lover is when the blinds are down and the door is locked. If your ideal man is a CIA agent, here's the one for you; he only whispers "I love you" from pay phones, sneaks into gay bars, and comes up with lots of code words and pseudonyms to run his covert operation—you. Touching or even looking at him with affection in public is out of the question; he may even feel uncomfortable about it in a room filled only with other gay men. You may find his idea of "forbidden love" spicy and exciting, or it may get real old real quick.

One time I was with a closet queen and didn't know it. He was completely passionate and generous and very, very sexy; but after six months he called to say, "I never want to see you again. I never wanted to be gay, but you talked me into it, you made me do it," and I was totally dumped. Ouch!

The Judge We all have our own ideas about how things should be done and how life should be lived; The Judge believes he holds the secrets to life and can't wait to make you, his special friend, very happy. You'll learn how to load the dishwasher, how to handle all troubles at your job, what deodorant to use, how to buy clothing, how to comb your hair, how to eat right, how to do every single little thing in life—and what a pathetic fool you are if you don't do it *his* way. Living with a judge isn't just a life of nagging; it's proof that when one is told, "You're an idiot . . . you're a moron . . . you're incompetent . . . you never do anything right" often enough, you'll even start believing it.

The Mean Geek It used to be we were surrounded by prissy queens, who were always on the lookout to make sure we didn't use the wrong utensil at formal dinners and frequently castigated our less-than-ideal French infinitives. As effeminacy has dropped in the polls, however, prissy queens have been replaced (in all but the most rural locations) by Mean Geeks. Just as escargot forks are no longer common in our dining retinues, so the Mean Geek has moved on, criticizing how we pronounce obscure *English* words, how we've partitioned our hard drives, how we wear our 501s, even our choices in lube. The Mean Geek always has the answer to even the most trivial question; life with him is an endless announcement of *en garde!*

Mr. Whims Mr. Whims is the man who lets his passing fancies and mood swings dominate his feelings for you. He doesn't know who he is and he doesn't know what he wants, and at 9:02 you're the man he's always dreamed about, while at 9:17 couldn't you lose about ten pounds? and at 9:31 let's just stay home tonight, while at 9:47 maybe we should go to that new leather bar and see what's happening, and at 10:12 oh just forget it, I don't have anything to wear. The following is absolutely true:

At a very convivial orgy I met a classically beautiful Brooklyn Italian, the man of one's dreams (if you dream of Martin Scorsese extras). Even though we could have had plenty of fun right there, he was adamant on leaving, but the minute our clothes were on and we were out the door, he insisted we made a big mistake, and kept insisting on this all the way in the car to my place. Things at home were awkward, since he wasn't "used to having sex one-on-one," but we arranged to get together again anyway.

Date Two: Things were much less awkward this time around, but the postsex chat was "You think I'm just a partyboy, but really what I'd like to do is settle down," and his ideas about what would happen if we were lovers (fat chance). Date Three: He called two hours after he was supposed to be there to say he couldn't make it. Date Four: He actually said, "How can I take you seriously when you don't have Call Waiting?" Date Five: Stood up completely, without a call. The following Tuesday at seven A.M. the phone rang: "WHAT IS THIS SHIT THAT YOU WON'T CALL ME! YOU CAN'T DUMP ME! I WON'T BE TREATED THIS WAY!"

If you've always wanted your life to be a Mexican soap opera, Mr. Whims will fill your every need.

The Egghead Since being manly in America means repressing emotions, practically every man that you will meet will hold back on how he really feels. The Egghead, however, utterly camouflages his feelings with a hard shell of rational thought and has a logical explanation for everything he does. If you had a crush on Mr. Spock as a teenager, you'll end up dating many of these, and if you love to solve puzzles, he may be the perfect man for you. You'll have to draw on all of your empathic powers to ignore what he says and unveil what he really feels; it's sort of like learning Braille.

Though the foregoing is of course sparked by cynicism, it will help you to understand what's going on the next time you tell a friend, "He's a wonderful guy in every way, but . . ." Refer back to this list of the most common "but's" when you're trying to decide what kind of man problems (and how much of them) you're willing to put up with to keep things going. More seriously, here are a few other issues you'll probably be running across in the great gay Dating Game:

HIV Apartheid

If you're HIV-positive, you may feel that you can never become truly intimate with an HIV-negative man since sex between you will always include the worry of infection and he can never really understand what you're going through. If you're HIV-negative, you may feel that a relationship with someone HIV-positive is impossible because of the risk of infection and because you may not think you're emotionally capable of caring for someone with AIDS and the eventual widowhood. To get these crucial issues on the table early on, men who refuse to be tested should wake up, and positives should let their partner know their status, the sooner the better. Here's how Howard, a forty-seven-year-old software designer with AIDS, described it:

> I can't believe some of the comments you get going out. I'll tell someone I'm positive and they'll say, "How dare you come into this bar!" or "Why do you think I'd be interested in you?" But then I'd ask about their status and it'd turn out that they hadn't been tested. The other comment I can't believe is "Well, since we're both positive, we don't have to use a condom," or "Well, since you're positive, I don't have to use a condom"—making me feel like damaged goods.
>
> Then there are the castes; if someone's positive but asymptomatic, they frequently don't want to have anything to do with someone with full-blown AIDS. It's gotten so that now I'm squeamish about bringing up my status; I hold back, even though I KNOW most of them must be positive as well.

Having such a large group of young men be suddenly confronted with their own death, it's actually a surprise that there hasn't been a grave social disruption. Pozzes, faced with a hideous, fatal disease, may react in any number of ways, turning hostile, saintly, abusive, willfully ignorant, medically expert, childlike, violent, or religious—and many can go through phases, being alternately any of these. Neggies, when their poz lovers are diagnosed, will also suffer severe depression, grief, and even "survivor guilt" (that he got infected but you didn't), but frequently they feel they have to cover up their own feelings for the sake of their lover. Negs frequently get wracked by conflicting thoughts: "I've got to get out; I can't handle it" versus "If I leave this relationship, I'm a coward." Or, "I'm terrified I'll get it from him" versus "Now he needs me more than ever." Both sides are whipped into a turmoil of emotions and will of course suddenly act in strange, unpredictable ways as their feelings twist and turn in the wind.

Besides being the legitimate cause of the terrible fear that you, too, may get sick and die, AIDS has poisoned many people's attitudes about relationships. "Why try to make things happen," they seem to think, "if he might be gone in a few years?" Some men have gone through AIDS widowhood once, twice, even three or more times; would it be a surprise to know they aren't champing at the bit to start over again and fall in love with someone new? While the overpowering trauma of AIDS has brought many men together into new families that care for each other, and has brought many more in contact with their spirituality and humanity, this plague has also driven others away from finding long-term relationships and trying to stay together as a couple.

One friend of mine who's positive was going out with a neggie when they finally had a discussion about the whole thing. At first the neg kept popping off with "Well, it doesn't bother *me,*" which of course my poz chum found offensive. But they kept at it, with the neg always having second thoughts about going forward and getting more serious and simultaneously feeling guilty about having those second thoughts and not rising to the occasion. The poz, thinking frequently about his pains, financial worries, and meditating on his life, his achievements, and what his death would be like, couldn't help but think in relation to his boyfriend, "It's an AIDS thing; you wouldn't understand." So even though both are working their butts off to keep things going, these small issues can build up and rock the boat, long and hard.

If you and your lover are both HIV-positive, you may think, "Well, at least we can now have unprotected sex." Unfortunately this isn't true. Besides the fact that some believe there are different kinds of HIV/AIDS, you can still infect each other with herpes, cytomegalovirus, and Epstein-Barr virus, among other things not so great to share. One poz I knew felt he didn't have anything to lose; he liked to get fucked without a rubber and yell, "Give me your garbage!" If you've got a similar attitude, talk to your doctor.

The Practicing Bisexual

If the kind of guy who gets your systems going is as straight as an arrow, you may find yourself frequently becoming involved with bi men. Besides the closet issues already discussed, you may feel troubled that you can never satisfy your guy completely, and you may feel doubly jealous if he's got a roving eye. If he's talking about this or that hot woman, it's a need you'll never be able to satisfy, and it's the fastest route to feeling totally inadequate.

The biggest problem in trying to have a relationship with bisexuals is that frequently they insist on having both a boyfriend and a girlfriend/wife, neither of whom is supposed to be jealous of the other since they're not the same sex (give me a break). But if you want to live as a Back-Alley Sally, it's your life.

If your bi would-be spouse is mature in other ways, don't fantasize that he's not yet completely come out and that if you wait long enough, he'll turn solely gay and forgo women (a common idea and prejudice gay men have against bis).

Christopher is a bisexual lawyer from Arizona; here's his story:

Every time I had a fight with my wife, I'd go out cruising. When that stopped, I became sexually compulsive. My wife knew nothing about any of this, but I met a bartender in a restaurant and had the best sex I ever had, and I realized I had to tell her. I told her I was going to seek psychiatric help, that I would try to go straight, and to please give me some time. It was our twenty-fifth anniversary. Three days later she admitted she was having an affair with my best friend. I stayed away from men for about seven months, but we began verbally battering each other, both of us so mad at each other. Three months later she told me I had to move out; I went to stay in the straight side of Fire Island, where I met my current lover, Robert. Two months later I met my current wife, Muriel.

It was my slut summer; I was hitting on every guy in the place, still being sex-mad; the deer weren't safe on that island. I closed the town every night at four A.M., and then cruised the walks to see who was available. So when we met, Muriel thought I was gay. Two weeks later she and I went out dancing; she noticed a man watching me, insisted that he was interested; she turned out to be right, and I said, "We'll be back in an hour." But instead I didn't see her until a party the next day, and she asked me what had happened and I told her and she said, "I wish I could've been there; I would've loved to have watched." One time she couldn't stay at her group house, so I let her stay at my place; we had sex for twenty minutes and laughed for an hour and a half.

Whenever Muriel has sex with another guy, I'm always involved, so I don't get jealous, and I don't get jealous when she has sex with women. My lover is dying to go out with my daughter, but I won't let him. I told him, "Don't put her through what I put her mother through." Muriel and I are completely secure with each other and we say exactly what we mean. All these people flying in and out, it's like living in a soap opera and I love every minute of it.

Bi men can be a heartbreaker for gay men; I don't think they should get involved. Socially and emotionally I need a woman to be with; sexually I need men as well. When I hold a woman and make love to her, it makes me feel like I'm giving power. Making love to a man is the exact opposite; I feel as though I'm gaining strength, getting recharged. But there's always going to be some element that a guy can't compete with. If you're utterly gay and involved with a bi man, the question is always going to be: Will he leave me for a woman? It makes things hard if you want to live a gay lifestyle and the man you love is fifty-fifty. My friend Harvey Fierstein once told me, "A bisexual hurt me once and I'll never have it happen again."

I always wanted my current male lover, Robert, to get married, and we could all go out together as a foursome. Then my longtime dream was to have Muriel, Robert, and me all live together, but now I think it's the craziest fucking idea I ever heard. Muriel is the main concern in my life, and my love for her grows every day. I couldn't handle the stress of having both of them living together.

If you think gays have it tough, you should try being bisexual; the gay men and lesbians don't want anything to do with you, and the straight people don't understand you. You can go through both worlds and be everything to everyone, but it's not a cop-out or an excuse.

Closet Depth

While much of the advice and ideas in this book could apply to straights as well, there's one issue that absolutely only applies to gay and lesbian couples: how out of the closet each of you are. If you're deeply apart in this category, coupledom will be extremely difficult.

Joe and Frank are two guys trying to make a go of it. Frank's completely out to everyone; when he meets someone straight, he feels free to let him or her know he's gay ASAP. Joe is much more conservative about it; his very close friends and family know, but he isn't forthcoming, and the subject is *verboten* at the office. For Frank, "What you see is what you get"; for Joe, "What business is it of theirs?"

At first they liked each other's differences on this issue. Frank made Joe feel liberated, and Joe made Frank feel steady and domestic; theoretically they're not really that far apart on the issue. Then Frank came by Joe's office and had to dress and act the straight chum; he saw that where everyone else had pictures of their families, Joe'd put up some snaps of his nieces. Going to mixed parties, Frank is proud of his lover and wants to show him off, but Joe has let him know it makes him uncomfortable, so Frank is often unsure of what to do and how much of a "couple" they can publicly be. Joe's starting to feel his privacy's being constantly invaded, while Frank wonders how important he is to Joe.

What can start as a small difference in closet depth between the two of you can, over time, result in a lot of pain and confusion. Getting back to the good feelings about this difference and working out the troubling ones isn't easy;

you'll really have to have everything else going great between the two of you to be able to overlook differing closet sizes.

Regular Guys

One of my Texas friends thinks that all of us fall into two categories: the professional gay man and the regular guy (sometimes called the nonscene). The professional gay man feels being gay is the most important thing in his life; it is first and foremost how he defines himself and is more or less his career. The nonscene regular guy, on the other hand, defines himself first by his job (or by a hobby that he wishes were his job), by his ethnic or family background, by his religious beliefs, by where he lives or comes from, or by something else I can't think of right now; being gay is number two, three, or four down the list.

Though this idea is simplistic, and in fact real gay men are usually a combination of these two extremes, the theory does help explain certain things. A couple acquaintance of mine is a mix like this: Pro-gay Richard works as a trainer at a gay gym, lives in a gay neighborhood, shops in gay stores, goes out on weekends to gay clubs, has few friends who aren't gay men, and vacations in Provincetown, Fire Island, and Key West. Nonscene John is an ad exec, lives in a mixed gay-and-straight neighborhood, sometimes goes to gay clubs, vacations wherever, and has mostly straight friends.

Surprisingly a nonscene/pro-gay couple is often a great mix, since their life together is much fuller than it would be if they were seeing someone of their own ilk. Richard knows when the newest club is opening, when it's time to make arrangements for a Pines half-share, and where to get advice and counseling when one of the couple's friends is diagnosed with HIV. John has a connection for discount theater tickets, gets the two of them invited for weekends at his straight friends' country houses, and always remembers Richard's favorite flowers and what he likes to eat when he's feeling blue. Richard, for the most part, keeps the couple an active part of the gay community and brings in lots of social spice; John, for the most part, provides the domestic anchor of day-to-day living.

The trouble is of course that in some ways the two men are living on opposite ends of the continent. If you and your lover are like John and Richard, the secret is to feel free to socialize in his world when you feel like it, and to let him feel equally free about yours. This also means feeling free to do things by yourself when he doesn't feel like coming along, and vice versa. Never use this difference against each other: "You're practically a closet case!" "You're such a superficial queen!" Remember, it was something that attracted you to each other in the first place, and it keeps your life together rich and full.

There is another major issue, though, when the two of them go out together. The pro-gay man feels very identified with other gay people, and his self-esteem stuff is usually about competition: a body he's seen at the gym, a kid he's seen at a club, his dumpy friend's gorgeous new lover. Regular guys, though, have a completely different idea; they commonly feel alienated from the gay community since most of what they see at bars, in the clubs, during a gay-pride parade or on *Sonya Live!* are scene gay men. One regular guy really felt strongly about this:

I've heard countless men over the years sum it up in the same turn of phrase spontaneously reinvented over and over. "I am gay," they say, "but not gay gay." I always thought I was the only one who hated gay parades; the *Advocate*; gay bars, clubs, and discos, and T-shirts that say "Hotlanta." I have a friend who even calls the gay-pride parade the "gay shame" parade; I actually think it would be fun to rename it the "I'm so proud to be up for two nights in a row on Ecstasy" parade.

The thing is, I always feel more alone and alienated than ever when I attend such an event, or when I "go out," or when I flip through the pages of a gay rag—and I know a huge number of people can relate to this feeling. There is just so much I feel at odds with in "the gay community" today. And I know there are a lot of people who don't participate in a lot of activities, or who perhaps even simply don't share a lot of the spirit or feelings chronicled in the gay papers and who feel somewhat oppressed by certain very basic popular "gay" notions of who and what they are (and how they think and act), and what for example, being "proud" entails.

I feel that the community is being led around like sheep to "Hotlanta" or whatever, I mean to me there is something that just *bothers* me about it. I think "we" deserve better. . . . (of course I'm totally ignorant of what Hotlanta even really is).

The real trouble for all "regular guys" is that in groups pro-gay men stick out; they're what you notice and remember, while nonscene regular guys fade into the background. Frequently other nonsceners aren't paying attention, and especially if they aren't attracted to pro-gay men, they start feeling alone and isolated—that there's no one out there like them. Personal ads are filled with the lament "Why can't I just meet a regular guy?"

So if you have this problem, pay attention, goddammit; regular guys are everywhere; you just aren't noticing them. The next time you go out, whether it's a bar, club, or just down the street, don't be distracted by the gay-gay man's magnificent hairy chest, remarkably tight butt, and Lorenzo

Lamas face passing by; pay some thought and attention to Mr. Castro Dreamboat's little friend, Lumpy. You wanted to meet a regular guy like yourself, and there he is, right in front of you.

Gay Guys versus Guy Guys

If you're indeed one of those who is always looking for a "regular" guy, or you're attracted only to those mysteriously labeled "straight-acting and -appearing," there's an issue you'll be bumping into over and over again. Just take this simple test:

→ Do you (a) pride yourself on being sensitive to others' feelings? Or are you (b) so puzzled by how people react to things that you've given up trying to figure them out?
→ When you're upset, depressed, or confused about something, do you (a) call a friend and talk till you're blue in the face? Or do you (b) go off by yourself and want to be left alone?
→ If your spouse is upset, do you (a) want him to talk about it in great detail? Or do you (b) immediately assume it must be *your* fault?

If you see yourself mostly as an *(a)*, you're a gay guy, and emotionally you're more or less similar to straight women, while *(b)* means you're a guy guy, who's emotionally somewhat similar to straight men. Of course once again this is a simplistic way of looking at things, and all of us are actually a mix of these two sides, but knowing about this issue can help you understand it a little better when your partner seems like he's from Uranus (and if the powerful "opposites attract" theory is proving to be true in your love life, you may be feeling this way often).

If you're a gay guy dating a guy guy or vice versa, the best way to learn all about the strange ideas they have and odd things they do is ironically to read a good het guide, such as John Gray's masterpiece, *Men Are from Mars, Women Are from Venus*. According to Gray:

▶ **The big difference between the two has to do with feelings of togetherness.** While a gay guy can sit around thinking of how much he loves his honey muffin for hours and be perfectly happy, if a guy guy falls completely in love, he gets so overwhelmed by his feelings for his main man that he starts thinking he's losing his identity, feels weak and powerless, and has to go off and be by himself. Then, after he gets his balance and strength, he comes back more in love than ever before. The gay-guy husband, however, flips out because of his guy guy running off; on returning, he is not in the mood for love but for a fight. Until both learn to see that the one running off needs to be left alone and the one left behind needs reassuring, this can be the start of a bad loop. As the guy guy withdraws, the gay guy will push to move in closer, or cry, "How can you treat me like this?" or dish out some punishment—making the withdrawal all the stronger. Coming back, the guy guy's ready for couplehood all over again, while the gay guy needs to be reheated and stirred.

▶ **If a friend offers a gay guy unsolicited advice, he'll consider it (taking into account the friend's expertise in such matters).** If a friend offers a guy guy unsolicited advice, he'll think you consider him incompetent and unable to solve his own problems.

▶ **When a guy guy says, "I'm okay," it means he's fine.** When a gay guy says it, it means he's *not* fine and you're supposed to say, "You don't seem okay to me, what is it?"

▶ **When a gay guy says, "I'm sorry," he means he sympa-**

thizes with your feelings. When a guy guy says "I'm sorry," it's only if he did something wrong and has to apologize.

▶ **A guy guy, for the most part, wants his lover to give him trust, admiration, acceptance, appreciation, approval, and encouragement.** A gay guy, on the whole, wants caring, understanding, respect, devotion, validation, and reassurance.

▶ **If you're having a heavy conversation and the guy guy turns silent, he's mulling over ideas.** If the gay guy turns silent, he's about to sob—or plunge shish-kabob skewers into your eyes.

The major defining symptom of guy guys is their reluctance to tell you what they feel. If your main man isn't coming across with the goods as much as you'd like, don't think having an honest talk will get him to be a Chatty Cathy —it'll only make him feel inadequate and that you don't really care for him as much as you say you do. Instead give him praise every time he comes through and learn to recognize when he shows his love in other, nonverbal ways. His idea of romance is when he does you a favor, or when you do things together you mutually enjoy—not very often the flowers-and-candy route. Guy guys aren't comfortable being romantic, or saying directly how much they love you; he'll be awkward and gawky and, if you have the right attitude, completely adorable when he finally feels compelled to express himself and his feelings for you. Everyone has his own style of showing his man how much he loves him, and if you can get used to translating, this won't be such a problem—in fact you might come to enjoy how he does it himself more than you would if he learned your own style.

What Color Is Your Collar?

> *A nuclear physicist could meet a plumber. Bath-*
> *houses were a great leveler, a common denomi-*
> *nator, a place where people did not have to be*
> *of similar social backgrounds.*
>
> —BRUCE MAILMAN

Though it's uncommon in het relationships, gay couples frequently cross the lines of class, race, economic status, and
cultural background. These relationships can be stormy but
rich and exciting, since each man brings something very
different to the table. Seeing your lover's country of origin
(or the neighborhood where he grew up, or even visiting
him at work) will be experiences you couldn't get otherwise.
You'll also be fighting over the *strangest* things.

Many times a white-collar/blue-collar mix is a great
combo, especially if the two feel free to pursue their own
interests separately and the white can make it clear to his blue
guy that the status difference doesn't matter. Commonly the
white brings in planning, education, smarts, and one set of
interests, while the blue brings in emotion, domesticity,
muscles, and a completely different set of experiences. One
night it's opera, another it's bowling; one weekend at the
doctor's friends' country house; another, eating your guts out
at an ethnic dinner with the carpenter's immense family. The
white may have the nicer apartment, but the blue can fix the
air conditioner.

The cultural differences, however, can be huge. One small
story: I was eating in a restaurant with a blue-collar guy and
came back from the rest room. He asked why I'd been gone
for so long, and I told him my stomach had been upset.
Disgusted that I had actually sat down on a public toilet, he

threw a temper tantrum and insisted I take a shower the minute we got home.

Another huge cultural difference happens when you are involved with someone from another country. A big thing you can do to impress him is to learn how to talk in his language, especially the language of love, sex, and romance. Having foreign men teach you their words is not such a terrible way to spend time together. Here's a quick phrase book for date emergencies:

Spanish

Quiero tenerte con la fuerza de un mil hermanos.
I want to hold you with the strength of a thousand brothers.

Veo tus ojos, y mi corazón vuela a la luna.
I see your eyes, and my heart flies to the moon.

Chíngame como un toro en la zapatería.
Fuck me like a bull in a shoe store.

French

Baise moi où le soleil n'existe pas.
Kiss me where the sun don't shine.

Ton beau visage me donne des idées.
Your beautiful face gives me ideas.

Je viens! Je viens!
I'm coming! I'm coming!

Italian

Te amo nudu in camera.
I love you naked in bed.

Il tuo dolce-doloroso incenzu pazzo facevi me con desidero.
Your bittersweet, innocent depravity fills me with desire.

Portuguese

Eu adoraria estar em casa com você.
I love just staying home with you.

Tesao.
I want you too much.

Eu desejo sua bunda linda.
I'm crazy about your beautiful ass.

Tagalog

Gusto kitang kantutin.
I want to fuck you.

Gusto kitan chupain.
I want to suck you off.

Nasa puso ko ikaw.
You are in my heart.

Polish*

Obey mooey e cha louie, meyood mishoo.
Hug me and kiss me, honey bear.

Die me tvooy pyanknee dupa, swodkey kozak.
Give me your pretty butt, sweet goat.

Yestem bardzo zadovolony chebya yebach, kotulek kohanie.
I'm so very happy to fuck you, love kitten.

How to Say "I Love You"

Te amo, Spanish	*Nagligivaget,* Eskimo
Je t'aime, French	*Aloha wau ia oe,* Hawaiian
Ich liebe dich, German	*Thaim in grabh leat,* Gaelic
Wo ai nei, Chinese	*Ani ohev otakh,* Hebrew

For many years I was with a man who'd emigrated to the United States from another country. During year six together he gave me some exciting news: His wife and grown children were moving here in three months! When I tried to explain how this wasn't my life's happiest moment, he had no idea what I was talking about; he'd lived for years with a family at home and a lover on the side, so what was the big deal? Besides, the wife would only be staying a year at most, and the kids would soon be moving out and establishing their adult lives.

Waiting for the family to exit, though, was hell. He had to jump back into the closet, of course, and could only tell me

---

* Since the actual Polish spelling of "hug me and kiss me" would be *Obejmuj i çaluj,* phonetic spellings are provided as a special service to the English-speaking reader.

the sweet things we all want to hear on payphones, in whispers, or at odd hours when everyone else was out of the house. Major holidays were always spent with the family, so during the most important moments to be with one's lover, our relationship was no touching, no holding, no kissing—it was utterly invisible. It was too much for me, but every time I tried to tell him that this was impossible and asked what else could we do to try to work things out, he thought I was out of my mind.

The difference in culture and expectation was too much to survive.

Heavy Stuff

> *Most people are about as happy as they decide to be.*
>
> —ABRAHAM LINCOLN

Everyone has his problems; some have ticklish feathers, and some have serious burdens. If things seem to be going well between you and your guy but he consistently acts strangely, with the same problems bobbing up over and over again, ask him about it. If his behavior remains a mystery, if he does things that just don't make any sense, it may be that something really serious is going on.

Instead of having the normal, quick, easy, and superficial response—throwing up your hands and thinking, "He's nuts!" and blowing town—you might want to try to figure things out. It may be that, with some professional help, you can get the problem fixed. Or perhaps you can accept this as his human shortcoming and stay together. Is it worth it? Only you, can decide, taking all his other qualities into account and considering your own needs and abilities. If your or your lover's problems are really serious, however, I hope you aren't reading lots of self-help and advice books like this one, but instead that you're seeking professional help *now*.

As I've said before, I'm no licensed therapist. The listing below is only a brief, introduction to common psychological problems you may confront in your romantic life. Since we Americans don't like talking about our troubles (except on *Oprah*), you may think you're alone if you discover these things happening to you; that only you and your boyfriend have a shameful secret in your relationship. Think again. This section may help you recognize patterns of behavior that are beyond being "just the way he is," and are, in their way, cries for help. If you find yourself living through one of the following with your man, you may end up learning how right Nancy Reagan was when she said, "A woman is like a teabag; you never know how strong she is until she gets in hot water."

The Bad-Love Rut Do you find yourself falling for the same wrong guy over and over again? Are you always with a screamer, a spendthrift, a problem drinker, a liar, or some other type who you know isn't any good for you? Bad-love ruts seem to come from having had a relationship in your past —whether a parent or a lover—that you never successfully got over. You meet someone who seems familiar, comfortable, like family—in fact a family member you actually needed to get away from. But if things weren't fixed in the past, you may constantly pursue someone like that in a misguided attempt at fixing it now.

Severe Depression There are many good reasons for feeling blue, from a "blah" physical sensation to troubles at home or work. But if his blues turn black and start interfering with his daily life, maybe it's time to get some help. With the onslaught of AIDS, and gay men frequently grieving the deaths of lovers and friends, severe depression may be our most common emotional problem today.

Grief over the death or loss of a close friend or loved one frequently lasts around five years; if his depression stems from that, let him have time to grieve. It's when many years go by and he doesn't seem to be coming out of it that professional help may be required. Following are some symptoms of chronic depression:

- Zero motivation (never wanting to go out and do anything)

- Constant fatigue

- Sleep disorders (either too much or too little)

- Talking and moving in slow motion (or pacing the floor and wringing the hands)

- Anxiety attacks, fearfulness, always being tense and uncomfortable

- Sexual compulsion

- Irritability (becoming easily upset over insignificant events)

- Headaches, constipation, indigestion, lack of appetite, or compulsive overeating

- Feeling guilty, unwanted, unneeded, worthless, at the mercy of others, that your life is not under your control, that you are separated from the rest of the world

- Emotional distance (not seeming to care about anything or anyone, including yourself)

Many men, when down, go off by themselves and try to wait it out. After a certain point, however, this is probably the worst thing your guy can do. Being with friends (or a lover) and feeling part of a family can help him tremendously, as can making an effort to be more active and more a part of life.

You can help him yourself by remembering that he needs an immense amount of affection at this time, especially hugging and stroking—far more than he does sex. In fact a common characteristic of depressed men is that they're distant and disappointed after sex, because deep down inside they didn't get the warmth and affection they were trying to get from having sex in the first place.

There are many drugs and therapies these days with good success rates combating depression, and at a certain point you may want to discuss the possibilities with your lover. If he's a guy-guy, he won't want any help, feeling he should be able to fix the problem himself, so you may have to make it clear that you just think he should give it a try and that you still love, admire, and respect him, regardless of his emotional troubles.

The Addict For whatever reason some men, including many gay men, feel very uncomfortable when they're around other people. They don't trust others, and they don't trust themselves; they are beset by inner feelings that leave them in turmoil. Drink or drugs can help them relax, feel friendly, and help them forget their woes; with the right dose they feel normal. They may turn to chemicals every time they want to get back those good feelings, but as their tolerance increases, they need more and more to get loose, and at some point the good feeling never returns. Others may start out using elixirs to boost their self-esteem, combat internalized homophobia, lessen the pain of rejection, or even join the "club" of others who use the drug of the season.

This is how alcoholism and drug addiction begins; with

luck it ends with intervention—Alcoholics Anonymous, Narcotics Anonymous, or a detox program. If your coupledom starts being completely focused on substances; if you can't have sex without drinking or drugs; if you or your lover have experienced blackouts, gotten arrested, had work-related problems, or have fights with friends over drinking, you might consider getting on the wagon with a gay AA group. If your lover goes to AA, you should probably try Al-Anon to learn how people who are in love with addicts cope —especially considering what's going to happen next:

Giving up drinking or drugs means he will be drowning in all the emotions he'd kept at bay with his chemical of choice, and recovering from addiction includes learning how to deal with these powerful feelings he was trying to avoid in the first place. He'll suffer from dramatic mood swings; be enraged, desperately sad, and overwhelmed by the feeling that life is meaningless. In the powerful, life-and-death drama of recovery, he also may suffer from "AA Graduate Disorder," becoming a zealot (disparaging anyone who has wine with a meal) or utterly self-absorbed (turning inward to heal and end the feelings of being a victim). You of course will be suffering right along with him, but many have healed themselves of addiction and many have kept their love going through this difficult time.

Adult Children of Alcoholics
If one or both of your lover's parents were drunks, he or an older sibling had to assume the role of an adult very early in life, and he learned to live with an out-of-control situation where a parent he loved and needed wasn't available. Your lover may have ACA stuff going on if

▶ The most important thing in his life is keeping things under control

- He doesn't trust you, or doesn't trust anyone but you

- He completely suppresses his feelings

- He feels he is completely different from other people and has to guess at what is "normal"

- He constantly seeks approval and affirmation

- He thinks that, deep down inside, he's an unlovable person and is terrified that at any minute you will abandon him

- He is extremely loyal, even when the loyalty is undeserved

- He seldom talks about what he wants and is only interested in what you and others want

Frequently ACAs find lovers who are alcoholic or drug-addicted, and create the life they had with their parents all over again. They're comfortable with a lover who's emotionally distant and erratic, who's personally abusive, unreliable, and treats them with contempt and ridicule, since they don't expect anything different from a loved one—or they don't feel they deserve anything better from life.

The Codependent   As counselor Amy Dean defined it, "Codependent behavior is exhibited by a loss of self within a relationship—a loss that's replaced by focusing on, reacting to, and taking care of all the thoughts, feelings, and behaviors of another. When you're codependent, another person's wants and needs—not your own—become all-important." If you're devoting your life to making someone else happy, it may seem noble and giving; but if that devotion means completely ignoring your own feelings, something's not working. Melody Beattie theorizes that "when we were children, someone very important to us was unable to give the love, approval and emotional security we needed. So we've gone about our lives the best way we could, still looking vaguely or desperately for something we never got." According to her, a lover may be codependent if

▶ He's had a relationship or history of relationships with alcoholics, drug addicts, gamblers, or men with violent mood swings, and their emotional chaos caused him great suffering

▶ He thinks he's responsible for another's feelings, thoughts, behavior, and well-being, and gets feelings of power and self-esteem by devoting himself to taking care of the other's needs

▶ He feels anxious and guilty when the other has a problem or is in a bad mood

▶ He's obsessed with the thought "Am I reacting the way he wants me to?"

▶ He thinks his own wants, needs, feelings, thoughts, and opinions are so unimportant, he doesn't even know what they are anymore

▶ He believes he's basically unlovable, and will settle for anyone

▶ He's constantly thinking something bad has happened, is happening, or will happen, and these obsessions put him in a state of mental and emotional chaos

▶ He's comfortable giving, but not receiving

▶ He picks on himself for every minor flaw (or imagined flaw), but when others criticize him, it's utterly annihilating, and he can't accept compliments or praise

▶ He feels love equals pain, and so often feels helpless, uncertain, frightened, and vulnerable that life becomes something not to be lived but endured

▶ He's overwhelmed with fear and anxiety when the other goes away, and literally feels he can't live without the other

▶ When his attempts to help, control, or "fix" the other don't work, he feels angry, unappreciated, a victim

▶ He thinks that good people don't get angry, he'll lose control and go crazy if he gets angry, or that the other will desert him if he gets angry

The Love Addict "You're Nobody Till Somebody Loves You." Just as some men become addicted to chemicals, food, or sex, others can become compulsive about a relationship. They will do anything to appear to be part of a wonderful couple, staying with their man no matter what—even when common sense tells them they should've gotten out years ago. If you wonder of a friend, "Why is he still with that creep?" this may be the answer. A love addict feels, underneath it all, "I am not enough," and the results are similar to codependency:

- His self-esteem comes from being part of a couple, not from himself
- He's terrified of being abandoned and panics when his lover has to go away without him
- He sees his partner's differences, including his other friends and interests, as a threat, and is constantly possessive and jealous
- He's so low in self-confidence and so afraid of failure, he has few friends or separate interests away from the relationship
- He's threatened by fully revealing himself and by really knowing his lover, so he doesn't discuss his or his lover's feelings
- Instead of growing together, he and his lover drag each other down
- He is so desperate about the relationship that he'll do anything to control or stay with his lover, including dishing out or putting up with emotional and physical abuse

Both codependents and relationship addicts need to detach, end their obsession, and start loving normally. This can happen with therapy or even an AA-like twelve-step program, giving up the fears and obsessions just like others give up alcohol or drugs.

The Sex Addict   Since many gay men have tons of recreational sex, the definition of "sex addict" is whether or not the tons you're having is more trouble than it's worth. Do you spend so much time arranging trysts that you don't see much of your friends? Are you having problems at work because you didn't get enough sleep Tuesday, Wednesday, and Thursday? Do you feel worse after having sex than you did before?

Sex is a great escape from the daily grind, but if you're using it to avoid confronting or solving your problems, or if you really want a relationship but are spending all your time in backrooms not speaking to anyone, maybe you should reconsider what really makes you happy in life. There is a very touching subtext to the issue of sex addiction, however, as David Crawford put it so eloquently:

> It's remarkable how much tenderness gets expressed in tearooms and parks and porno movie houses. This is the sexual compulsive's most shameful secret: he wants to caress, to hold, to kiss, to nuzzle a warm neck, to express affection— even to hold hands. The hard-core compulsive may consign these secretive gestures to "foreplay" or "afterplay," but— again secretly—they often constitute the most important component of the whole "act." The barely acknowledged sense is, however that these are dividends—subsidiary to the Main Event. We usually don't allow ourselves to accept these passing, furtive, tender gestures as "important" or "the point." The point, we tell ourselves, is mechanistic sex.

You can contact the following organizations for further assistance:

Sexual Compulsives Anonymous
P.O. Box 1585
New York, NY 10013
(212) 439-1123

Sex Addicts Anonymous
P.O. Box 3038
Minneapolis, MN 55403
(612) 339-0217

Here are the questions they use to help a person determine if
this is a problem:

▶ Do you keep secrets about your sexual or romantic activities
  from those important to you? Do you lead a double life?
▶ Have your needs driven you to have sex in places or situations
  or with people you would not normally choose?
▶ Do you find yourself looking for sexually arousing articles or
  scenes in newspapers, magazines, or other media?
▶ Do you find that sexual fantasies interfere with your relationships or are preventing you from facing problems?
▶ Do you frequently want to get away from a sex partner after
  having sex? Do you frequently feel remorse, shame, or guilt
  after a sexual encounter?
▶ Do you think other men have a "magical" quality and that
  once you have sex with them, you'll have it too?
▶ Are you always finding yourself attracted to men who aren't
  available, or who will reject you or physically or emotionally
  abuse you?
▶ Do you feel shame about your body such that you avoid touching yourself? Do you fear that you have no sexual feelings, that
  you are asexual?
▶ Without a relationship do you feel empty, incomplete, like
  something is seriously missing? While you are in one, do you
  constantly fear being rejected and abandoned?

- Even when you're in a relationship and know that you're wanted and loved, do you feel it's never enough and are constantly lusting for others?
- Have you been arrested or are you in danger of being arrested because of your practices of voyeurism, exhibitionism, prostitution, sex with minors, indecent phone calls, and so on?
- Do your sexual activities include the risk, threat, or reality of disease, coercion, or violence?
- Has your sexual or romantic behavior ever left you feeling hopeless, alienated from others, or suicidal?

One of the most insightful things I've ever read about the pleasures of anonymous sex was posted, anonymously, on an electronic bulletin board:

Perhaps, just for that one small moment in time, standing in a dark, cramped, sweaty and hot room with bodies pressing all over, you *might* be able to forget that you don't look like the cover of this month's *Playgirl*. The guys in there want you, and however small and animalistic that want is, the fact is that you are *wanted*.

I thought about this one long and hard, because I've been there too many times. When I walk into one of those back rooms, video stores, bushes in the park, or wherever it might be, I don't have to worry about the fact that I've never been picked up at a bar, never had anyone proposition me, never been invited to dance. I'm an anonymous person with a dick, he's the same, and we indulge in sex. There's a thrill to it that can't be described, and a deep depression afterwards, when I think about how wonderful it could be with someone to love always, and not just for 10 or 15 minutes.

I think a lot of people, including a lot of gays, see anonymous sex as something that gays do just because they can't control their sex drives. I personally think that it's an indirect result of the way gays are treated in our society today, no matter how many advances we've made in the last 25 years, teaching us that we are second class citizens, combined with this worship of the "perfect" body. Deep down inside myself and those "anonymous" guys, for just a few fleeting moments, however dark, seedy and disgusting it may be . . . we are loved.

The Abuser Everyone gets frustrated and everyone gets angry. But if your lover's rage starts being consistently uncontrollable and involving emotional, sexual, and/or physical abuse, you need to get help immediately. This issue may be obvious to anyone if they're going to work with a black eye, or if they're being sexually raped and assaulted. What many men don't consider just as damaging (even though it may be the most damaging) is mental abuse. If your lover is constantly putting you down, humiliating you in public, making you feel sexually incompetent, calling you names, treating you with sarcasm and contempt, making one accusation after another, or intimidating you, it's as serious as any physical violence, and you should again seek immediate help.

Batterers are almost always relationship addicts, and fit the above profile. Additionally

▶ He tries to take control over every aspect of his lover's life, tries to socially isolate him, and belittles his lover and his lover's friends
▶ He denies that he's a batterer, claims that the abuse is minimal, and blames his lover for instigating the abuse
▶ He feels his lover should instinctually know how to make him feel good, and when this doesn't happen, he lashes out

After his rage is exhausted, the abuser commonly showers his spouse with love and affection; they usually have fantastic sex; and he promises it will never happen again. But unless a batterer learns to be responsible for his behavior, learns how to cope with conflict and disagreement, and learns how to see his lover as an individual human being instead of a "thing," the cycle of abuse won't end.

If you have a tendency to become furious and abuse your lover, the very least you can learn to do is recognize when you're about to blow and get out of there. Go for a walk, go to the gym, just get away from him and do whatever it takes to calm down before going back. Learning how to deal with extreme anger requires professional counseling, but you can at least figure out how to absent yourself and stop the abuse.

The Battered I had a cat named Vicki that I rescued from the streets, not knowing at the time that she'd been seriously abused. For the first two months whenever I came home, she'd hide behind the refrigerator; for years whenever another person came into the apartment, Vicki ran under the bed. Finally, after years of treating her as gently as possible and only doing what made her feel comfortable, she became okay being around other people. Vicki could never stand being picked up, and couldn't sit still to be petted by anyone but me; she "paraded" back and forth in front of other people, just out of reach.

If you meet a guy who's been abused, he'll be damaged like Vicki and will react similarly. You'll reach out with tenderness, and he'll act like he's about to get hit; you'll offer love and devotion, and he'll be afraid and mistrustful.

Abuse comes in many forms. There can be childhood sexual abuse, with suppressed memories bubbling up to the surface (in the 1994 *Advocate* gay-sex survey, 21 percent of the men responding said that they had been sexually abused by an adult before the age of fifteen—about the national average). There can be physical abuse, where someone has been taught that love means bodily pain. There can be emotional abuse, such as that suffered by children of alcoholics, whose parents were never emotionally present for them and who now constantly fear abandonment. There can even be bad-luck abuse, where, for whatever reason, your lover has had a series of relationships with men who are screwed up and emotionally unstable—and he's now expecting more of the same from you. An abused spouse can be characterized by the following:

- He was supported financially by his battering lover

- When in an abusive relationship, he was cut off from his friends and didn't receive any support from his family

- He was terrified of being left alone

- He thinks he doesn't deserve a decent relationship with a good person

- He insists it wasn't real battering, or that it wasn't so bad, or that he caused it

- He thinks that if only he'd done or said the right thing, his lover wouldn't have battered him

- He felt completely powerless, never having the strength or will to walk out, insist on change, or react in any way that might have ended the battering

Battered men have particular ideas about love and relationships. They may feel that no one has ever loved them for themselves, but rather for what they could do, what they could pay for, or what they could provide in bed. If your lover has been abused, his idea of love is that it's manipulative, painful, rejecting, angry, and with conditions that he must meet.

When you reach out to him, not knowing any of this, is it any wonder he runs like hell? The closer you move in, the more he pulls back.

Invisible Therapy

You are not a therapist, you are a regular Joe, but you are in love with a man who has some inner stuff going on, and you want to keep things going as a couple, and you want to help. Whether or not his trauma is serious, whether or not he's getting professional aid and treatment, there is something you can do, something any human being with fears, worries, and problems (i.e., everyone alive) wishes his lover would do for him.

Use empathy to become sensitive to your lover's inner desires, and give him the emotional support he needs. "Invisible therapy" is being mindful of your lover's sensitive areas, building him up, and making him feel good about himself. Don't Bee an evil queen who uses someone's personal demons against him; do Bee the kind of man whose love is generous and forgiving.

Many gay men focus on their weak points and belittle their strong ones; so feel free to compliment your lover on his talents and abilities. If you know he has body shame and it's unwarranted, say something good about the parts of his body you know he likes. When you suddenly realize something about him that you especially love, blurt it right out.

If self-esteem's the problem, the answer is to use your own empathy to know when he's ready to listen to you and when he's not. When you think he is, compliment him on something that you can be completely honest and serious about; make sure you don't sound like you're "just talking." Make him focus on his strengths; learn how to sincerely say why you love him, what specifics about him you find so attractive.

When he starts talking about his bad points, insist that they're insignificant compared with all his good points. If the situation is serious enough, be self-deprecating and try to point out your own weaknesses so that he'll feel more of a sense of balance and equality between the two of you.

Besides the aid of an experienced therapist, you can help your ACA lover by building his inner strength as a human being. Give him all the room he needs; have him lead and make the decisions on everything from dinner to sex; treat him with respect; make sure he understands that he is your equal in every way.

The very difficult part about all of these invisible-therapy techniques is that your love bunny can't just understand what you're saying logically; he has to *feel* it inside. In order to reach him there, you will have to communicate your feelings in the way that he communicates his. How does he tell you he loves you? Does he say it directly, does he write notes, does he bring gifts, or is he the most emotional on the phone? Many ACAs, codependents, and abused men, for example, are extremely empathic, since they trained themselves to constantly monitor other people's moods from their facial expressions and vocal tones so that they'll know when trouble's coming. If you want to reach an ACA sugarpuff's insides, you'll have to be physically present to do it and you'll have to make sure your feelings of love and compassion are honestly reflected in your eyes, your voice, and your touch.

When a lover has been abused, the psychological damage may never completely heal. You will have to be extremely patient, waiting for him to learn to trust you and then waiting again for him to realize that you are very different from what he knows from his dreadful past. You'll be walking on eggshells as he learns, from scratch, what it's like to be part of a couple with someone who's healthy, devoted, and sincere about his happiness, inner strength, and well-being. If you're strong enough to live with his growing up, you will find that giving your love to someone who needs it so desperately and being with a man who's healing and coming back to life is an utterly deep and profound experience, albeit one filled with rough patches and bumps.

> *If I were to choose between pain and nothing, I would choose pain.*
>
> —WILLIAM FAULKNER

Chapter 8

· ·

♂ # When Things Start Getting Serious

The supreme happiness in life is the conviction that we are loved.

—Victor Hugo

Maybe it started with someone you were seeing as a fuck buddy, a date set up by mutual friends, a neighbor across the street who walked his dogs with you twice a day. Date three . . . date five . . . all of a sudden it strikes: "Hey, this could really be something!" You're excited and happy, but you're also nervous and frightened: "Should I start thinking 'lover' thoughts? Does he feel the same way?"

The most common thing that happens at this moment between two men is that nobody says anything; each guy is waiting for the other to spill the beans. Cough up "I really, really like you" too soon and you might get "I like you too" said flatly and without real feeling, or "I'm so madly in love with you, it makes me want to scream!"—quite a bit more than you expected.

Taking the Plunge

Let's say you are the one who's madly, devotedly, utterly in love. Isn't it great . . . and isn't it terrible? You flip-flop between heaven and hell, and many times can you do nothing but think of him, him, him. What did he mean when he said this? What did he mean when he did that? What did that twinkle in his eye *really* mean when he said this and did that? He sounded annoyed on that last phone call—was it something *I* said? You're just like some twelve-year-old girl waiting breathlessly by her Princess phone: "Let it please be him, oh, dear God, it must be him." Either you want to sleep all the time or you have insomnia; either you're high as a kite or the wind's been completely knocked out of your sails.

Right now I myself am truly, madly, deeply in love. The minute day-to-day life stops fully holding my attention, I think of him; the minute times are tough, my head is flooded with memories of his body, his kindness, something funny he said last week. All my emotions are right on the surface: I ache and ache to see him, strain violently to express how much I love him, live in terror that something will happen to break us apart, have my stomach twist in knots of jealousy when he seems interested in other guys. My emotions are so overwhelming that sometimes I squirt a few tears, not from happiness or sadness but just from my body trying to do what it can to relieve this immense tension.

He has become a bible of fetishes for me: the way his shirt rides up, showing off his stomach at the gym; the salt-and-pepper at his temples; his baby-tender bald spot; the body-builder strut in his walk—all make my catalog of desire. I love him when he's smooth and suave; I love him when he's gawky and awkward; I love him when he does exactly the right thing; I love him when he doesn't know what the hell he's doing; I love him when he tries so hard. After sex, while he sleeps cradled in my arms, I feel that I've reached the pinnacle of achievement as a human being. Nobel laureate? Instant Lotto millionaire? Nothing else could make me feel so deeply happy, so deeply content.

How did this happen? How did you and I become utterly obsessed love junkies? John Money, a sexologist, has an interesting idea: He says that as children we associate certain people's physical and mental qualities with the feeling of being loved—he calls this a lovemap—and we look for those maps from other people later in life. When you find a guy with the map you go for: Bingo! Others think that if you're emotionally ready to fall—if you've just gotten out of a relationship, if you're bored and want something new in your life, if you're finally mentally and financially ready—love can smack your face just like that. Then there's the "Romeo and Juliet" theory, where one tends to get excited and obsessed about someone when there are big obstacles in the path to coupledom. My own idea is that a twosome is an intricate and complicated seesaw of similarities (shared interests and outlooks) and differences (which bring excitement and newness to each other); if you meet someone with just the right mix that you're comfortable with and excited by . . . you're dead meat.

There's also a chemical explanation for falling madly into passion. The middle of your brain houses the limbic system, where all the basic, core human emotions occur. At the end of your limbic nerve cells is a chemical, phenylethylamine ("fennel-ethel-amine," or PEA—also found in chocolate), which helps move neuronal impulses between cells, is a natural form of speed, and is the culprit when you feel exhilarated and euphoric. When you fall into love, deep lust, or psychoinfatuation, PEA levels soar. Some people are even addicted to its amphetaminelike effects, jumping into one relationship after another to get that high—usually with disastrous results. PEA researchers feel this is why infatuation always ends after one and a half to three years; your brain at some point becomes oversaturated by the chemical, your ecstatic, biologically induced bliss wears off, and the man of your dreams becomes the guy who leaves the bathroom looking like a rhino pit.

The other chemicals involved in making you a lovebug are pheromones; perfumes that were once the primordial key to getting laid and that are found in a person's sweat, semen, and urine. Everyone's pheromones are uniquely his own (like a sex fingerprint), and no matter how much soap, antiperspirant, and other cosmetic odors we may lather on, that subtle, very personal smell remains.

A group of scientists now believe they've uncovered, deep in the nose, the human vomeronasal organ, which uses its own, specially designed nerve cells to detect pheromones, making them far more significant than previously believed. There's now a perfume made from the stuff—*Realm*—with an infomercial insisting it will enhance your "positive feelings of romance, confidence, attractiveness, and self-assurance." If you're seeing someone but it goes sour, moving from "There's *something* about him" to "What did I ever see in that guy?"—it may be that elusive aroma of prehistory at fault. When he's away and you can't get his stink, attraction plummets.

America's most famous pheromone saga took place in Dallas: Candy, a housewife who taught Bible school, was playing volleyball one day with her best friend's husband. At her trial a year later for the ax murder of said best friend, Candy testified that the husband raised his arms at the game, she got a whiff, and it led inexorably to uncontrollable passion and cold-blooded killing. She was acquitted.

The most plausible explanation for the simultaneous "thrill of victory and agony of defeat" roller coaster of infatuation is of course when most if not all of the above get combined. You're ready, your PEA's on the march, and you meet that big, hunky guy who's got some obstacles, as well as the lovemap, the pheromones, and the seesaw. Smitten, kitten? You're crazed and you're paralyzed by doubt, worry, and dreamy feelings. What will I say the next time we talk? What will I do the next time we're together? You're blinded by love, seeing only what you want to see and hearing only what you want to hear, with all his faults and disabilities melting into the background.

We all know that emotions have nothing to do with rational thought and very little to do with concrete reality, and when you're drowning in love, you are in effect completely out of your mind. You start having thoughts about Him and ideas about Him that have absolutely nothing to do with anything in the material world; you'll talk yourself into the craziest things. Then when you finally do see Him in real life, your mind is lost in the haze of the stories you've been telling yourself and the imaginary conversations you've been having with Him and all those nonsensical ideas that your love for Him has been endlessly generating. It's like that story about the traveling salesman:

A traveling salesman gets a flat tire smack dab in the middle of nowhere. He opens the trunk of his rental car, and realizes he has no jack. Off in the distance, he sees a farmhouse, and starts walking toward it, talking to himself all the way, and getting angrier with every step. "I bet they don't even have a jack," he thinks at first, but keeps walking. "If they do have one, I bet they won't let me use it." Then he thinks, "Maybe they'll let me buy it, but they'll probably make me pay as much as they can get out of me!" As he gets closer, he thinks, "I bet they'll screw me out of money and won't even give me a glass of water if I ask for it!" He approaches the farmhouse, boiling, and knocks on the door.

The farmer comes out the porch and asks, "Can I help you?" The salesman says, "TAKE YOUR FUCKING JACK AND SHOVE IT UP YOUR ASS!"

In love you're overwhelmed—but you're probably overwhelming him as well. One of the most important abilities when you're coupling up is empathy to the other's alternating needs for intimacy and for solitude. We all want to be loved, but too much of a good thing can make anyone feel smothered, and it is very unusual (if not chemically impossible) for two human beings to love each other with the same degree of ardor at the same time. The tired cliché "I need my space" is completely true; everyone needs a sense of himself as well as time alone to think. Knowing when to emotionally move in and when to back off will keep you and your beloved from feeling like you're drowning in coupledom.

A lot of men get scared when things start turning serious. They're afraid of the power of their own feelings; they're afraid of falling in love, being dependent on someone, getting dumped, getting hurt; they're afraid of doing or saying the wrong thing; they're worried about what's going to happen next. So they perform, just for you, that wonderful dance we all know so well: Moving closer, moving back, moving closer, watching every step. Some pull back with shocking haste and head-spinning abruptness, leaving you, the "axis bold as love" kind of guy, bewildered and wondering what you did wrong.

The best way to handle things? "Leave them alone and they'll come home, wagging their tails behind them." Take it easy. If things are going well enough, you can never hurt the situation by going slowly and letting things proceed at their own level. Too often we get anxious and start moving in for the kill; but if he's not ready, it'll only kill off his interest. Assume that if you're dating someone into double digits, he likes you very much, and relax; you don't have to completely plan out your future together this very second. Don't be gamy about it, but learn the rhythm of moving in and pulling back that makes him feel simultaneously loved and free.

This period, between casual dating and marriage, is filled with pitfalls and traumas. You're both getting serious about each other, but things aren't settled yet; you're in one of those "in-between pictures" moments in life where things are unstable and there's no set way to act or know what to expect. It's when both of you are at your most vulnerable, not completely sure if you're ready to take things farther or what the other's thinking. Each of you had important relationships in the past that didn't work out, and the pain of what happened then is coloring what's happening now. You feel that things are supposed to be proceeding in lockstep: from seeing each other occasionally to once a week, twice a week, spending weekends together, moving in together. But the timetable has to be negotiated from scratch for each couple; don't try to make it happen all on your own. If it's going to, it will.

What you are both doing right now is one of the great tragedies of love: taking everything personally. When you realize that he may be HIM, you start constantly monitoring what he thinks about YOU YOU YOU. You spend five nights in a row together and he says he's tired and doesn't want to screw on night six. Even though anyone in his right mind would accept this, of course you know the secret truth: *He doesn't think you're sexy anymore and it's all over.* One Friday night he says he can't see you since he's got relatives in from out of town, but he'll see you the rest of the weekend. You know the secret truth: *He's getting tired of you and it's all over.* You call him at work and he's tense and irritable on the phone, explaining that he's having a shitty day, but you know the secret truth: *You make him tense and irritable and it's all over.*

Did you ever think that maybe even if his world *does* revolve around you, it's not every single second of every single day? Stop thinking ME ME ME and give him a break. Remember, just like on that TV show *Tricks,* we are all slow to believe in another's devotion yet quick to hear (or think we're hearing) the worst. If that's your regular habit, try to get some perspective, and if you really start getting paranoid, ask your friends for a reality check.

The Naked and the Pseudonaked

If you are one of the many gay men who've had an infinite number of one-night stands, there's a funny thing that happens when you first start seriously seeing someone: Your life has a history of finding yourself naked in bed with a stranger, and by now you've got a whole "naked in bed with a stranger" act down pat. You kiss and touch and look and fuck in a certain way that attempts to be warm and intimate—but really you're faking that intimacy (since you've developed all this with people you don't know and who don't know you). Now you're with someone you want to be really close to but you find yourself falling into that "auto-intimate" mode all over again.

Some call this the Closeness Game; I call it being pseudonaked. You've got the warm, human look in your eyes; the deep, whispering compliments in your throat; the tender hugging and caressing in your hands; the postcoital satisfied smile on your lips. You can turn it on at a moment's notice, and if you're really good at it, you deserve to feel proud of being able to help set a mood and give someone else pleasure for an evening. But when you *really* are falling for someone and when you *really* want to get close to him, being pseudonaked gets in the way. After a while you'll know you're faking it, and he'll know it, too, or at least he'll know something's not right.

How do you get over it? When you find yourself going pseudonaked, think hard about how being with this guy is different from all the others; remind yourself of how you really feel about him. Then upend your act; if you're normally romantic at night, get sincerely naked with him when you first wake up or before taking an afternoon nap. When you find yourself falling into auto-mode, stop it right then and there and do something completely different from your act. Recognize when you're playing the Closeness Game and learn how to turn it off for him.

The Opiate of the People

> Love is the power within us that affirms and values another human being as he or she is. Human love affirms that person who is actually there, rather than the ideal we would like him or her to be or the projection that flows from our minds. . . . Love is utterly distinct from our ego's desires and power plays. It leads in a different direction: Towards the goodness, the value, the needs of the people around us.
>
> —ROBERT JOHNSON

If things are going well, you and your guy will move into the next stage of romance: attachment. Differences between you are, as much as possible, stifled, and similarities are buffed to the max; some days you are so in tune with each other you just cannot believe it. The hysteria of infatuation is over, and a sense of calm, comfort, and warmth settles in. The researchers who treated the PEA addicts believe a new chemical is welling up in your brain at this point: endorphins, the body's own version of morphine, which soothes, kills pain, and relaxes.

He is sitting next to you; it could be in the car, a movie, eating dinner, whatever. You can sense both his body heat and a slight humming that is only felt when one is deeply in love. Your breath becomes slow and even; tension melts away; your whole body fills with a warmth, a contentment, a peace, and you think, "This is exactly what it's supposed to be like; this is exactly what's supposed to happen." I'm sure you've met couples who're getting a good shot of opiate; they never want to go out or even have much to do with their old friends since they're so content just to stay home with each other. Night after night of Chinese food, cable TV, and being together makes them so happy, they can't even come up with a reason to get out of the damn house.

This nesting period is when you really start creating the private world of you as a couple. You know things about each other that no one else knows, secret jokes and stories that no one else can share; your home becomes a refuge from the storms of the world. As Nathaniel Branden so eloquently put it,

Whether it is a universe shaped by happiness or one that is merely a fortress against pain, it is—by its very nature—an emotional support system, a sanctuary, a source of nourishment and energy, apart from the outside world. Sometimes it is experienced as the only point of certainty, the only thing solid and real, in the midst of chaos and ambiguity. . . . Indeed, this is one of the needs filled by romantic love: The need for the support provided by that private universe, the fuel that it offers for the outside struggles of our existence.

Relationship isolation occurs when you overdose on endorphins and have absolutely nothing to do with the real world. Your relationship becomes your whole life; you spend as much time together as possible and as little time with other people as you can; you find the grocery store and laundry that delivers so that you don't even have to go out for that. Kurt Vonnegut called them *duprasses,* the couples who are so sucked into each other, they become completely obnoxious. If you and your lover start turning into a pair of whales and dressing exactly alike, watch out: You may be getting an endorphin (and togetherness) overdose. You may also wake up and find out you've lost all your friends.

Having a love-drugged brain incurs other consequences, too. When separated, lovers tend to suffer greatly—since they're not getting their medication. When a relationship ends, a major part of the grief process is a form of withdrawal. Certain people in fact are low in natural endorphins and become so addicted to the doses they get from their spouses that they'll put up with anything—even physical and psychological abuse—in order to hold on to their beloved drug dealer.

The Terrible Twos

At about this time is when you discover an odd thing: Now you are three. There's you, there's him, and there's that intersection/overlap/negotiated position of you two, a.k.a the relationship (God, is that a repellent word—your partnership? your pairing? your couplehood? your team? your twosome? your dyad?). As you merge closer and closer together, the intersections, overlaps, and negotiations become stronger, more detailed, and more complicated; as each of you changes, your pairing changes as well, in ways you can't expect.

Being a twosome is like having a child, with your baby growing up and developing through obvious stages. Couples who've been together a few years are very different from those who've been together for twenty. For example, when a survey asked, "How long do you two expect to stay together?" most of the gay couples in the first few years said, "Forever"; most of those who'd been together around five years said, "A long time," and most of those who'd been together ten years or more say, "A while"!

When there are problems at home, you worry and fret like any parent, wondering what you did wrong, are you inadequate, is there an answer? In each stage there are predictable troubles and balancing acts; there may be problems because one of you is at a different stage than the other; and instead of a common progression that we can all anticipate, couples tend to move back and forth between the stages, even combining them at various points.

The first few years involve merging, creating your overlap. You'll find yourself using your lover's expressions, talking in his voice, constantly remembering something he did or said, taking up his hobbies, his interests, his schedule, even his tastes in food. You'll each be commenting, delightedly, on all the things you have in common and overlooking, minimizing, or even totally ignoring all the things you don't. Each man's idiosyncratic traits and habits (which later on will drive you both nuts) are seen as cute and endearing; you're so much into each other that other human beings fade into the background; and of course you're fucking like bunnies on speed.

Merging also takes place on the level of contribution; what you each bring to the other. A very funny thing usually happens: In the areas where one of you is more expert than the other, typically the less-adept will become more and more incompetent, letting his lover take over completely. For example, a good cook paired with a great chef will push on the differences, letting his chef spouse show off his abilities while his own cooking skills fade away. Things you could, with a little effort, work out for yourself now require his aid and attention, and the once perfectly competent man now finds himself always asking, "Could you help me with this?"

Another issue with this stage is that when it ends and you no longer are mutually obsessed, you might think you're no longer in love and should call the whole thing off. But falling out of hysteria and into a calmer tightness is a universal phenomenon; if we remained crazy in love forever, just think what a soap opera that'd be.

The Psycho Hour

> Love and attachment can breed such painful feelings as jealousy, fear of separation, a special kind of loneliness, heartache, disillusionment, loss of affection, rage, insecurity, loss of identity, a sense of being smothered—the list goes on. The only surprise is that we are often surprised when love's dark edges come into view and that love rarely fits snugly into a calm and ordered life.
>
> —THOMAS MOORE

Love's whimsy is sometimes completely overwhelming because of a very strange thing that happens to practically everyone. You've fallen like a rock, no one could be more perfect for you than him, you're moony and glowy over your new guy—and then suddenly your mind fills up with junk. You've pursued him like gangbusters, then the minute he responds completely, you have second thoughts. When he does something wonderful, instead of being thrilled, you can't get it out of your head all the times he *wasn't* so wonderful. You know that everything's going just great, but some little tiny thing happens and suddenly you think: Divorce.

This terrible quirk of human emotion is wildly common, but exactly why it is so is subject to debate. One camp believes that when you're single, you only have yourself to satisfy, and being content with your life is relatively straightforward. With another man in your life, however, there's a whole new host of expectations, wishes, opinions, and judgments to take into account, and you can't help but worry that you're not measuring up. Falling in love throws your image of yourself and your life into disarray; issues that are important to your new man will become important to you, even if you've never cared a whit about them in the past. Even the most loved man on the planet can suddenly find himself woefully insecure, calipering his body fat and wondering, "Did I say and do the right thing?"

The other theory about the psycho hour is that the minute we fall in love, all the garbage that happened to us in close, intimate relationships from the past (parents, siblings, important relatives, and prior b.f.'s) comes rising to the surface like pond scum. It's as though we let our guard down to be close to someone new, and that drop brings back everything nasty from the old.

Some therapists believe that the strong emotional pull of love triggers these memories (but this doesn't explain why they're usually only bad memories). Some, like John Gray, believe that "love thaws out our repressed feelings, and gradually those unresolved feelings begin to surface in our relationship. It is as though your unresolved feelings wait until you are feeling loved, and then they come up to be healed. We are all walking around with a bundle of unresolved feelings, the wounds from our past, that lie dormant within us until the time comes when we feel loved. Then, when we feel safe to be ourselves, our hurt feelings come up." The more love you feel, the bigger and badder the emotions that rise.

Did something happen between you and your mom, your dad, or an ex, that you're still sad or angry or regretful about? If so, you may start having all those emotions toward your new guy. If your parents treated you in a critical, demeaning manner, you'll be on the lookout for every little thing he says and does that implies the same treatment. If his ex suddenly dumped him, he'll be on edge trying to figure out if you're about to do the same.

During the psycho hour, you and your guy will have sudden shifts, being sexually passionate one part of the week and couldn't-care-less another, feeling "let me give you my house keys" one moment and wanting to run for the hills the next. If the two of you have terrible past histories with your families and lovers and don't watch out, you'll fall into a severe love-hate kinda thing, glued-to-the-hips on Monday, throwing furniture by Wednesday, kiss-and-make-upping for the weekend, and starting the whole cycle all over again during *60 Minutes*.

Knowing the significant moments in both your pasts will help the two of you realize when this is happening. Remember things that you wanted but didn't get or bad things that happened, and try to keep from imbuing him with the same fears and pain. Get to know about his history, and keep it in mind when he turns sullen, numb, distant, scared. Find out, especially, why things ended with his previous lovers; if there was one especially dreadful relationship, it may be all you need to know.

Try to remember, every relationship has completely different and complicated dynamics. People change, and the problems you had with your evil exes will probably have nothing to do with the many, many problems you're going to have now.

Nothin' More Than Feelings

Therapist Rik Isensee, in *Love Between Men*, has some remarkable points to remember about emotions (especially if the two of you are opera queens), as paraphrased here:

- You don't have to justify feelings, they simply exist.
- There's no right or wrong in how we feel.
- Feelings want to be recognized, and they continue to push into our awareness until we acknowledge them.
- Feelings are transitory and, once acknowledged, will frequently change.
- Unacknowledged feelings tend to be acted out, and the less aware we are of our feelings, the more likely we are to act them out. Besides behavioral problems, those unexpressed emotions can also pop up as psychological or physical symptoms.
- Anger often masks hurt, sadness, or fear.
- Expressing feelings to each other enhances intimacy.

Secret Desires

- You're going out every Saturday night, but something comes up and he can't make it one time. Instead of being mildly disappointed, you spend the weekend enraged.

- ▶ You have a family emergency and suddenly have to leave town; he goes nuts and acts like you're running off for a wonderful vacation and deliberately leaving him behind.

- ▶ Usually he calls you every morning, but then for whatever reason he stops. Instead of calling him, you think he's a jerk and he doesn't really care about you anymore and maybe you should go out and meet someone with some real human feelings for a change.

Does any of this sound familiar? All of us get used to patterns with another guy that make us comfortable and secure; but when the patterns are disrupted in some area where we deeply and secretly need consistency, we go completely nuts. These secret desires really are hidden; it's not until you get far more upset than the situation merits that you know you've got 'em.

When they hit you or your manchild, first try to keep a perspective on what happened in real life instead of in your emotional life. Is it really time to call it quits just because he didn't make a date or a phone call? Does he really feel left out not going to Akron to see your granny in a coma? The answer is always no. Then try to figure out what secret desires made this nothing item pop for you and him. Did the "every Saturday night" date make you feel you were a couple? Do you want to be spending more time together than he does, so that A.M. call was your substitute? Does he need to feel you're there for him—and suddenly taking off across the country takes that feeling away? Bringing secret desires to the surface will help you understand that it's not the other man's fault when you get upset over trivial events, and maybe you'll each be able to do a better job of meeting each other's needs if you just know the truth.

In the Arena

Men are taught from the get-go to be competitive, but that competition can really be a stinkeroo when you're trying to make coupledom work. While comparing yourself with the man you're closest to in developing your own sense of self makes perfect sense, if your boyfriend feels insecure about himself, he may try to prove his self-worth by beating you in as many arenas as possible.

When you go out together, he may be looking to see who gets the most cruisey looks. He may know exactly how the two of you stack up in income, job status, handsomeness, cock size, and washboard-tummy definition. Some men will go out of their way to fuck around outside of the relationship and let their lover know every gory detail—to prove that other guys think they're hot and to gain a competitive edge. If both men in a couple are like this, they may even pull a "can you top this?" rondo of sexcapades, surely one of the quickest paths to divorce. Besides the obvious conflict, a couple stops developing together when they're in competition, because how can you show your full self—warts and all—to a rival?

Who has the upper hand in a pairing—who has the power —is one of the richest, most confusing issues between a couple, fluctuating back and forth, up and down, as wildly unpredictable as a T-cell count. After the two of you've been together for a while, power may appear to fall into predictable cycles, with one of you being the boss and the other always compromising. Usually, though, things are not so clear under the surface, especially when it comes to martyrdom and victimhood. Frequently, for example, the one who appears to be the less powerful will use his veto power (on sex, dinner plans, even housework and conversation) to equalize things as much as he can.

Anthony and David come to mind: David, even though he's madly in love with Anthony, will never be Mr. Monogamy; he just has to cat around. Anthony will suffer through him running off, complaining to all his friends, but ultimately forgiving David and keeping the relationship together. The simple view of this story is that David is the one in power (and at fault) while Anthony is the mistreated victim (noble and pure). Under the surface, however, Anthony uses David's infidelity and guilt about it to his great advantage, making David "behave" and do whatever he says, as part of his "forgiveness"; the power cycle is decidedly to Anthony's advantage in the long run.

If you have competition problems, you need to go back to the self-esteem issues above and develop a sense of your worth and good points that has nothing to do with your lover's worth and good points. Learn to enjoy what you can learn from your lover's expertise; ask him to teach you what he knows. When he has a success, learn how to be proud of him, and think how his success reflects on you as a couple. Stop putting yourself down and making inane comparisons with other guys; if your lover thinks you're terrific, well, maybe you are.

Especially learn how to equalize yourselves in bed. If you're both versatile, and one is always being the top or the aggressor in getting things going, switch. If you follow very defined top-bottom roles, try upending the positions so that the bottom's riding on top, or set up your foreplay so that the bottom feels worshiped and adored. If your "love leagues" aren't making you even as a couple (or if it's obvious that one of you can't *feel* how well matched you are), get to work, or you may soon be going into battle.

Keeping Score

Love makes some of us give and give and give until we're exhausted, but that isn't so common. What's really common is keeping score.

He goes out of his way for you and does something special and then waits for you to do something he considers equal. If you do, he'll keep going out of his way and doing things; if you don't, he'll get chilly and distant. It may not happen right away, but if a guy's thinking the score's uneven for any length of time, sooner or later you're going to hear the classic lament, "HOW CAN YOU TREAT ME THIS WAY AFTER ALL I'VE DONE FOR YOU?!"

Scorekeeping wouldn't be such a problem except that *nobody* does it in the same way, and that difference in point-giving makes everything really unfair and means that small things can accumulate into serious obstacles. Figuring out your love sprocket's point method will help explain a lot of why he is alternately groovy and not-so-groovy.

On the whole, guys give points when you do something special; they give you small points for things they think are easy for you and big points for things they think aren't so easy. Of course his judgment on this is very different from yours; something that looks easy but isn't gets small points (so make sure he knows when you're going out of your way). Keeping special things special is also part of the trick; if you make him breakfast in bed, you'll get big points the first couple of times, but if it becomes a regular feature, you'll get fewer points, 'cause then it looks easy. If something is hard for him but easy for you, when he does it, he gives himself big points, and when you do it, you get small ones.

Most men also take points away based on what they think is important. If someone you're seeing is ultrapunctual and you're usually not so timely, you may think it's a small thing and he'll get used to it—but he may be deducting big points each time you don't beat the clock, and you won't find out about it until it's the last straw and he throws a fit. If he keeps telling you he's going to call and doesn't, he may think he's just forgetting and it's no big deal. You, however, may be giving him penalties for each instance, and over time start wondering what you ever saw in someone with such a major character disorder.

The biggest points of all, though, come when he does something wrong, makes a mistake, or hurts you in some way —and you forgive him without inflicting guilt or punishment. It can be a small matter, like when you're a neat-freak and he's a slob and you don't tell him to pick up after his pig self. Or it can be a big deal, like when he backs out of doing something he knows is really important to you, or doesn't follow through on doing what you think any decent human being would do.

Many men, especially guy-guys, feel completely heinous when they do something to hurt someone they love; some can barely even get out the words "I'm sorry." For these men this is the very point when they are most vulnerable and when they desperately need to know you still love them. I'll never forget two guys I dated who were both like this; they'd do something, I'd get upset, they'd get ten times as upset because I was upset, and it'd always end up with me having to console *them*—another way that the point system is grossly unfair. Telling men like this that it's okay and everything's fine and don't worry about it (and not following your natural impulses to seek revenge and dispense compensatory damages) will earn you megapoints and make you look like a hero. And you'll be able to get away with murder for a month.

"Gimme!" "No!"

The core conflict within any couple is when one wants something he thinks is crucial and the other says, "I don't think so." You want it badly but he can't do it, finds it very hard to do, or just doesn't want to do it. This desire isn't a "you do the laundry since I did it last month" kinda thing; it's something that's way up there in your priorities (but usually not in his); something that, if it isn't satisfied or addressed or negotiated in some way, will make you question your staying power as a couple.

Jason has been living with his lover, Eric, for two years. Jason's gotten tired of always being the one who initiates sex; it's getting too one-sided and he's made a point many times of asking Eric to do the honors. Jason's turned this issue into something critical in his head; he feels that if Eric can't start things off, he doesn't find him attractive or exciting in bed anymore. He thinks it's his turn to be seduced for a change, and his patience is running out. "Never being asked" has turned into "Maybe we're not meant for each other."

Eric is very sexually passive, shy, and needs a lot of reassurance about his looks. He's never been the one to initiate sex with another man. Jason's turned it into "his duty," pulling out all the stops and using all the classic lines: "If you really loved me, you'd take the lead sometimes"; "Don't you like sex with me anymore?" and the ultimate, "I don't know about us if we have this kind of problem." If Eric was shy about starting sex in the past, you can just guess what he thinks about it now.

The way Jason's going at this is the way many of us do it: setting up an obligation and wheedling, demanding, and threatening until the other guy gives in. There are many men who bully their lovers like this all the time: "Just do *this* and *this* and *this* and then I'll be happy with you," they'll say, but then are never happy; they just come up with a new list of tasks and demands. Jason thinks that if his lover does what he wants, it really means something; but if someone's forced to do something against his will, *what* does it really mean?

There's a whole other way to go about getting your lover to do what you want when he doesn't really want to do it: Set it up so that he can give of his own free will. You tell him directly what it is, but in a way that makes it clear it's something important to you personally and doesn't mean anything about him as a lover or a person or whatever. Don't threaten, wheedle, nag, whine, or bully; just explain that it's something you want. You can even go to the extreme and try taking all the blame, even when he's obviously being the stinker: "I know it's nothing to normal guys, but sleeping together regularly and cuddling in bed after sex are these *weird* quirks of mine." If he's got a lot of reasons why he can't or won't do it, try to listen, come up with compromises, and explain ways that would make it okay even if it ends up being not exactly what you wanted.

Then be patient. Be very patient. If nothing happens, remind him gently, jokingly, or in a way that makes this something that's clearly your preference, something that's important to you personally, and something he can do for you as a gift. Nine times out of ten he'll eventually come through and be the caring, thoughtful, and generous person you fell in love with. You can then convey that you know the effort it took for him to do this for you, and how much you appreciate it . . . and him.

Jason finally snapped out of it. He told Eric that this wasn't such a big deal after all, it was just something he wished Eric would try sometimes. He explained how Eric must know, after all their years together, how steamed up he gets just looking at him naked and what a hot man he is and how, if he ruled the world, they would stay in bed twenty-four hours a day; how the only reason he really wanted to switch over is that sometimes he feels iffy about whether or not Eric's in the mood, and he's always stuck being the one doing the guessing and maybe getting turned down. With the pressure off and a couple of weeks gone by, Eric tried; he was awkward and hesitant and completely clumsy, and Jason fell in love with him all over again.

By making it clear that you two can tell each other what you really want (or think you really need, even if it's something completely goofy), that it's up for some negotiation, and that each is free to choose and act on his own, you'll be amazed how often you'll both get just what you want and how thrilled each is to come through. Doing something for your honey that you don't really want to do but that's done completely of your own accord will make you feel like Gandhi.

The Waver of Second Thoughts

Honesty, as anyone in a couple will testify, is one of the biggies. "Something that really turned me on when Daniel and I first started dating was that he was so utterly guileless, so *completely* honest with me," Richard vigorously declared. "Sometimes it hurt, because he really would say *anything,* but I'd never felt so close to someone before, and I think it was because I never thought that he was holding anything back. I feel like I know him completely, to the core; that I know him exactly the way he is, and not as some facade he presents to the world like practically everyone else I know, including me!"

There is, however, a lot to be said for not telling your spouse every single thing that pops into your head. Some couples break up because they have been too honest, while many lifers think their staying together over the long term has to do with understanding how honest and intimate they can be—and knowing those things better left unsaid. One of those things is love's big secret: the fact that, as much as we'd like to be a constant spouse, it's just not within the scheme of being human.

In love we are filled with ambivalence, with warring emotions of strength and fear, comfort and nervousness, love and hate—and we are all working like demons to hide this fact from our boyfriends. We all want someone who loves us unconditionally and forever. At the same time we are all constantly wavering inside between "This is really it; he's really the one for me" and "Shouldn't my lover be someone who doesn't [insert any of your boyfriend's qualities you don't like here]?" Should you always be honest in discussing these second thoughts, or would that make both of you, in the midst of wavering, merely undermine each other's already shaky sense of security? When one says, "I have to think about us" (which is of course exactly what both of you are doing much of the time), doesn't it always mean at least a trial separation?

The answer is to accept that everyone has these second thoughts; there's no one alive who doesn't waver. As Michael Broder says, "Far too few couples acknowledge that reevaluation of their commitment is a constant and ongoing part of every relationship." Expect that you and he are human, and not constant, but don't feel compelled to penetrate his wavers or drown him in yours. If he's seeming especially distant and preoccupied, or if you're really overwhelmed by needing to think about things, you can go to "The List" to think things over (see page 189). If those second thoughts continue to bear down, a "trial separation" might be in order—and you don't even have to leave home to do it.

Creating some distance from time to time, even when you're living together, keeps you from drowning in coupledom, makes you fresh for each other, and helps you remember all the reasons why you're together in the first place. Frequently, for example, a man is overwhelmed with grief when his dog or cat dies; the pet had been so ubiquitous that the human had taken it for granted and had forgotten how much he loved that sweet companion. To effect a miniseparation, just get busy with your own solo life. Do more work on your own; go off and see friends by yourself; take care of some normally mutual errands without him. Think single for a period, then get back together for a date night or weekend. Remember, you can quickly help yourself and your lover not take each other for granted, especially during stressful periods, by getting away from each other from time to time. Absence may not make your heart grow fonder, but it will help the heart remember, and stop thinking of the other as just another piece of furniture.

If, on the other hand, you're the kind of annoying guy who's constantly wavering and wavering, never content with what you've got and perpetually thinking the grass is always greener on the other side, there's a Chinese fable you should memorize:

There once was an old stonecutter; every day he chipped away at some huge stones and boulders. One day the local prince came riding through town, and the stonecutter watched as everyone kowtowed, trembling in fear. The stonecutter thought, "The prince is more powerful than me . . . Oh, if I could just be that prince."

Suddenly he was the prince. He rode far and wide, checking out his subjects, bringing terror and awe into their hearts. He knew he could do anything he wanted with them. But the sun beat down upon his head and he became hot and miserable, and he thought, "The sun is more powerful than me. If I could only be the sun." And he became the sun.

He hung in the sky, shining down on the world, and he shone hard and burned up all the crops, and the prince and the people cried out in anguish. But suddenly a dark cloud floated by and blocked out the sun and brought rain. The stonecutter sun thought, "The rain is more powerful. If I could just be that rain." And he turned into a cloud and started to rain.

He went everywhere, raining and bringing floods and destroying crops. But suddenly a strong wind blew in and blew the cloud away, and the stonecutter cloud thought, "The wind is more powerful. If I could only be the wind," and he became the wind.

He blew down buildings and people and wreaked havoc. Then he slammed up against a giant boulder, which would not move, and the stonecutter wind thought, "The boulder is more powerful. If I could be that boulder," and he became the boulder, big, huge, immovable.

He stayed there watching things change all around him. But he remained the same. Until one day, he felt a "tink, tink, tink" on his body, and he looked down and saw . . . a stonecutter.

The List

Even if you're the most sophisticated, savant kinda guy, all of us are infected with "The One" fantasy to some degree or another, and one result is that we commonly don't know what to do when we're hit with serious second thoughts about our men. A couple is two different people, and in certain ways they're going to be *very* different people, and while we're expecting "love to conquer all" and to live "happily ever after," when we meet someone who seems absolutely right, of course that's not the way of the world. We all fall into moods, and one of those moods for anyone who's part of a couple is "He does this and this and this; why should I have to put up with it? Maybe this isn't going to work."

Some of these things he does are nuisances and some of them are serious and where do you draw the line? How much of someone else's shit are you supposed to take? I think when you find yourself constantly falling into this mood (or when you're planning on moving in together), it's time to prepare "The List":

▶ On a sheet of paper write down what you want your life to be like in five and ten years. Ask yourself, "Does my guy fit into these plans? Will he help me move toward my goals? Or is he an obstacle?"

▶ On a second sheet of paper write down the five most essential qualities you feel your life partner should have. Then think, "Does he fit or come close to what I'm really looking for, and in what ways does he not fit or not come close?"

▶ Take a third sheet. On one side write down everything that you like and love about him, and on the other, all the things you don't like and hate about him. Put stars next to the things you really love and the things you really hate.

Take some real time and put some real thought into this; keep working until you really feel you've done as well as you can, and be as specific as possible. If done right, "The List" will cover the same issues that come up between you for the rest of your life together. We all tend to work on our Lists only when we're pissed off; to make it really accurate, try also thinking it over and refining it when you're filled with love.

You're finished; look it all over. Is it worth it? Many successful couples feel the proper formula is "60 percent plus spark." This means if your guy is 60 percent of what you think a lover should be, and there's a real feeling of love and affection between the two of you, this is really as good as it gets. Demanding 100 percent is unrealistic; putting up with less than 60 percent won't work; and with no spark there's nothing to tide us over the 40 percent we're not getting. Only you can decide; but when you find yourself falling into "Maybe this isn't right" moods, take out this exercise, look it over again, and think about one of your life's most crucial decisions.

One very interesting psychological theory is that the parts of our mate that really bug us are the things that we (perhaps secretly) don't like about ourselves. It's the Shadow Lover, rising once more. If you've struggled all your life to stay fit and eat well, but secretly deep down inside you're dying to spend the dinner hour polishing off a tub of Ben and Jerry's and a big box of doughnuts, you may become enraged when you see your zaftig boyfriend innocently chowing down. If you're the reserved, polished sort who's seriously worried about saying the wrong thing, it may drive you up the wall when your bigmouthed love bucket pops off with socially inappropriate comments. If this idea is true, you might want to carefully look over the "hate" parts of "The List" and think, "Why does this put me in a frenzy?"

Rising to the Occasion

When trouble strikes, it's always tempting to follow the golden rule of that eighties mega-bestseller, *Looking Out for Number One,* and move into the all-time biggest couple loop in the history of the world. He's done something you don't like, so you're going to make him pay, but he thinks he didn't deserve punishment, so he's going to make you pay back. Or, he's unhappy with you about something and goes off pouting and sulking; you think it's not fair that he's unhappy, and you likewise pout and sulk; your pout-sulking makes him even madder, so he starts not coming home till all hours; you go off to spend the weekend with your sexy ex in Provincetown; he fucks your best friend and lets you know about it; you go gun shopping; he's putting cyanide in your protein drink. . . .

From a distance you could just smell the infinite loop coming, with each guy trying to outbrat the other, but in the thick of it your emotions may easily overwhelm your better instincts, and you fall into the tired patterns of accusations and squabbling that everyone could do without. We're in love, and everything tough that happens grinds right into the pit of our stomachs. We're a couple, and everything bad that happens makes it look like we're not going to make it. With so much hanging over our heads, problems throw our emotions into a hurricane; little tiny nothings blow up in our faces.

If you can try to keep in the back of your mind the feelings you had starting out together as a couple—that your relationship was bigger than the both of you, something inspiring and great—you might be able to rise to the occasion and stop looking out for number one and instead start looking out for us. Instead of immediately reacting emotionally, step back, cool off, and stop thinking *Me Me Me Me Me*.

This idea is especially crucial for guys. Since many gay men think at least a little bit deep inside that gay couples are doomed to failure (or even that they don't deserve love and a loving husband), getting both of you to accept your coupledom as a solid, present, longtime arrangement can be harder than it is for married-with-kids hets. We all tend, in the emotional heat of the moment, to think: "This isn't working . . . this isn't worth it . . . he's impossible . . . I should just call it quits." Rising to the occasion means that you step back a minute, stop reacting personally, and think, "What would be the best thing for us?" Stop thinking as an emotion-filled little boy and start thinking as an adult whose future is at stake—since you are, and it is.

Rising to the occasion is especially important when the two of you are out of sync. Say you're in the mood for unconditional love, but he's feeling cranky and out of sorts; his not responding to your overtures makes you take it personally and get offended. Rising to the greatness of the two of you means you'll step back and see what he needs and what you need, right now. If he can't be your loving companion at the moment, maybe tonight the two of you should go out to dinner with some close friends. Perhaps they'll distract him from his problems, and perhaps you'll get the warmth and affection you wanted (after the decafs).

Chapter 9

· ·

♂ Fidelity?
What's Fidelity?

You know, of course, that the Tasmanians, who
never committed adultery, are extinct.

—W. Somerset Maugham

What is possibly the most universal element in human societies worldwide? The fact that people pair up and get married. The urge to merge is so strong that, even in the nineteenth-century Oneida utopian community, where everyone was supposed to have sex with everyone else and there was to be only one giant, communal marriage, couples kept falling in love and pairing up in secret.

If you think there are plenty of cultures far afield from this idea, think again. One study of 1,154 human cultures in history found that, although about 1,000 allowed a man to have more than one wife, due to economics and need, only 5 to 10 percent of the men in those "harem" cultures actually had more than one wife. Pairing up, in twos, seems to be part of our worldwide genetic code.

What is the other universal element in human societies

around the world? After getting married, people commit adultery. In a study at Yale of 185 human societies, only 5 percent insisted on monogamy and disapproved of all nonmarital sex. Another anthropological survey of 853 current human cultures found only 16 percent believing in monogamy. A 1987 survey of straight, married Americans showed 70 percent having extramarital affairs—and those were the ones who'd admit it. Apparently in monkeys and apes, the ratio of testicle to body size directly correlates with the incidence of monogamy, with the bigger the balls, the more promiscuous the female. As Diane Ackerman has said, "In humans, because we're right in the middle of the spectrum, you can ask yourself, does that mean that sometimes we're monogamous and sometimes we aren't?"

There were two other studies, focusing on American gay couples, done in the mid-1980s. Even though it's common knowledge that many gay marrieds fool around (discreetly and not), the survey numbers were pretty surprising: The first found 82 percent forgoing monogamy, while the second saw 95 percent doing so. Both found that for gay couples together longer than five years, *all* of them had made some kind of special arrangement for sex with outsiders. As David McWhirter and Andrew Mattison put it, "Sexual exclusivity is not an ongoing expectation among most male couples." One of the studies found that those couples who were monogamous for the first two years together had a much greater chance of making things last than those who had an open relationship from the very start; both, however, found that none of the couples, whether monogamous or non, were utterly satisfied with their own arrangement.*

* Of course all study percentages—especially those whose topic is something "forbidden"—are subject to debate. In 1992 the University of Chicago surveyed over three thousand Americans, and they insist that over 75

Those studies were all done in the 1980s; that was then, and this is now. Fifty-two percent of the *Advocate* sex-survey couples reported being monogamous, and even if that's a huge exaggeration, my own very limited research found a broad upswing of monogamy (or at least sincere attempts at monogamy) among gay couples. AIDS is the obvious reason; the baby-boom generation hitting middle age and growing out of our urban gay sexual Olympics may be an equally powerful factor. The American cocooning trend apparently doesn't stop with the hets.

Monogamy-or-not is probably the least-discussed issue for gay couples, yet the huge majority say extramarital fucking is the most difficult problem they face. In fact 85 percent of the couples surveyed above say it's what's caused their biggest fights. The struggle is the gay version of the old double

---

percent of the men and over 85 percent of the women report being utterly monogamous. Why are these results so inconsistent with the other studies? Let's take our own most difficult example—surveys of the percentage of the population who is gay—which have been reported anywhere between 2 and 10 percent. All of us know that a huge percentage of the guys in the sleaziest sex haunts, especially public toilets, are married. How would they respond to a questionnaire or interview about their sexual preferences? Similarly, how do you make someone respond in complete honesty about being a wanton slut who can't even keep his own wedding vows?

The same study, widely publicized, had another interesting conundrum in its findings. As *Time* magazine reported,

> Several readers questioned a figure in the University of Chicago survey of sex in America: over a lifetime a typical man has six sexual partners, whereas a woman has only two. . . . Sociologist Edward O. Laumann, who led the research team, said the 6-to-2 ratio is possible because "it is a median figure, not an average. This type of gender inconsistency has been found in other sex surveys. There are several logical explanations for it: men may be having sex with other men with more frequency than women are having sex with women; men travel more broadly and would have more opportunity for casual sexual encounters; and, yes, they may very well exaggerate."

standard: "I've always played around before, and giving all that up will put a huge burden on him. But if I can play around and he can play around, what will I think and feel when I know he's been out getting plowed? What will happen if either of us meets someone new and exciting and things move beyond fucking for fucking's sake?"

We all seem to feel the same way; if we go out and pursue random acts of meaningless sex, it's completely unimportant as far as our commitment to our lover is concerned; but if he does it, doubts nag and worries fester. What if he meets someone he likes more than me? What if that other guy is more exciting, more satisfying than me? Why can't he be happy just with me and what I can do? At certain moments the idea of our honeypots getting fucked and sucked and kissed and loved by another man can set our stomachs a'churning, while when we do exactly the same thing, what's the big deal?

Why is monogamy so tough? Helen Fisher, in *Anatomy of Love,* thinks it's Darwinian. For men, spreading your seed to produce as many offspring as possible means a greater chance for your DNA to survive through the ages, while for women, adultery means a kind of insurance. Nisa, a !Kung woman living in southern Africa, commented, "One man gives you only one kind of food to eat. But when you have lovers, one brings you something and another brings you something else. One comes at night with meat, another with money, another with beads."

When It's Wide Open

You are two men in love. You've learned all about each other's special wants and naked soft spots; you've learned exactly what to do where and when to get the other happy and excited. You are both aching to take your lover to the very apex of physical pleasure, and you've been educating each other all this time to accomplish just that. You've now been together long enough that all the fear of not measuring up, all the inadequacies we might feel about ourselves, naked with another man, have vanished. You can think, "Trick sex is nothing compared with this; why bother?" You can also think, "Trick sex is nothing compared with this; why be jealous?"

Just like anyone, gay men use sex for a wide variety of purposes. You can see if beautiful strangers find you attractive, hunt for the hunt's sake, take a fantasy break from day-to-day life (which of course includes your lover), or just do it for pure physical pleasure. Sex with outsiders can boost self-esteem and can even integrate you more into the gay community. We want casual sex as something novel and fresh for ourselves; to do something we can't do with our lover; to reassure ourselves of our attractiveness; to have sex purely as a physical act, without the romantic and historic intensity that comes with it when it's with our partner. Sometimes a guy we couldn't have screwed in the past for whatever reason is suddenly available, and we've gotta have it. Sometimes we meet someone who really ignites us emotionally and in bed, but he's in no way a threat to our main man.

If you're a gay man in urban America, you're living in a sexual Disneyland, and many think of random sex just like Dad thought about bowling. One man was really to the point: "I have a lover, and my heart is not available . . . but my mouth and dick are public property." Good sex with the right attitude and the right strangers, after all, can be the perfect antidote to whatever ails you. As one man told McWhirter and Mattison,

"I see sex with [my lover] Peter on a whole bunch of levels. At times it's been the most important way we say how much we love each other. Sometimes we've made love in anger and then again to relieve our urges for sex. We've never felt that either of us should be sexual only with the other. From the beginning that was absurd. He knew as well as I that we would trick out, so why start our relationship by making rules and denying that probability? We do lots of things alone together, and we share those same activities with others. We share pleasant meals with others. We dance and party with others. And we have sex with others. Sex can be like a recreational sport and still maintain its specialness for us between ourselves. Our relationship is maintained by our love and willingness to make it work, not what we do with others in bed."

You do, however, have to feel extremely secure about your relationship before you can explore the delicate art form of infidelity and openness. Even the most perky three-way can provoke tremendous jealousy and feelings of inadequacy if it isn't handled just right by guys who are at just the right amount of comfort with each other. In fact here's the great paradox: When you're completely secure and committed to your lover is when you feel most okay about sex with other guys. It's when they're no competition, and the sex is totally insignificant, that it has no emotional impact.

Essentially, the more attracted to and in love with someone you are, the more jealous you get. As time goes on and you fall out of hysterical passion and into more relaxing feelings of companionship with your stud lover, you frequently don't give a damn about whatever he's doing on the side. When your wanting your lover to have pleasure outweighs your insecurities about his commitment to you, all those worries vanish, and if he craves sex outside the relationship as a real need, sooner or later you'll start feeling that being jealous of that craving makes about as much sense as being jealous of him having the mumps.

Famed sex researchers Masters and Johnson have discovered that there are a number of benefits to spouse-free sex:

> There are many situations in which [an extramarital affair's] positive aspects outweigh its negatives by a wide margin. Affairs can help keep a marriage together by reducing sexual tension. . . . Affairs sometimes turn out to be personal growth experiences. Affairs don't always provide better sex or more happiness than a marriage; because of this, they can help a person appreciate the quality of his or her marriage at a time when this may have been in question. . . .
>
> Although common wisdom has it that affairs often lead to marital dissolution, we have encountered hundreds of marriages held together and solidified by affairs. . . . Marriage maintenance affairs are convenient arrangements that provide a key ingredient that is missing from one or the other partner's marriage. By supplying this much-needed element, the affair actually stabilizes the marriage and makes a breakup less likely.

On the other hand, being completely monogamous and faithful to each other, against all the odds, can give the two of you an immensely strong bond. It's very comforting emotionally, ties you together strongly, and can make you each feel secure. Some couples get HIV-tested, pledge monogamy, and drop safe sex, which can make bedlife easier—but if this is your decision and one of you is irresponsible with outsiders, it'll feel to the faithful partner like an even greater betrayal. Pretending to be monogamous while either or both of you are out cheating undermines your trust as a couple and will eventually make you feel distant and isolated from each other. Over time it's also common for monogamous couples to start feeling tied down, trapped, or taken for granted. If this happens, you need to reimagine your sex life with each other, start dating all over again (even if you're living together), or reread the "Sex Tips for Guys" ideas. Many men pursue fantasy and role-playing games with each other, for example, going to a bar and picking each other up as if it's for the first time, or one being a businessman and the other being a hustler he's found on the street. You'll have to work at keeping your monogamous sex life together great and new, exciting and fresh.

If handled just right, an open arrangement can even make a couple just as strongly bonded as the utterly faithful. You can feel completely honest with each other (at least sexually) since you have nothing to hide, and you can feel completely secure in knowing your commitment to each other is a bond that goes far beyond mere screwing. But if you or yours uses your open status to make the other jealous, run off after a fight, or as an act of vengeance, things can turn real nasty real fast. You'll have to work to keep your open status from being a source of jealousy, competition, or hurt feelings. One man described it this way:

About twenty years ago, my lover walked into a college toilet near our apartment, and found me having just completed a blow job on another man. I freaked; I couldn't explain what had drawn me there, I felt awful, I had betrayed him and our barely begun relationship, but I knew I loved this man.

We went outside and sat on a staircase and began to talk. And it dawned on me he was probably coming to this notorious john for the same reason as me—to get some action! I asked him if that was the case, and he admitted it was. We both grinned. It took us a while to work it all out (to be honest, we're still working it out), but we've maintained an open relationship for over two decades. We've met hundreds of men, had a lifetime of experience, and are completely and totally dedicated to each other.

Neither of us were raised in this sort of lifestyle—we had to work together to *create* a life that worked for us. Until both members of a couple are willing to be honest enough to face the issues confronting them, the relationship will remain a tenuous one.

If you want monogamy and your spouse wants open, then imposing limits and trying to make him toe the line is a recipe for trouble. By making them forbidden, his outside quickies and affairlets will seem all the more exciting and erotic; you'll create a situation where he'll be constantly tempted to sneak and fib; he'll probably even use sex away from you when he's unhappy with your home life and wants revenge. If you can try to feel secure with his love and stop fearing that sex with others means he'll dump you at any second, your easy-come-easy-go permission for his catting around will make you all the more loving in his eyes and take away a great deal of the fun of straying. You might give it a try sometime yourself. Here's what happened to one couple:

I was in a relationship where I insisted on monogamy. Well, he was "weak" once or thrice. He did finally tell me. I was surprised that it didn't make me want to kill, or dump him right away, or anything I *thought* I'd feel. However, the thing that hurt the most was that he kept it a secret for so long. It really was a symptom of a deeper problem in our relationship. If he had spoken up when it had happened, instead of almost a year later, things might have turned out very different. But the secret undermined the trust more than the "trick" did.

Louis, a retired architect who's been with his lover, Randy, for over forty years, had an affair that ended with a twist:

Randy and I had been together about fifteen years when I met Paul, this gorgeous kid. He was twenty-four, and we were working together. Things with Randy were fine; I wasn't unhappy, in fact I was pretty content with things as they were; he's a really solid, dependable guy, incredibly sweet, easy to live with. But Paul came after me like no one's ever done before; we had lots of things in common (lots more, really, than I had with Randy) and Paul was fun, drop-dead handsome, lively—I couldn't believe he'd even be interested in me.

He lived in San Francisco while I lived in L.A., and every business trip or other excuse I could make I'd go north. At first it was all one-sided, with him really interested (obsessed actually) and me feeling completely guilty and confused. After about a year of this he started pestering me and hectoring me to give up Randy and move to San Francisco to be with him. I thought about it for months and finally decided that yes, I'd do it. I told Paul I'd decided to live with him, and he said, "Oh, you're too late. I've met someone else."

I was really stunned, and I'm still pretty bitter about it. But coming so close to ending everything with Randy made me realize just how much I wanted to stay with him. From then on I was the most married guy in the world, and now that I see what we have together after so many years, I know I made the right decision.

That there's a big difference between sex and love gets played out hard and strong for open couples, and it happened vividly in my own life. One lover I was with for six years ran a demanding business; frequently he'd have eighteen-hours-a-day seven-days-a-week jobs that'd last for one, two, or even three months. During those periods we'd never see each other, and at first I was very bitter about it and wanted to give him up. Then I decided I could stay with him and put up with the situation by feeling free to run around when he wasn't available. So I did.

For five years I was completely unfaithful physically, but emotionally I was utterly monogamous—my heart never strayed. Even though I was meeting plenty of other men through various pickups, I never gave any one of them a second thought. The deep bonds I felt from spending years with my lover completely overshadowed anyone I might meet for a few hours; the quickie insta-sex I was getting on the side was pleasant, but I never pursued these fuck buddies beyond a few convenient and mutually satisfying evenings or mornings or afternoons or teatimes. When our relationship started falling apart in the sixth year (due to external factors having nothing to do with sex), I started giving the other guys I was meeting a second thought; it was only when I'd completely given up on continuing with my lover that those second thoughts turned serious.

Sex Deals

Getting resolved how the two of you want to handle sex apart early on is a very good idea—unless you have a thing for tears and screaming. What bothers each of us when it comes to extramarital sex can get really complicated; everyone has his own "limits." Here are one man's thoughts:

> I've noticed this in myself: If I want to trick out outside of the relationship, it's okay because I know it doesn't mean anything. But if I find out he's been fooling around, whoa. When it comes right down to it, I'm just too jealous to be

able to deal with a wide-open relationship. And there are other variations on the theme. If the guy that my boyfriend has been fooling around with doesn't do anything for me, I kinda go "have at it." But if it's someone that I like, too, that's *entirely* another matter. Also, I can handle someone straying once in a while (that doesn't mean I have to like it), but persistent promiscuity is another matter.

You can avoid trouble and misunderstanding by agreeing to a set of guidelines that will help reduce jealousy before it becomes an issue. Have a serious heart-to-heart, and come up with your own rules that both can live with. Here's how other guys've done it:

- Only having outside sex with three-ways, where both men are involved

- Only having anonymous, sex-club, and bathhouse encounters, no sex with friends

- Sex with a regular outsider is okay, but if any emotional involvement happens, the fuck buddy gets dumped

- Only having sex when out of town, not at home, and never in one's own bed

- Okay to have sex at home, but not in the bedroom

- Never having outside sex that interferes with the pair's regular or planned times together

- Never having unsafe sex with outsiders

- Never having sex with outsiders when things are going wrong with the couple

- Always discussing and being completely honest about sex outside the relationship

▶ Agreeing between each other that "What we don't know won't hurt us"

The last technique is probably the worst way to go, since it is based on lying to each other and covering up affairs—turning your relationship into something of a French sex farce. If the two of you can learn to talk about sex outside your relationship without using it as an arena battle, making it clear that you are emotionally monogamous and committed to each other, you can overcome one of the biggest problems gay couples face.

Jealousy

In the sixties we were all told not to be possessive of our beloveds; just a few years ago even Mr. Sting preached, "If you love somebody, set them free." Well, welcome to the real world. If you really care about someone, of course you're going to get upset if you think you might be losing him, and feeling jealous has in fact some benefits: It wakes us up to the fact that someone is important to us and we want to keep hold of him.

Jealousy can also be an element in how we all want to protect our lovers from the world's bad side—and this can of course include the bad side of gay men. When guys with infectious herpes or hepatitis are cruising the sex clubs (while others, simply speaking, are mean as a plate of snakes); when gay friends are fickle and irresponsible and less-than-friends . . . we want to draw our lover into the haven of ourselves and away from the unpredictability and pain of the Real World.

While hets don't normally have social events that include a constant undertone of carnal potential, it certainly is common for gay men, even if most of the room is coupled up.

The number of friends' boyfriends who've tried to pick me up more or less right in front of my friend's very eyes is truly astounding, and it seems many gay men have the idea that if another man's gay, he's available, and what's the big deal? Getting used to all this—especially in the early stages of an open relationship—means having to learn all about how jealous you are and what you can do to tamp those worries down.

If you think an all-gay-man party is filled with erotic confusion, just try an all-gay resort. One of my friends, Luther, spends every summer on Fire Island, and here's his typical evening:

> You're eating dinner with someone you've been seeing a few times, and you're flirting with each other. Then behind him is sitting a really hot guy, and he starts looking you over, so you try juggling and flirting with both of them. Then the guy you've wanted for months comes in and goes and stands just in back of the second guy, so you're trying to keep all three on the line. The third has a friend come in and they hug and kiss and go off to an intimate corner table, so he's done for; the second, piqued by your interest, comes and sits down at the table—but immediately he hits it off with the guy you came in with originally. You realize it's hopeless, so you leave the restaurant, meet someone completely new, go off and screw in the dunes, and forget about *all* of them.

Twinges of jealousy that wake you up are one thing; paralyzing jealousy that fills you up with crazy thoughts is another —those times when you start really getting paranoid and think that every moment he's away from you is spent making passionate love with someone else. Frequently these overwhelming feelings come from more than just wanting to keep someone special in your life; they mask another emotion that's the real problem. If you feel shaky about your lover's commitment to you, if you've got ideas that he only loves you for sex (or status or money or anything but for you yourself), then of course you'll be going off the deep end when he looks at other guys.

Feeling jealous when he's fucking someone else is probably genetic, but in fact, according to those surveys above, it's extremely rare for an open couple to break up over what happens from being open. If you get upset about it on a regular basis, stop thinking of the four days a month or whatever that he's out getting his rocks off without you and start thinking of the vast amount of time you spend together and what your plans are. Is what he's doing depriving you of anything? Does it really detract in any way from you two as a couple, or from the life you have together?

If you're still having trouble on this front, see if he can help make you feel okay. Could he be more discreet? Could he make you feel more secure, special, cherished so that you know, emotionally, that his outside activities are snacks while you are haute cuisine? Maybe if he makes it clear that sex with others is just sex, but sex with you is something else, you'll see that you're no longer in the arena.

You can finally help yourself by helping yourself; don't stay home and mull when he hits the streets; do something without him that's far more fun than what he's doing without you. Take yourself to a great movie or play or out to a wonderful dinner; go barhopping with some wonderful friends; hit the dance floor, or just get laid yourself. If you're really bothered by it, the answer may be not to live together; that way you won't be confronted so often, and you can know as little or as much about his meaningless trysts as you want.

Of course if someone serious appears and offers him something you can't or won't, there'll probably be some self-assessment in order. If things get really out of hand, you are of course completely justified in calling the other party and asking, "I don't understand what's going on. Can you fill me in?" Make the interloper take responsibility and make it clear that he's nothing but a cheap home wrecker, then make it clear to your b.f. that you had this conversation and that you're afraid of losing him, especially after all the wonderful things you've shared together, like that night when you accidentally locked yourselves out of the apartment and had to call the super and sat and kissed out in the hallway.

If he's getting looks and laid and you're not, your jealousy might be a case of bitter envy. If you're a Run-Around Sue and you can't stop yourself from constantly thinking about sex with other guys, you'll probably feel guilty and perhaps think your lover's the same way and, at the same time that you want to be free, you want him to stay home and do the dishes. You may also have the kind of lover who gets feelings of love if he sees you jealous—Mr. Flirt—and if you want him to cut it out and he won't get therapy, you may have to go overboard to let him know your feelings and get him to calm down. Constant flirting may also be his attempt at telling you, "I feel like you're taking me for granted and not giving me enough attention"—and even if you have been giving him all the loving anyone should ever want, sometimes it's never enough. So if you're overwhelmed by jealousy, try to think it over and see if there's other stuff going on underneath.

When I'm out with my boyfriend and interested parties approach, I expressly let my guy know that I'm out with my boyfriend. Touching him, whispering to him, laughing with him, impulsively kissing him, and keeping my distance from any pursuers usually lets both them and him know the score. "I'm so much in love right now, I can't really have sex with other guys" can get you out of lots of trouble, as can "Have you met the love of my life?" said at appropriate moments. My flame of desire hasn't quite learned the various nuances of these crucial techniques, but as he's sincerely interested in retaining the use of both testicles, I know he'll develop this talent in the very near future.

Chapter 10

♂ Keeping It Together

Gays must work twice as hard for people to think we're half as good. Fortunately this is not difficult.

—RUPAUL

You Better Work

Contrary to popular beliefs, mating for life is very rare in nature; it happens only with some kinds of birds, a couple of species of beetles, a few fish, the Nile crocodile, the American toad, and certain types of wood lice. Among mammals, only 3 percent settle down with a single companion; all wild dogs mate up, for example, but besides the canines there's merely a couple of kinds of antelopes, some monkeys, certain seals, muskrats, beavers, a few bats, the clawless otter, the dwarf mongoose, and the deer mouse.

In fact many anthropologists, sociologists, and other societies think it is bizarre and unnatural that most Western countries base coupledom and marriage on romance. As Denis de Rougemont wrote in his classic *Love in the Western World,* "To try to base marriage on a form of love which is unstable by definition is really to benefit the state of Nevada. . . . Romance feeds on obstacles, short excitations, and partings; marriage, on the contrary, is made of want, daily propinquity, growing accustomed to one another. Romance calls for 'the far-away love' of the troubadour; marriage, for love of 'one's neighbor.' "

We'd all like to think that "love conquers all" and "all you need is love" and "love is the drug"—that two people in love will never have any problems if their love is strong. Of course, if you have a little couple history under your belt, you know how naive this is, but even the most sophisticated man is usually surprised at how much work it takes to keep two guys, aflame with devotion, from killing each other. Love may be the inspiration to makes things work out, but by itself it's a lazy little thing that can't accomplish much.

Everyone wants to be loved with consistency, strength, and utter devotion. Unfortunately love is whimsical, capricious, and obnoxious. You can go out on the town with your husband and think, "He's the greatest guy who ever lived," get into bed and remember something he said you didn't like, wake up the next morning and be furious at him, and then completely reverse yourself and fall in love all over again while you're slicing the prosciutto for lunch. There's nothing specifically that happened to make you fall in and out and in again; it was just love being the imp that it is. But that impishness is exactly what keeps us on our toes, and makes marriage so difficult.

The Tao of Elmer

"There is no society in the world where people have stayed married without enormous community pressure to do so," said Margaret Mead. Not only do straights get tax and insurance benefits that gay marrieds don't, but gay men don't really have much social pressure to keep coupled, and this is one of our many problems in staying together. We have a collective glue deficiency.

Wouldn't it be great if your friends and family accepted the seriousness of your relationship the instant that you see it that way? Unfortunately this seldom happens, and for a very good reason. Even the most gay-positive and supportive colleagues are familiar enough with the instability of gay relationships in general (and perhaps yours in particular) to not want to get emotionally tied into your lover if your current beau doesn't stick. When a breakup comes, they'll get hurt too.

As one mother told therapist John Driggs, "I don't want to get attached to one of my son's lovers until I'm sure that he will be around for a while. It's exhausting to get to know one and like him, only to find out a year later that you'll never see him again because the relationship is over." Of course as couples we need all the support we can get. But if your friends and family aren't instantly warm and inviting to your new guy, try to remember they may have a valid reason and don't hold it against them. How often does it happen that when a friend mentions a gay couple whom you haven't seen in a while, your first thought is, "Oh, are they still together?" How rarely do you have the same thought about married hets?

An additional problem is all those times when you feel uncomfortable with Public Displays of Affection (PDAs). While waiting in a movie line, while the het couples are kissing and touching and holding each other, we're usually doing none of the above, no matter how long and how solid a pair we may be. As Betty Berzon put it, "The need to stop one's self before the spur-of-the-moment kiss or touch of the hand often took its toll in the couple's ability to be spontaneously affectionate, even in private. Love so diminished often did not survive."

Additionally how often does one partner of a gay couple, in the middle of a fight, say something like "I don't need this shit; I'm leaving!'' They don't necessarily mean it; they're using the prospect of divorce to win this battle, or make their lover wake up, or as a threat to get their way. But if it's a constant refrain in our fights, it only helps undermine us even more.

Sometimes it's obvious that two of us are in it for the long term, yet our families continue to make us feel that our relationship doesn't count. It can happen in many little ways that pile up, such as the mom who remembers all her children's spouses' birthdays but not her son's long-term lover's. Roger got a call from his grandparents, announcing there'd be a big family reunion in a couple of months. They made sure to mention that perhaps his lover, Joel "wouldn't feel comfortable attending"—even though Roger and Joel had been together longer than any of Roger's straight and married siblings.

Also, while het sex and romance roles are often strictly defined into stages of acquaintance, friend, boyfriend, fiancé, husband, and ex-, gay men live with more ambiguous positions. For example, there's the fuck buddy who's more than an acquaintance but less than a friend and maybe we're still having sex but maybe not. There's the "We've been seeing each other for a long time now, but who's ready to discuss real estate?" situation. There's the ex-lover who's sort of a friend but both of us are hoping that maybe things will bring us back together again in the future.

While it's great being fluid, it'd also be nice sometimes knowing where we stand with each other. Having things vague means your relationship isn't as rock-solid as it could be, and a little shake could turn the boat over. As Tina Tessina noted,

> We do not see thousands of images of gay couples meeting, dating, falling in love, and living "happily ever after." We do

not see examples of how two women or two men can divide up household chores, handle finances, and deal with emotional stress. We have no way of knowing who is supposed to initiate sex, who makes the financial decisions, or how these power issues are resolved. As a result, each of us has had to attempt to reconstruct role models and certain behavior codes from scratch, never knowing whether we're doing it "right" or not.

Do you know hets who've lived together for years and years yet refuse to go the final yard and get married? This is usually what happens when at least one of them wants to have it both ways: They have the security of being part of a couple, and they feel free to leave at any minute. They never get beyond the ambivalence we all feel about our better halves and make a final, solid commitment. Unfortunately since most gay couples aren't tied together by the legal bonds of marriage and the emotional bonds of children, we are often in exactly the same position: part of a couple, but not fully committed.

Since it's so easy to meet guys (especially if you know the tricks in the foregoing chapters), it's always tempting to look elsewhere when trouble appears. Every relationship goes through rough periods; without children and social pressure it's extremely difficult to keep it up. If you want to stay with someone, plan on working like a dog. One man put it this way:

It seems that many people I have talked with seem to overlook what I consider to be the single most important thing that contributes to a long-lasting relationship. Terry and I have been together four and a half years. It has been a very interesting time, with many difficulties, and lots of ups and downs. The thing that has gotten us through everything has been an unwavering commitment to the idea that we are together for the long haul. It sounds very simplistic, but it is amazing how helpful it is to approach problems with the assumption that breaking up is not an option. You figure out ways to compromise and work things out when you simply don't have the alternative of walking away. We have each given the other cause to break things off during the last few years; we're still together because we know that we belong together, we know that staying together requires effort and determination in addition to love.

I wonder how many gay "relationships" are more equivalent to going steady than to marriage? The whole point of dating is to try things out, be free to move along; the whole point of marriage is staying with someone for a very long time. We "dated" for quite a while before we decided to stay together always. Having made that decision, we are able to work through a lot of things that "boyfriends" would have little reason to.

Words, Words, Words

With all this trouble, helping to define and solidify what's going on between the two of you isn't such a bad idea. Let's say that one fine day you and he are out shopping and you run into a very good friend whom you haven't spoken to in a while and you say, "Carla, this is John," but what you'd like to add is, "my———." Filling in that blank may seem insignificant, but it's something you both should give some real thought to.

Throughout the decades, we've called ourselves (and have been called) "urning," "Uranian," "invert," "friend of Dorothy," "pansy," "orchid eater," "nelly," "nancy-boy," "nance," "swish," "light-in-the-loafers," "fruit," "faggot," "fag," "queer," "queen," "homo," "mo," "girly-man," and "gay." Since Stonewall, "gay" has been the most popular, but some think it makes us sound light and insubstantial; they want more politically confronting labels such as "queer" or "faggot." Each name has a different spin and tone to it, and what you call yourself and want others to call you says a lot about who you are.

The same holds just as true for a male couple. To date, the longtime favorite term is "lover," but it looks like public opinion is starting to sway. Many men think "lover" makes their relationship sound too sex-oriented, insubstantial, and short-term, and are starting to prefer "spouse." Others think "spouse" sounds too Barbara Billingsly; they like "paramour" or "comrade"—which to others sounds like you're living in eighteenth-century France or are some pair of retro Muscovites. Being from Texas, I think "partner" sounds serious but friendly; my sweet dream, however, thinks it sounds like a corporate merger, and prefers "boyfriend"—while two middle-aged men calling each other "boyfriend" smells a little goofy to me. "Inamorata" should be reserved for special occasions; "mate" is for Popeye, "lifemate" is for therapy addicts; "main man" is for seventies refugees; "stud-muffin" will confuse the literal-minded; "special friend" is for delicate relatives.

If you're in a 1940s mood, "beau" is good; randy teens (or those who merely act like them) can be "steadies"; "swain" is nice, but sounds a little too much like "swine"—which may be perfectly appropriate at times; "husband" brings up the "which one of you is the woman?" issue for your less-educated straight friends; and there's always "sweetheart" and "other half" when you've completely given up on everything else. In the 1994 *Advocate* sex survey the most popular terms were, in order, "partner," "lover," "life partner," "husband," "companion," "significant other," "boyfriend," "spouse," and "mate."

My suggestion? Use them all—find out what terms each of you likes, but don't be afraid to try on others for size, especially when your coupledom changes for the better (or worse). And don't be afraid to make up your own nicknames; "Carla, this is John, my honeypot," has a certain direct charm. If you get confused or just plain forget, this handy clip 'n' save chart can be yours:

Lover	Boyfriend	Sweetheart	Partner	Husband	Spouse
Other Half	"Friend"	Swain	Comrade	Roommate	Mate
Fiancé	Intended	Betrothed	Beloved	My Guy	My Man
Spark	Flame	Companion	Lifemate	Buddy	Love God

Moving In—Arrggh!

One of our society's biggest pressures is the belief that lovers must live together, and if you don't, there's something wrong with you and your relationship—you're just not "serious." Since we don't get many of the benefits of traditional heterosexual courtship and marriage, why bow down to the traditions that don't fit? There's a natural inclination to want to move in with the guy of your dreams, but before you do, think hard: Is this really the right choice for us?

Joseph Harry studied gay couples, and discovered that those who didn't live together and preferred it that way felt just as fulfilled with less constant companionship as those who did live together. One of my friends had a long-standing *Who's Afraid of Virginia Woolf?*–style relationship with his lover until they stopped living together; things started really clicking for them the minute he moved out. This may be just as true for you and yours, so give "alternative living arrangements" some serious thought before leaping into that U-Haul. Taking time to really get to know each other's good and bad points (especially those bad points) before moving in together can't be recommended highly enough. It's all in the timing, since discovering his petty irritations and troubles all at once (with the same happening on his end) can make you both want to run for the hills. If you learn, over a period of months, that you have to wear earplugs to get some sleep because of his thunderous snoring; that he won't have much bedtime snuggling since you wake so early and go to sleep so late; that cleanliness is godliness since he's a total neat freak; and that your ten years' age difference means he likes sex every other day while you're ready for it every other hour, this isn't so much to bear. If you find out all this within a few days of living with a stranger, however, it could make the future seem less than bright.

Before the big decision, try weighing the benefits and liabilities of joint real estate very carefully:

- Combining paychecks means we can live better than we do separately, but it also means handling financial problems together as well.
- We'll be able to see each other whenever we want, but we'll have to figure out what to do when we want to be by ourselves.
- We'll know each other more and become closer, but we might start taking each other for granted and lose the spark.
- We'll feel more secure about ourselves as a couple, but we'll

have more pressures to deal with, and there'll be a lack of privacy and independence.

Making the Commitment

Congratulations! You've taken the plunge, moved in, and things are going pretty well. You've joined the estimated 40 percent of gay men who share a household with a partner. Remember those old-time marriage vows? "I promise to love, cherish, honor, and obey, in sickness and in health. . . ." You must make a similar commitment to your relationship—that your being together is one of the most important things in your lives—and remind yourselves of it on a regular basis.

You've looked at each other and thought, "This is the one." It may be the corniest advice you've ever heard, but I say, *Have a ceremony.* For plenty of gay men "gay marriage" is an immediate turnoff, but there are many reasons to think it over.

Since the dawn of human culture we've used ceremonies to signify something very important in our lives. Deciding to become each other's spouse, s.o., lover, main man, and long-term stud muffin is a crucial step that deserves the serious attention and memorable celebration that only a ritual can provide. It gives your vows to each other a public cementing and concretely symbolizes the wonderful fact that you two found each other and are committed to making it work. Gay marriages in fact have a long history, with notable precedents including Roman soldiers, Native Americans, and Ming-dynasty Chinese. In 1993, two thousand gay couples were wed at the climax of the Gay and Lesbian March on Washington.

The biggest news about gay marriage has come from across the seas. In May 1993 the State Supreme Court of Hawaii ruled that refusing to give marriage licenses to gay couples deprived them of financial and legal benefits (including lowered taxes, inheritance rights, Social Security benefits, and cheap hunting licenses), violating the due process clause of the Hawaii state constitution. As reported in *The New York Times,* "The Supreme Court sent the case back to the trial court to determine whether preserving the marriage ban was 'a compelling state interest,' the highest level of judicial scrutiny and one that legal experts say is rarely met unless public safety is at stake." As of this writing, it looks as though the only solution is for the legislature either to legalize gay marriage or to provide such a sweeping domestic-partnership law that marriage licenses restricted to straights wouldn't include any compelling benefits. Either way there'll be no more needing to go to Amsterdam.

The real question, though, is: Why can't we take the best parts of marriage for ourselves and drop the boring junk? Why not give your very serious relationship the approval and validation it deserves—the same kind any het duo gets? It can be as churchy (or as synagoguey or as mosquey) as you want. I myself, for example, have always wanted a *chuppa,* even though I'm not Jewish, because they are so excellent.

Having your union spiritually blessed may make you strive harder to keep things together when it's not so easy, and most religious organizations insist on couple counseling before going through with the vows—not such a bad idea, even if you've met the love of your life and are human society's first perfect couple. The religions that are open-minded about all this include Reform and Reconstructionist Judaism, the Metropolitan Community Church, the Quakers, and the Unitarian Universalists, as well as some Methodists and Episcopalians.

On the other hand, your service can be completely secular, with a bunch of friends and relatives, all dressed up in your living room. Just as weddings come in all shapes, sizes, and religious beliefs, you and your squeeze can decide and negotiate exactly what you want for your ceremony. And since there aren't any burdensome traditions of same-sex-union rite precedents, you two can do absolutely anything you want (though don't be surprised if mom tries pinning something borrowed and blue under your tux).

If the words "wedding" and "marriage" bother you, there are plenty of other names to try: "holy union," "lifetime commitment," "rite of blessing," and "union ceremony" are the most popular alternatives. Depending on what each of you think, you can either have or forgo all the traditional elements: formal announcements; shower; special site; rings (engagement and wedding); clergy; photographer; reception with food, favors, and dance band; and of course the honeymoon (though whoever heard of dropping the honeymoon?). A full, all-out formal wedding for two hundred will cost you around twenty thousand dollars—so that may be reason enough to forgo some of the tradition.

Engraved invitations—or ones you do yourself on a computer, a laser printer, and some yummy cream-stock paper? Exchanging vows at dawn with a breakfast for your twenty closest friends—or the Cathedral of Saint John the Divine on the anniversary of your first date? One couple's preceremony presentation included a slide show of each partner's development, from childhood to the present. You can call the gay cruise lines listed in "Where to Meet Men" and even get hitched on board.

Planning all this out together doesn't have to be the trial by fire of a traditional wedding either; spend some time with it, make sure you're ready, and savor the planning and the moment together. Don't you have a favorite song, or a poem you've known all your life, or epigrams on life and love that are important to you? Even if they're bittersweet or downright bitchy, include them in your service. Don't be afraid to have fun and show your joy. Isn't there a special place that's important to you? Try that first; you may be surprised at what's available for your celebration.

Union ceremonies commonly include the following elements: a statement on why this is a special occasion, a promise and a commitment, a symbol of that promise, and the whole thing sealed with a gesture. Your symbol and gesture can be the traditional rings and kiss, but cultures around the world have used different means (such as exchanging food and sharing a glass of wine) to mark the same moment in a couple's life. A terrific Jewish symbol is the *mizpah*, a charm that's been cut in two and says, "The Lord watch over me and thee while we are absent, one from the other." Let your imagination roam.

Your commitment vows can be equally expressive and of your own making. Here's one that shows just how far afield from tradition you can freely go:

Like many of my ilk, one of my beliefs was always "so many men, so little time." So it was quite a shock for me to meet you, and after many months to fall completely in love with you, and many months after that to realize that I wanted to spend my life with you. You are so sweet, and you are so smart, and you are so sexy, and you are so kind, and you are so special, and you are so lovable that I still can't believe this is happening—that we are here together.

In front of all of these witnesses, I now promise you, in two ways, that I will work to the very best of my abilities to be the man of your dreams. I will honor you as an individual, guarding your freedom to pursue the life that you want for yourself. And I will be constant and steady, the friend, lover, and partner who is always there to celebrate when things are good, and help when things are not good.

I will do all I can to make you feel cherished and supported, trusting and honored, inspired and comforted, loved and free. Having you in my life is the most important thing in my life, and to help both of us remember this promise, I give you this ring.

♂

All het couples have anniversaries, why not you? The fun here is in picking what your annual day refers to: when you first met, when you first dated, when you first slept together, when you started dating regularly, or when you moved in together. All of them are perfectly appropriate; just pick one and celebrate. Have a second honeymoon; have all your mutual friends over for a big party; show off to each other that you're making it as a couple. Take over this straight tradition and make of it what you will. You'll have plenty of moments to feel hopeless and morose about your future together; set aside time to consider your accomplishment and your great good luck as well.

Behind Closed Doors

The first big problem you'll run into after moving in is—surprise—your damn privacy. You're on the phone talking to your best chum, Margie, all about his good and bad qualities —when you suddenly realize he's sitting in the next room and could've heard every single word. He's borrowed your laptop for the weekend—and, too late, it dawns on you that there may be some things in there you don't want him reading. You get ready to go out for the night—and he's wearing your not-cheap tuxedo shirt. You're in the bathroom with the door closed; he walks right in anyway. Are you ready to reveal to someone else all your secret fetishes—or will you throw away that priceless collection of erotic Bolivian-soccer-team-in-their-underpants Polaroids before he sees them?

It's the stuff of every wacky sitcom since *I Love Lucy,* and it's also major trauma. You will each have ideas about privacy that the other thinks is nutty, so just get them out in the open and allow each other to be gooney in this respect. Maybe you need separate answering machines . . . maybe you can't read his magazines without checking first if he's read them or not . . . maybe he can't invite friends over without asking you first. Don't do the "It means he doesn't love me if I have to ask to come into the bathroom when the door's closed" bit; realize it just means that you have to ask to come into the bathroom when the door's closed, and do it. In day-to-day life you'll have far more exciting stuff to fight about than this.

Some guys think one of the most wonderful parts of living together is that it instantly doubles their wardrobe options. If the two of you even remotely share sizes, you'll constantly find yourselves trying on each other's things at crucial moments. This is one sharing issue that needs to be addressed fast; some guys can't stand giving you the freedom to wear their prized outfits. As Dorothy Atcheson noted, "*Borrowing* underwear is one thing, but if you're throwing it all in one drawer and sharing it indiscriminately, you're pretty merged. In the 12-step program of gay cohabitation, underwear-sharing is a major boundary issue."

The Big Shuttle

The second big complication you'll probably see on moving in is that you'll both have an *immediate* need to be by yourselves. Before joint housekeeping you spent a lot of time and energy on how to be together—coordinating schedules, making reservations, planning the day or evening, deciding which place to spend the night—but living together means you'll be spending just as much time and energy on being apart. As you merge your individual daily routines into a joint operation, each of you will be staking turf. Partially it's also the old "the grass is greener" sensation: When you were single, you dreamed of finding a great man and sharing your lives together; now that you're married, you think everyone in the world who's single is having the time of his life whereas you're being stultified.

There is one balancing act that, no matter who you're with or what stage you're in or how much you love each other, will always be present, and it explodes when you move in: You are each individuals *versus* you are both part of a couple. There are times when you'll each want to be by yourselves, when there are friends you want to see that your partner doesn't care for, jobs and hobbies that can't really be shared, family obligations that everyone knows would be better off handled solo.

Dr. Charles Silverstein thinks all men (and gay men in particular) are ruled by two opposing passions: We want the security, comfort, and stability of a home and steady lover; simultaneously we want to be able to go out and have the adventure, excitement, novelty, and freedom of being single. Some men are more on the Nest Builder side, others are more in the Excitement Seeker mode, but all of us swing back and forth, our erratic emotions and muscular whims pulling between these two poles.

Trying to force your coupledom down each other's throats and thinking you have to do every single goddamn thing together has been tried by gay couples throughout the centuries with the same result: They all ended up hating each other's guts. Two ultraindividuals making a go at it and pursuing so many separate job, family, and social situations, however, end up living *around* each other. You fall into routines, taking each other for granted, becoming more and more distant, perhaps even having separate bedrooms, bathrooms, phones, closets, and home offices. Some couples get so distant being joint individuals that they literally end up making special arrangements to see each other for romantic evenings and weekends—living together, but back to dating.

Successfully juggling he, me, and we is tough, and it's crucial. If you're in the mood for love and he wants to go do intense yoga breathing for an hour, you have to stop thinking, "He doesn't love me anymore!" and start thinking, "Later, when he's in the mood, we're going to make up for lost time." If you're in the middle of some endless phone call trying to calm your hysterical friend, Alice, and he keeps coming in every two minutes to give pointless shoulder rubs, you have to stop thinking, "He's an obnoxious pest," and start saying, "Wait'll I'm done on the phone and you won't be sorry."

Contemporary philosopher Thomas Moore thinks that our very souls have an insistent need both to be with other people and to be on our own, and at this stage you may really learn that lesson. The trick for both guys is to have enough security so that you each feel fine when the other's off on his lonesome. Don't Bee a nervous Nellie who thinks it's the end of love and marriage because you're not spending twenty-four hours a day together; do Bee a man who respects his lover as an individual, wants him to feel happy and free, and knows you each bring unique qualities to your life together.

Basic Tenets

Why do we pair up and move in together? To fulfill our dreams of home and family; to create, as a couple, a "haven in a heartless world"; to have love, passion, and the secure comfort that someone else is always there. We move in together hoping to have this constellation of desires become a core, basic element of our daily lives . . . and instead spend practically all our time negotiating, arguing, and manipulating each other over the niggling, irritating problems of mundane existence. We never have time to create that world we always wanted; we're too busy dealing with garbage (and laundry and dishes and money and . . .).

As early as possible in your living together try to work out the core day-to-day issues, and stick to it. How you pay the rent, grocery bills, utilities; how you cook, wash the dishes, and clean the house; taking care of pets, doing yardwork, evenings spent together and apart, even vacation planning— all are issues that should be resolved before emergency strikes.

Household chores: Try to talk first about what things you like doing, and that'll make the fifty-fifty divvying not so fraught with "mopping is twice as hard as dishwashing" analyses. If he likes to cook and you like to set the table and clean up afterward; if he likes to go to the Laundromat while you like to vacuum; if you both like doing windows together (and who doesn't?), you're halfway home. Couples who don't have a pattern of likes they can fall back on frequently develop a point system, negotiating what each chore is worth and divvying up that way. Others alternate, with each doing *everything* for one week or month (this is a good technique if you're having lots of master-slave issues popping up), while others have one doing more chores and paying less rent. The best solution? Hire a maid, and don't clutter your life with such trivial matters.

♂

Money, like chores, has many problems and many solutions—except for the maid part. You can split everything equally, or let things fall along the percentages of each one's income. You can have utterly separate banking arrangements, a joint checking account with each contributing monthly for household expenses, or a piggy bank with each contributing a set amount every week.

A joint checking account can be used by either of you separately (and if this is so, make sure you keep accurate records and balances), or it can require both signatures on every check. You can even have joint credit cards—though of course if one of you goes on an insane shopping spree and can't afford to pay, the other will be stuck with the bill.

Many couples start out completely separate moneywise, but as time goes by, finances merge and merge until everything is combined—"your" and "my" become totally "ours." When this emotional and financial mingling is finally reached after years of being together, many guys think it's a real proof of their commitment and trust in each other; they feel solidly together as never before. Starting out $$ separate, though, isn't such a bad idea, since you won't be arguing over each other's mysterious shopping habits, such as your seventy-fifth salt-and-pepper collectible, or his must-have ten-CD set of Annette Funicello's greatest hits.

If you're splitting along income lines and you're the one with the bucks, don't think your paying extra will automatically make him feel loved and taken care of. Most men feel inadequate if they think they aren't pulling their own weight. One guy with a rich boyfriend said, "At times I feel like he's trying to buy me. I feel like I can't measure up, since I have not been nearly as successful in my own life. I also feel bad because I can't buy him the kind of expensive presents he gives me."

If, on the other hand, he's got the bigger income, don't think it's nothing that he's contributing more than his fair share; he may feel you should be putting up with a lot more from him in other ways than he has to put up with from you. Inequality as far as money goes is fraught with potential land mines, so try to strike a bargain that everyone is comfortable with and everyone thinks is fair. If you're having screaming fits over who should pay the $17.50 laundry bill since he's got massive quantities of dress shirts while your cat is always spitting up on the silk divan slipcovers, get your financial act together and get a life.

♂

Legal Matters: At some point you both need to go see lawyers. We do not live in a society wholly supportive of gay couples, and not every gay man's blood relatives are compassionate and understanding. If your lover is hospitalized, you may be kept from visiting him, and if he's seriously ill and uncon-scious, you may be kept from participating in the decision about what to do next—unless you have a *durable power of attorney*. A regular power of attorney expires when your bet-ter half becomes incapacitated; a durable power keeps you on the visitors' list at a hospital and allows you to make financial and medical decisions in your lover's stead. When serious trouble strikes, this document should be shown on admission to a hospital to prevent "misunderstandings" from occurring later on.

Just as today there's no such thing in the United States as a legal gay marriage, there's also no such thing as a legal divorce. If your relationship ends unhappily (and how many relationships end happily?), you won't have any court protection over your finances and property. Especially if you and your partner have complicated business and financial arrangements, you might want to prepare a *relationship* or *living-together contract*. It may seem really nerdy, but many couples have found it incredibly useful to think carefully about and express in words exactly what their expectations and needs really are. You can write about money, sexual fidelity, division of labor, career plans, how to settle fights, even "prenup" stuff in case you decide to call it quits. Some couples include when they plan to be together on a regular basis, consultation strategy on major shopping decisions, pet-care negotiations, provisions to go out of town for a romantic weekend every other month, even arrangements for when they plan to quit smoking together. Figure out the crucials, and use this informal agreement to let each other know just what is significant in your new life together.

If you're buying a house together, the deed can be specified as *tenants in common* or as *joint tenants with right of survivorship*. "Common" means that you own the property jointly; "right of survivorship" means that if one of you dies, the other will retain title no matter what a will, if one exists, says. Either form should be accompanied by a *joint ownership agreement,* which will state what percentage of the property each of you owns, what will happen if you decide to dissolve joint ownership, what happens when one dies or won't pay his share, and other contingency matters. You should consult a lawyer in the appropriate state to make sure your needs are met.

♂

Should a terrible accident or sudden death occur and your property issues aren't settled in writing with a *will,* you might find yourself plagued by locusts—a.k.a. his relatives. Without a will a legally unrelated lover has far fewer rights than the dreaded Uncle Irving, and when it comes to money and property, even the most gay-positive in-laws can turn rapacious. If your family is homophobic, expect them to take their final vengeance on you for being gay by trying to violate the terms of your bequest. Do your will ASAP, no matter how young or how healthy you are; who knows when you or he will suffer some horrible accident? Maybe the example of Gertrude Stein and Alice B. Toklas will clue you in: When Trudy died intestate, her blood relatives yanked the couple's staggering art collection and magnificent apartment completely away from Alice . . . who was left in utter poverty.

When creating your will, you'll need to think about all your valuable possessions and sentimental items and where they should end up, as well as who you want to be the executor of your estate. A will is also where you should state your preferences for your funeral, burial versus cremation, and all those other pleasant thoughts. You can specify who should organize the service, and how much money from the estate should be used to pay for your final party. Don't assume everyone will have your desires in their hearts after you're gone; can't you just hear someone saying, "I know John wanted marble, but these plastic urns are so much less expensive and it'd look so nice in Uncle Todd's guest bathroom." A will can be fought in three ways: that it was improperly executed (with weird bequests, or written in lipstick), that there was undue influence involved, or that you were incompetent when it was drawn. A good attorney will make sure none of these issues will be lurking around after you're gone.

A *living will* states your preferences for what extraordinary measures should or shouldn't be taken in the event you are medically incapacitated, a decision you should only make for yourself. In both cases forewarned is forearmed.

Love in Translation

The different styles between you and your guy are never so clear as when it comes to how you each express your love. How does he let you know he loves you? Does he talk, does he phone, or is it in the way he touches you, volunteers to do favors for you, or pops up with presents?

How we saw our parents treating each other, the romances we watched in the movies and on TV, our own daydreams of romance, the chapters in our inner Books of Love, and what happened in our past affairs and marriages all affect the way we act in love today. With all these different origins, it shouldn't be any surprise that we all show our love in very different ways, but it usually is—in fact frequently a couple needs a translator until they get used to each other's *langue d'amour.* You may go off to work each morning with a "Have a good day, honey; I love you," and when he doesn't respond the same way (but shows you in plenty of other ways that he does indeed love you to death), you'll get unhappy—unless you are actively translating. One guy put it this way:

> I think saying "I'll love you forever" is usually used more to convince oneself than to communicate anything of substance to one's partner. By that I mean the men who have been the most glowingly "lovey" in their talk have been the

ones who have fallen out of love the most quickly. The man I am currently with is more reticent with such love talk, but seems to mean it when he says he loves me. It's interesting to note that in traditional marriage vows one doesn't promise one's partner permanently lasting love (the emotion) but permanently lasting commitment (the actions). When a man tells me, "I love you," my gut response is to ask myself, "Yeah, but what does he *mean* by that?"

Neurolinguists believe that, though we use all our senses, each person has one sense that's dominant. According to this view, you can be primarily visual, auditory, or kinesthetic (feelings/touch-oriented) and that'll be the way you send and receive love. Which do you enjoy the most about your lover: touching and holding him, looking at him, or listening to him? Does he love getting hugged, like to see you dressed up, or is he always calling on the phone and singing you love songs? Do you spend lots of time listening to music, going to art museums, or having dinners at home and just being together?

Following this idea, you can say, "I love you so much!" to a touch-feelings guy, and if it isn't done with a hug or some other kind of touch, it won't have much force. Say it to someone over the phone who's visual, and it doesn't have the impact that a face-to-face would. Try figuring out what his dominant sense is, and use it to really let him know your feelings.

One man I know would get upset if we didn't talk on the phone at least twice a day; those phone calls meant love to him. Another could barely say the words "I love you"; he would instead rub my arm with his fingers, which to him meant exactly the same thing. A third always wanted me to decide what we'd do for the evening or weekend, what we'd eat, what we'd do in bed, everything; giving over all the decisions to me was his way of expressing his devotion. One man told me this story:

> I'd been seeing Alan for a couple of months, and things were really good between us, but I felt like something was missing. There was still some rockiness; things weren't smooth. He wasn't very emotionally expressive, and I'd gotten used to that; still, I felt like there was something troubling him that was keeping us from really being together in some serious way.
>
> He was always doing these favors for his friends, and lots of times it annoyed me, because I thought some of them were taking advantage of him, and you know, I'm Mr. Self-sufficient. Then I suddenly woke up: This was his way of showing someone he cared about him, with all these favors. So I started consciously asking him to do minor things for me, errands that I could've done just fine but that were easier for him to do because of his schedule, and the change was unbelievable. Suddenly he was completely comfortable, and that rocky feeling that'd been worrying me was gone.

Anthony and David are also a great example. Anthony grew up with a bunch of hugging, kissing, and fanny-patting Italians who did everything together. When he was growing up, David's folks were on top of him all the time, wanting to know where he was and what he was doing and who he was with, second by second—with lots of criticism and commentary about every bit of it.

Anthony's style of love is just like his family's, with lots of physical contact and lots of togetherness, while David's is just the opposite (in reaction to his parents being so overbearing) —he shows love by giving his guy lots of freedom and independence. It may look like Anthony is the more loving of the two (and that's exactly what he thinks), but in fact it's just a matter of style, not quantity. There was a happy ending: Anthony got used to David's way of demonstrating his love and gave him lots of room; David, at first very awkwardly, learned to enjoy being together more often and even being more physical with his lover.

One of my protospouses was immensely empathic; I could say "I love you I love you I love you" a thousand times, but if I didn't do it with the right look in my eye and tone in my voice, he thought I was just blabbing and not sincere. I could likewise talk to him about the most difficult, soul-grabbing troubles between us, and if I used a compassionate tone, it'd turn out okay (while his ex, who never figured this stuff out, could say something only mildly critical and it would drive him crazy for days).

Another man and I had completely opposite styles when it came to being troubled. If he got upset or mad, he wanted to be left completely alone for as long as it took him to pull himself together. When I'm upset, I usually only want to be by myself for a little bit, but then I want lots of distracting (and loving) company. So I'd see him unhappy and rushed to be the loving company, he'd think I was overbearing and suffocating. He'd see me upset and leave me utterly alone, and I'd think he was a butthead. As you can guess, it took some time for us to get used to this.

Tina Tessina, in her book *Gay Relationships,* has a fantastic list of "what love means to me." If you and your lover are frequently in conflict over romantic misunderstandings or think the other is from another planet when it comes to expressing love, make two photocopies of this list, have each of you check off the items that are crucial to you, and compare. You'll be amazed.

I Feel Love When My Man:

- Fusses over me when I'm sick

- Brings me flowers

- Calls me at work

- Cleans the house

- Lets me make a mess sometimes

- Greets me and talks to me about his day when I come home from work

- Gives me space when I come home from work

- Buys me presents or takes me out on birthdays and anniversaries

- Kisses, hugs, and touches me often

- Lets me know I turn him on

- Lets it be okay if I don't want to make love

- Phones me if he is going to be late

- Gives me time alone

- Doesn't seem to notice if I've gained a few pounds

- Encourages me when I have a problem at work

- Helps me to forget work and relax

- Celebrates my successes and achievements with me

- Is nice to my friends

- Does some of my chores if I'm especially tired

- Tells me when something is bothering him

▶ Holds me when I cry

▶ Makes me laugh

▶ Doesn't take it personally if I'm feeling crabby

Vulcan Mind-Melding and You!

In researching this book there were two subjects besides infidelity that practically every couple I interviewed wanted to mention. When I asked long-termers, "What's the secret to staying together over the years?" the answer was always the same: *communication and trust.* But don't just think, "Communication and trust are good"; that's like saying, "World peace is good." The crucials are in the specifics.

Everyone's been in a situation where you and he are out of sync, your moods aren't congruent, your wants don't match up, the evening is filled with tension, and bad feelings are in the air. You feel like everything you do is wrong and everything he does is wrong and none of the patches either of you tries will put it all back on track. When you've been with someone long enough, and when you've become close enough and trusting enough, however, you can have times that are the exact opposite—being utterly in sync. You both move and operate in tandem; everything is smooth and easy; when trouble rears, it's quickly fixed.

Is anything more comforting than the feeling that you can trust another person utterly and without reservation? Many feel that this is the ultimate goal of being part of a couple, and taken in the larger sense they're right. If you are able to make plain your unconditional love for him and receive that feeling in return, your life together can transcend petty difficulties and tiny troubles and last for the big haul.

Getting that Vulcan mind-meld going is no snap, though; you'll have to confront many things you don't like about yourself, and you'll have to take risks over things that you feel iffy about how he's going to react. It means getting to a point where you're willing to give more than you want to give and ask for more than you expect to get, a point where you're not afraid to look foolish, stupid, weak, wrong, or even less than a man in front of the person who's the most important human being in your life. It means that both of you think you can say or do just about anything and the other won't swerve.

Intimacy is a deeper need than many want to believe; you can live without it, but you can't flourish. Connecting with another person, growing closer and closer, feeling more and more comfortable, until finally you are both able to be completely honest and reveal your innermost desires, fears, and hopes is a process that nourishes your soul with meaning and significance. As we talk to each other, caress each other, complain to each other, share significant experiences with each other, fuck each other, and hold each other, love, understanding, and trust all deepen into richness. We stop wasting our time creating Band-Aids for our existential loneliness; we stop being cynically convinced that "Life's a bitch and then you die."

By being part of a strong couple with the right soulmate/lover/spouse/partner, we are deeply connected to each other and to the human race as a whole. In love we are better human beings: patient, kind, generous, considerate, selfless, tender, giving. In love we are richer human beings: desperately trying to hold on to something that is crucially important, yet maddeningly evanescent, something that floats all our worst emotions—fear, jealousy, competition, revenge, bitterness, anger, suffering—right to the forefront. We go out into the world, knowing someone is there for us; someone who's hoping our day is wonderful; someone who's thinking we're great lovers, important people, terrific guys. When life on the outside is hard, we can turn to each other for inner strength and emotional recharging; when life is good, we can enjoy it even more together.

Achieving all this, however, is no Hallmark card. "Getting to know you" means sometimes thrashing out differences, fighting to find common ground and make ourselves understood, facing the possibility of losing him and what the consequences might be. The struggle to connect may become so intense that one of us may need to withdraw for a while, getting strength as an individual before returning to the arena and fighting for each other another day. Being able to get away from time to time is in fact a key part of growing towards being together.

To make matters even more difficult, a great many men are very uncomfortable with making that deep, close connection with someone meaningful. They believe that if they reveal their fears, their worries, their doubts, or their troubles, it'll make their b.f. have less respect for them and think less of them as men. Many others feel, when they're completely in love and deeply enmeshed with another guy, that they're losing their own identity, becoming dependent and not in control of their own life. Many are truly frightened that if they let themselves fall in love and then get dumped, it would be worse than not letting themselves fall in the first place.

If this is what's going on with your lover, the burden may fall on your shoulders by default. At some point take a deep breath and try asking for something that you think he may not want to give. You can then try fantasies, dreams, and ideas you have that others might consider weird. The final piece of the cake arrives when you've done something you know he won't be happy about, and you admit it, say you were wrong, and ask him to forgive you.

If he's not responding in kind, it may or may not be your own doing. Ask, and try to be patient. See if he knows why he doesn't feel ready to trust you yet. Talk about the things in your separate lives that weren't exactly your happiest, strongest, most admirable moments. Work it up.

Everyone has a different style of communicating, and especially if you two are on the "opposites attract" spectrum, you probably will have style troubles. The clues:

- Every time there's a problem, you end up fighting

- When one is upset, the other usually has no idea why

- One always feels misunderstood or ignored

Here, then, are the key communication hot spots:

- **Remember to talk when things are good.** Is there anyone alive who's heard "I love you" *too* often? No way, and no matter how clear you think your feelings of love and devotion are, this is one rerun that no one ever gets tired of. If a wonderful memory of something you did together suddenly occurs, say so. If the CD player's on and a love song suddenly pops out and inspires you, sing along with Mitch. If you're attempting seduction, explain precisely why he's the greatest sex you've ever had. When he does something especially smart, witty, helpful, charming, or just plain wonderful, tell him—and tell his friends and relatives too.

- **Remember to talk when things are bad.** This advice isn't intended for those of you who are professional whiners and naggers; you people can learn to shut up. This advice is needed when either of you is so scared or mad that you won't talk. Scared is scared of rocking the boat; he's doing something (or a number of things) that bug you, but you don't mention them, trying to get over it. You hold back and hold back, getting angrier and angrier, until the final straw breaks the camel's back and you blow up with a torrent of accusations and complaints that he's hearing for the first time. This scenario ensures that it's good night, Irene.

That torrent (and the hidden, simmering resentment that led up to it) can be a real couple killer; some therapists believe that resentment is the all-time biggest threat to a relationship. If one of you thinks the situation is consistently lopsided and unfair, the other will start looking less like a lover and more like the enemy. If he's bugging you about the same thing(s) over and over, work it out before you blow, using the "Gimme!" "No!" techniques mentioned on page 184. You may not get him to do exactly what you want, but you might get close enough to make both of you content.

There are any number of men who grew up being told that their opinions and feelings didn't matter, and they commonly have "simmer" problems. If that's the fish you've hooked, he won't be forthcoming or talk about his feelings easily, and you may have to put in some overtime to get him thinking that these things do matter to you. You know what your lover is like normally; if his behavior suddenly changes, it's usually time to have a talk, and you may have to be the one to get that talk started.

▶ **If one of you is acting up, try talking instead.** Many guys are taught from the time they're little sweet tiny baby children never to express emotion except as "action," so they learn all this terrific passive-aggressive stuff instead of just coming out and telling you what's going on. You walk in the house to find Mr. Sweet Stuff sitting at the dinner table in icy silence and you say, "What's the matter, honey?" and he says, "NOTHING." Or he says he's coming home late; it's ten, it's midnight, it's two A.M., and still he's not home and he didn't call. Or suddenly he has many social obligations . . . and you aren't invited.

If this is happening, you have to be the grown-up and ask specific questions until he comes through with some talking. Instead of "What's your fucking problem?" try "Why are you mad at me?'' or even ''Are you mad at me because I can't go to Herman's party this weekend?'' and keep asking again and again until the truth is out.

If you're the one who's acting up instead of coming out, try practicing with small, not-so-important emotions first, and then build up to the biggies. If you think it's unmanly to cry, for instance, try to realize that when a man feels free to cry in front of someone (and he's not doing it to manipulate), it's actually a compliment; it means he trusts the other person enough and feels so close to him that he thinks it's okay to look weak and not together.

- **Remember to listen aggressively.** Use empathy to really tune in to him when your guy's talking about big stuff. Make sure he's following what you're saying by watching his reactions, and listen to what he's telling you with your entire body. If he starts getting really distant, it may be a good idea to time-out and talk about it later; if he gets really bent out of shape and completely defensive, you should try some reassurance and the ''This is all my problem, not yours'' approach. Be responsible when you talk, and responsible when you hear.

- **Talk together about your childhoods.** Lots of times, things we find Martian about our lover become utterly clear when he talks about how his brother treated him, or what his parents were like, or what things he loved to do as a kid. Yet it's astonishing how many boyfriends know nothing about each other's formative years, as if we'd each sprung full-blown from the head of Antinous. If you're the shy, not-so-socialized type, ask him anytime you want about what his friends and family were like when he was young; it's always illuminating (at least).

- **Remember that sometimes the answer is to shut up.** When your lover is upset, most of the time he doesn't want you to analyze his problem or come up with answers or point out to him that his position is either valid or illogical. He just wants you to listen and to be there with him; he just wants not to be alone with his troubles.

Another time to shut up is when you're therapy abused and you tend to give more prominence to minor issues than they deserve. One couple I know, Robert and Bob (yes, it's confusing), have both been seeing psychiatrists for many years, and they communicate beyond any couple therapist's wildest dreams—in fact they communicate too damn much. They tell each other precisely every single feeling that, minute by minute, pops into their hearts. Like everyone, sometimes those feelings are loving and sometimes they are "I'd rather see you hit by a speeding bus than have to look at you over the Wheatina this morning."

Remember that you have the right as a human being to have moods, but your man has the right not to have to know about all of them all of the time. Give it some thought before popping off; you may feel completely differently in a matter of minutes. Each of you also has the right of privacy; maybe there are some things you really *don't* need to tell each other. Therapists demand for couples to "Communicate! Communicate! Communicate!"—but sometimes it just goes too far.

We may wish to have a domestic life as pleasant and harmonious as any Disney cartoon, but it's when we go through fire, pain, and hell together that we are pulled more tightly to each other. In order to achieve the love, the closeness, and the bond we all dream of, and be able to fight the fight to make it happen, we have to be as self-assured, brave, solid, and powerful inside as we can be. We have to be tender enough to open ourselves, nakedly, to another man, yet man enough to weather the storms that always come with the territory.

The Fun House Mirror

When you are in love and your love is returned, it's like living in an echo chamber; each's personality becomes magnified by his lover. The masks we've each created for our polite appearance in society get worn away by our lover's presence and his wanting to know us more and more deeply. Our best qualities rise to the surface, but so do our fears and traumas. Being with another man will automatically stir up your deepest emotional conflicts. Trying to bandage them over with a quick fix of communication and compromise instead of really exploring why such issues cause you grief is in fact running away from yourself.

When trouble strikes, we immediately want to think, "If only he'd change, things would be okay." But you can turn this beat around by remembering your love is an echo chamber or a mirror and asking instead, "Why is it that when he does this, it bugs me so much?" Stop seeing yourself as right and him as wrong and instead learn to see the two of you as cocreators of the problem.

I've used this idea myself: My boyfriend is far more experienced at working out at the gym than I am, and when we go, he wants to spend time with other guys at his level—which I found piglike and irritating, especially when I saw all the other couples who do work out together. Why did I care so much? After a while, thinking it over, I remembered phys. ed. in high school, when I was one of those legendary last "pre-fags" anyone wants on his team, and I realized immediately what was happening at the gym now. He is still a pig, but the conflict isn't all his doing, and the solution isn't for him to change but for me to have a different attitude (or join a different gym).

Let X = X

> *In former times, if people wanted to explore the deeper mysteries of life, they would often enter the seclusion of a monastery. . . . For many of us today, however, intimate relationships have become the new wilderness that brings us face to face with all our gods and demons. . . . Intimate relationships force us to face all the core issues of human existence—our family history; our personality dynamics; questions about who we are, how to communicate, how to handle our feelings, how to let love flow through us, how to be committed, how to let go and surrender. If relationships are difficult, it is because being human is difficult.*
>
> —JOHN WELWOOD

Being part of a couple is like learning to dance. We each have our own dances as individuals; we then take those separate movements to make a new, theme-and-variations dance as a couple. We can be awkward and clumsy and step on each other's toes . . . or maybe he wants to mambo, while you're ready to waltz. If you're very, very lucky, however, sometimes the two of you can sweep across the floor in perfect rhythm, each doing a great job at making just the right moves, reading each other's minds to create perfect synchronization and harmony.

For all the obvious reasons, award-winning dancing is extremely rare, yet we too often think that every day of our life together should be filled with blue-ribbon moments. Because of this fantasy we get obsessed with the clumsiness, with the toe stubbing, with the minor frictions, becoming emotionally overwhelmed when things are out of sync and the dancing isn't perfect. Sometimes couples are like Jell-O that squishes together with just a little nudge; and sometimes they are like billiard balls and no matter how much merging force is applied, they bounce off each other in ricochet.

Every pair sooner or later hits a patch o' weeds. In the early evening you're in the mood for love while he's thinking about pulling together all the stuff for your taxes; later he's in the mood for love while you're mad that he wasn't in the mood earlier on. In the morning he thinks you're childish because you were mad and you think he's selfish because he wasn't on when you were . . . and this can go on for days.

With het couples, women are usually the ones who're required to be flexible and adapting, since men are so notorious for being "set in their ways," creatures of habit, and lovers of routine. If you've got two men who are both stubborn goatheads, merging and compromising into a couple will be especially difficult. One of our major complaints as couples is always "things shouldn't be this difficult," but the more goatlike each of you is, the more difficult things will be.

Long-term couples usually get to discover this issue the hard way when phase three of most relationships begins. You've been infatuated; you've nested; but now it's the cold light of dawn, and everything the two of you *don't* have in common is making a dramatic reappearance on the stage. You'll discover that his slobdom is genetic, a force impervious to your sarcastically pointing out the pigsties he leaves in his wake. He'll learn that your need to have random acts of meaningless sex with strangers is something you're not willing to forgo, no matter how much begging and nagging he tries. You're both constantly trying to change the other, and you're both constantly asking yourselves the age-old question: How much of this shit do I have to take?

This phase can last a couple of months; it can come and go for a lifetime; or it can even become the centerpiece, the touchstone, the great-item-in-common for you as a couple. Some guys never "accept the things they cannot change" and nag and gripe until they drop dead; others, terrified of splitting up, stifle their complaints and worries into one big seething, unexpressed hostility. Some men even turn into the gay version of Tracy and Hepburn, their lives taking a backseat to endless rounds of bicker, bicker, and more bicker. This is of course the time when both of you are thinking, "Gee, that grass over there is an awful lot greener; maybe I deserve better."

Just knowing that this is the phase where most couples fall apart can give you the foresight you need to keep going. Knowing that you need to go out of your ways to remind yourselves (and each other) why you fell in love in the first place will help smooth over this period. Maybe you are too dissimilar to make it work, but maybe it's time for both of you to stop looking for the "perfect" guy and love the one you're with. Don't let the heat of the moment determine major life decisions; if you start thinking serious thoughts of separation, try to back off and get some perspective. The couple that survives this phase and doesn't turn it into a lifelong drama is in for a big treat (see below).

The great line "Accept the things we cannot change" can even go farther: Accept what is. As our old math teachers always said, "Let $X = X$." Learning to understand what's going on between you two and accepting that this is the way things are will make you a lot happier than constantly trying to make your twosome fit a fantasy pattern from your inner Book of Love (which has probably nothing in common with the pattern he's got anyway). Stop thinking, "If only he'd change!" and start thinking, "X."

To do this, you have to learn to *step aside*. Here's how it works: He does or says something that throws you into some emotional turmoil. You don't like being upset and you try to talk yourself out of it, but the more you think about what happened, the more horrible thoughts appear in your head: "How can he do this to me? . . . I don't deserve this. . . . If he really loved me, this would never have happened. . . . We're just not right for each other, this isn't working . . ." until you're enmeshed in a hurricane of emotions.

By trying to focus your analytical mind and step aside from this tumult, you can stop making yourself more and more upset and actually solve much of the problem. To step aside, take some deep breaths, do whatever you can to relax your mind, and try to be in an observing instead of a feeling mode. Think about why he did what he did and why, especially, it upset you so much. When your emotions are in chaos, your mind is overwhelmed by the irrational; you're jumping to conclusions, taking what's probably a small matter and extrapolating it into universal significance. "He forgot to make dinner reservations" becomes "He doesn't really love me." Stepping aside means bringing back the rational function. It's extremely difficult to master this technique, but with lots of practice you will be able to do it. By stepping aside when trouble happens, your coupledom will become greatly strengthened, and you will become one of the world's great boyfriends.

The Decline of Passion

Infatuation is when you think that he's as sexy as Robert Redford, as smart as Henry Kissinger, as noble as Ralph Nader, as funny as Woody Allen, and as athletic as Jimmy Connors. Love is when you realize that he's as sexy as Woody Allen, as smart as Jimmy Connors, as funny as Ralph Nader, as athletic as Henry Kissinger and nothing like Robert Redford—but you'll take him anyway.

—Judith Viorst

Every couple says, "It won't happen to us," yet it seems to happen to everyone. After a few years of living together it's universal for romantic love and sexual passion to dwindle. Your PEA's falling off, your mind's on taking care of day-to-day life together instead of "dating," you're in the mood on Tuesday, while he's anguished over a job problem, and then he's in the mood on Thursday, while you can't decide whether or not to fire the maid.

Most couples will have trouble now, since each is feeling less attractive to the other and each is seeing the problems and limitations of the relationship that the romance and sex helped them overlook in the past. The honeymoon is over, and you may start finding your day-to-day life seeming utterly repetitious and mundane. Your lover may start looking like the most boring man you've ever met (and he may think exactly the same about you). Both of you will start feeling taken for granted, and outsiders will start having more and more allure. Many men don't know what to do next; unless you become good buddies and develop a sense of teamwork, can this marriage be saved?

Don't think that you will be the first couple in history to confront this fate; romance is based in great part on mystery and distance, and it's pretty impossible to keep up romantic illusions and ideals about your man when you see him day after day after day. Also, you're getting tired of being madly, soap-operatically in love all the time; fatigue has set in. The intense early feelings of love drop, as does the desire to have sex as often as possible, and this combination leads many guys into serious depression.

Some therapists believe that if the hump of disappointment

that happens at this stage can be overcome, your relationship will enter its strongest phase. They say that you are no longer *in love* and that you can now start truly *loving*. Your differences as individuals may be reemerging, but at the same time you start being more selfless and more caring. What's probably going on is that the tension and nervousness of your early dating days is over, and a sense of comfort and long-termism has settled in; you are in fact taking each other for granted, but in a good, solid way. As one man said, "Things do get stale. What I have found is that when you have separate interests, and take separate vacations once in a while, what you bring back to the relationship could spice it up. After twenty-one years we find that we are more like best friends; the sex thing has sorta taken a backseat. You get real comfortable together, and just the closeness becomes the center of the relationship."

When this happens to many men, however, a whole host of fears arise. Most guys don't feel confident that they can keep a relationship going, and it's at this stage in a couple's life together that those feelings can sabotage everything. If this is happening to you, remember: All long-term couples have gone through the exact same thing. You and your spouse will be closer than ever before in certain ways, while in others you'll feel strange and awkward, since this phase isn't exactly a highlight of love stories and romantic myths.

It's also common for this period in your coupledom to be accompanied by either or both of you going through a nice, knock-out midlife crisis. You're singing along with Miss Peggy Lee, constantly wondering, "Is that all there is?" as you reassess your life, run around like a dizzy teen, and torture innocent bystanders with your yo-yo mood swings. Many couples don't survive the combination of midlife trauma with bloom coming off the rose, but if you both remember that these are natural developments that happen to practically all marriages, maybe you can see that it's okay and that in fact you're tighter together than ever before.

Part of the reason you're tighter now is because typically you've finished with the "merging" stage and now both of you are reemerging as individuals. You each feel free to go off and do things without the other; you go back to interests that you had alone before you met; you discover new interests that are yours alone. You're practically reading each other's minds at this point, knowing in advance how the other will react, and there's a great comfort in going off on your own and then coming back together again.

Because you're so comfortable with each other now, you feel free to be more honest; you don't have so many fears that if you say the wrong thing, he's outta here. You may feel like you're both in an endless therapy session, with him saying, "And another thing I don't like about your friend Morton . . . ," and you saying, "And another thing I don't like about how you fuck . . . ," day in and day out. You're also so comfortable that you aren't paying enough attention to yourselves as a couple, and sometimes that taking-for-granted bit isn't such a good thing.

There's no reason to feel that just since this is a predictable stage in coupling, there's nothing you can do about it. You can try rekindling those early days of feeling completely in love by remembering what worked for you both in the past and re-creating that now. Try some "sex tips for guys" and "little things mean a lot," or whatever else will remind your man how important, how special, how crucial he is to you. Remember the lengths you used to go to when dating? Making plans, buying small gifts, coming up with special surprises? Keep it up; take the time and make the effort to be romantic and passionate, loving and sexy. Set aside an evening for dating when both of you are expected to turn it on and not let mundane life intrude; get away for the weekend, or just throw off all the world's responsibilities and spend a few hours together in bed. The hard-core passion may have ebbed, but the joy of romance is always in your hands (or wherever). Feeling safe and secure can get boring; bring back some novelty and excitement. You've got plenty of comfort, so hit the delight.

Commonly a couple now become coworkers. Working together on something—taking care of a house or a garden, redecorating the apartment, planning a series of weekend trips, even taking lessons together—will help tighten and maintain those bonds and can often mean greater intimacy between two men than when they were fucking five times a day.

How to Have a Fight

Never go to bed mad. Stay up and fight.
—Phyllis Diller

No matter who you are, you are two very different people trying to make a go of things together. You will have conflicts. If you avoid and ignore them, they'll just sit around, haunting your house. Unspoken angers and resentments can destroy the most committed relationship; but if you bring them out in the open, have a big fight if it's needed and work things out, you'll be even more in love with each other than you are right now. Not talking about "It" in order to keep things in harmony won't keep the music playing for long; usually a dramatic confrontation is the only way many of us really get our true thoughts and feelings out on the table.

A good fight sometimes easily, but more often very painfully, can be effective in generating a solution to the problem or in helping one or both of you adjust your attitudes and see things in a new light. Most of us don't have good fights; what we usually do instead is to start to discuss something rationally and quickly devolve into screaming, accusations, cruelty, and completely absurd statements that you wish you'd never said in the first place. Try to remember the following points, however, the next time a fight starts and you may be able to have a good confrontation that really does something:

▶ **It takes two to fight, and one to stop the fight.**

▶ **You know you're angry at him, but until you know specifically why, don't talk about it.** Starting to talk without having a point to make means you'll just flail around and break the Limoges.

▶ **Fights usually start out about an issue, but within minutes turn into being about how each person is fighting.** Remember, style is everything. How you say it is far more important than what you're saying; watch out for your eyes and voice.

▶ **Learn how to make criticisms that aren't personal attacks.** "I like things to be tidier than you do," for example, will work better than "You're a real pig, aren't you?"

▶ **Learn how to talk backward and take the blame away** ("I'm the kind of person who likes . . ." or "Wouldn't it be great if . . .") **so that he doesn't get offended and defensive, which will get you nowhere fast.**

▶ **You don't always have to be right.** Pull out all the empathy stops and don't just be obsessed with your own point of view. See if you can figure out why this issue is such a problem for the two of you instead of just trying to get your own way for a change. Make an effort to understand why he thinks and feels the way he does.

▶ **Try to have perspective:** How crucial is this fuss? Are you causing lots of agony over something that's really no big deal?

- **We Nancy boys are famous for our irony, sarcasm, and wit.** Now is not the time to practice; curb your tongue, knave.

- **We fagelahs are also brilliant at mimickry, at hitting below the belt, and at going for the throat, using ridicule and our enemy's most sensitive personal points against him.** Not now.

- **If you're having a fight and one or both of you becomes a crazed bitch, back off and time-out.** You'll only make psychotic pronouncements, which you should be saving for the next time you go to a sale at Bloomingdale's.

- **Try to only fight about one issue.** Don't bring up every single thing you don't like about him every time you want to fix something ("And another thing I'm sick to death of . . ."). Stick to the point.

- **Say what you think and feel** ("I'm really angry about this") **instead of blaming** ("You really make me mad when you do this"), **or saying what you think he thinks and feels** ("If you loved me, you wouldn't make me mad like this!").

- **Don't make threats, especially ones you don't really mean ("Either you clean up after Miss Tweety . . . or we're through!").** Just because you're really, really upset doesn't mean you're ready to call the whole thing off, but it may come out that way if you don't watch your mouth. Threatening to end the relationship when you don't really mean it but just want to win an argument is the coward's way out. If, however, you get so mad that you do in fact have to get out for a breather, make it clear you'll be coming back.

- **Try to have the fight end with some kind of resolution, an answer.** Say what you'd like him to do to make things better, or if he's the one who's mad, ask what you or what the two of you could do to work it out.

If you have to discuss something really crucial, make an appointment (when you both have time and when you're both going to be in the right mood) and set an agenda. This'll give you time to think about what's earth-shattering and what's not, and solutions that would be okay for you. When the time comes, say what's on your mind, with as little threat and attack and accusation as you can muster. Let each other explain how important this issue is to him and what solutions he can think of. Negotiate.

Keep in the back of your mind, "We're a team, and together we can solve this." If you feel like you want to launch World War III, take a few deep breaths and calm down. Don't threaten, don't coerce, and don't be afraid to say what you think. Lighten things up with your sense of humor (without using it against him). If the solution isn't in sight, maybe you can come up with something that'll work for the time being; you can always talk about the issue later on.

Infinite Loops

One of the reasons fights that could potentially be constructive instead degenerate into something more debilitating is that couples start to have predictable responses to each other, creating bad loops that are difficult to break.

Your lover comes home depressed and frustrated about something and is cool and distant to you because of it. Instead of asking him what's wrong, you take his mood personally and become off-putting and cold yourself. This makes him feel more removed, which makes you more distant, and the cycle spins and turns, unless one of you makes a concerted effort to break it.

Serious infinite loops, though, involve qualities that are specific to a couple, and they're practically a m--'

"He does x, so I do y, so he does $2x$, so I do $3y$, . . ."
Louis, for example, is a chilly kind of guy. This really bothers
Randy, his lover, who compensates by spending as much
time together as possible—he attaches to Louis like some big
leech. Louis likes having lots of time alone, and when Randy
overdoes the togetherness, he feels smothered and withdraws
even more. This makes Randy more leechy, so he attaches
harder, making Louis more distant, making Randy more
smothering—until they drive each other completely insane.

If you find that your lover is consistently making you nuts
over the same issues again and again, try to be empathic and
talk out the matter. If you had asked and understood that
your b.f.'s bad mood had nothing to do with you in the first
place, if Louis could figure out that his distance made Randy
feel unloved, if Randy could get the idea that constant togetherness wasn't accomplishing anything, these loops would
vanish. Backing off a little from your coupledom may give
you some perspective in working out this kind of trouble.

Empathy, Again

If understanding other people emotionally doesn't come naturally to you, the "Empathy 101" discussed at the start of this
book really needs to be worked on when you're part of a
couple. Do you have "gaydar," that is, do you know another
gay man when you see him? The nonverbal clues of gaydar
are the keys to empathy, so if you can figure that out, you can
learn to figure out your lover.

In traditional, straight relationships the woman usually as-
sumes the burden of being the empathic partner, interpreting
her lover's feelings and keeping the couple together by reading her man and knowing when to move in emotionally and
when to pull back. Mother-infant bonding and the old chest-

nut of "women's intuition" imply that females are naturally more adept and sophisticated at empathy than males. Biologically the neural pathways between the two hemispheres of women's brains are actually more fully developed than those of men's, so it may very well be that women are innately better able to interpret body language, vocal tones, and facial expressions. In a relationship between two men, empathy work is frequently required to compensate.

Empathy plays a crucial role when you start seriously seeing another guy, and being able to pay attention to your lover and really listen to him is easily the most important thing you need to learn to do to understand each other and thus keep yourselves together. Once you're empathic, you'll know not to take it personally when he's feeling less than amorous because his mind is focused on something else, and when he's more upset about something than it seems to deserve, you'll know to try to find out what the real problem is.

Though the ability to read tone and nuance is crucial when your lover is upset or angry, that isn't the best moment to practice—instead see if you can pick up what he's thinking and feeling when you're eating dinner, watching TV, or having sex. Just as before, empty your thoughts and only "receive," trying to make an emotional picture from the look in his eyes, the tone of his voice, his gestures and facial expressions. During these special moments it's possible that the only things you will pick up are "I'm starving," "Change the channel," and "Blow me," but you may get other insights as well.

A common thing that happens between men when they're not being empathic is that they turn a talk about emotions into an argument about ideas. If your man talks to you about his feelings and you respond by attacking the logic of what he's saying, this isn't a conversation, it's two monologues.

Feelings have nothing to do with logic and everything to do with expression. So if you just shut up about your own damn opinion and get him to talk, the problem may fix itself.

The other common nonempathic moment is when you're discussing important, heavy stuff and you spend all your time thinking of what you're going to say next instead of listening to him and seeing how he's reacting to what you're saying now. If his reactions or body language don't mesh with what you expect, you're not being empathic, and you're not communicating either.

One technique that many therapists use when a couple is out of sync and having a hard time can have incredible results. You and your guy arrange to be together for twelve hours—an entire day—with absolutely no distractions. No TV, no books, no magazines, no computer, no phone calls, no relatives, no friends, no nothing, only each other. At first you'll feel awkward and strange; then for a while you'll open up and really talk about things that've been on your mind but pushed to the back burner; you'll feel great together and will think you might as well call off the rest of the experiment. But then you keep going and all of a sudden you find yourselves talking about stuff you've never even mentioned before; many couples who've tried this end up feeling like they know each other (and themselves) in a whole new way.

Couple Therapy

When you're in trouble as a couple and it isn't just him and it isn't just you and the advice from your friends isn't getting you anywhere, you should probably consider getting therapy together, as a team. Couple therapy is designed to solve problems that happen between people, where neither is to blame. Some recommend couple therapy as a means of safely talking out serious issues, even if everything's going great between you. If you've got the following issues going on, though, you should seriously look into it:

- Conversations about problems always turn into fights that go nowhere. You have the same fight about the same thing over and over again, and it never gets resolved.
- Both of you avoid discussing certain things, since you're afraid the issue is so delicate, it could blow you apart.
- You are so far apart on certain issues that you can't even come close to understanding how each other feels.
- Either of you is compulsively drinking, eating, drugging, fucking, gambling, going into debt, or being a workaholic; either of you is severely depressed.

The Lonely Couple

One of the big surprises I found when researching this book is how many men go into coupledom and wind up lonely because they lost all their friends from their single days. The gay community-center bulletin boards and on-line computer services are filled with notices from couples looking for platonic friends; it's as if they woke up and suddenly realized they were together but alone. How did this happen?

Friends get dropped for all the regular reasons, but there are additional pressures when male marriage comes into the picture. If you once had lots of single gay friends, the bar- and bath-hopping you may have done with them probably isn't going to be as much fun as it used to. If some of your old friends spent lots and lots of time with you, they may feel you don't have time for them anymore. You may be so engulfed in nesting with your new guy that you don't go out of your way to keep in touch, and your friends may be tired of initiating everything you do together. Some friends won't mesh well with your Mr. Right, and it may be difficult seeing them; others may make your lover jealous, especially if you've had something going on in the past. Many guys make new gay friends after having sex with them first; if that's no longer an option, you may not know what to do.

You can of course use the "Where to Meet Men" ideas of chapter 4 to make friends instead of sex dates, but you could also learn new ways to be with your single friends. Maybe you, the b.f., and two of them can go out dancing as a foursome; maybe you could be having them over more often for dinner and TV; maybe a threesome to the theater or a museum would be just the ticket. If your lover doesn't care much for some of your friends, why not just see them by yourself? It's a great excuse for when it's time to get away.

If you get a lover, don't become such a love addict that you disappear from your friends' lives. Make sure to make time for them; include them in events with your spouse; draw them (especially your single friends) into your new family life. Don't take them for granted.

Reading His Poetry

Wouldn't it be great if other people were simple, consistent, easy to grasp, and a snap to understand? Wouldn't life be easy if your new s.o. always and forever remained his personal ad —"Italian GM, brn/brn, stache, lean and trim, smart but open-minded, seeks fair-haired lover of all things (including me)"—and you could always tell just what he was thinking?

Well, too bad. People are a mass of many things, and you won't believe just how many things until you make that commitment and live together. One minute he's passive and impulsive; the next he's authoritative and can't wait to boss you around. One minute he couldn't be sweeter; the next, if you don't get away from him immediately, knives will fly.

Marriage means you'll be learning detail upon detail about another man, as well as a great deal about yourself—but at a certain point there is the unknowable. Practically everyone at some time or another complains about being misunderstood, but how well do we really even understand ourselves? Are we utterly consistent and logical in our emotions and thoughts; do we have an overriding character that forever remains constant? After years of practicing psychoanalysis Jung in fact felt that "In the end, people don't want to know what secrets are slumbering in their souls. If you struggle too much to penetrate into another person, you find that you have thrust him into a defensive position." So try to understand enough about yourself and him to keep you together, and for the rest —enjoy the puzzle, and allow yourself to be amazed (or amused) by the mystery.

Living together, you'll discover how both you and your s.o. are deep, complicated, and living with lots of personalities and subpersonalities jumping around inside. So instead of being angry or confused that he changes and moods around and gets so strange you never know what to expect, enjoy it! Just as poetry is a few words that bounce off each other to evoke greater things, you can stop trying to figure out every inch of him and instead learn to read his poetry and marvel at the vast, inner life of another human being.

Just to have a feel for how complex a marriage can be, try considering this simple form of Transactional Analysis (T.A.), a theory of relationships that basically says we all fall into family roles with each other. When you're doing something together that he knows a lot about and you're unsure of, he's like a dad and you're like a son. It can reverse, with you being the dad and he being the son, and when you're equals, you can be brothers together:

You		Him
father	↔	son
brother	↔	brother
son	↔	father
father	↔	father
son	↔	son

Conflict, according to T.A., happens when you're both competing for the same roles, such as if you're being dadlike and childing him off, but he feels demeaned or slighted and also wants to father. The biggest conflict usually comes when he's being childish, and instead of dadding up, you respond by being equally childish, and it all escalates as you each try to brat off the other. So even in this simplistic diagram there are five very different roles with five very different styles of behavior you can both fall into—and it's all just on this one small aspect of your life together.

Too often, self-help books and articles have a harsh, reductionist attitude about being human. A man who doesn't talk all about his feelings and is slow to move a relationship forward is "afraid of intimacy." A spouse who constantly feels overwhelmed with bad feelings when his lover's not at the top of his game, throws himself so totally into the relationship that he becomes obsessed with his lover's every mood, and works constantly to make his man happy is "codependent."

Troubles that make you and your mate run to a therapist are all based on a "failure to communicate."

These labels and definitions can be helpful, such as when you're talking about big, complicated problems that seem unmanageable or when you're trying to address a constellation of hard-to-understand behaviors and fix endless conflicts. But when it comes to romance, the pleasures of love, and the joys of marriage, focusing on labels and behavior patterns can make you forget the poetry. When things seem to be going less than great, what you as a couple need as much (or even more than) therapy is to get back to the powerful, mysterious, overwhelming pull that brought you together in the first place.

Re-igniting that pull is a matter of comfort and delight, as well as creating the moments that allow each of you to feel completely free to be yourselves and completely tuned to each other as individuals: taking a long walk in the park or out in the woods by yourselves, letting your conversation wander wherever it will. Writing letters that express your attachment, or your wants, or your fears. Telling each other your dreams.

So why not try enjoying the complications, the magic, the mystery of two people who are ultimately unknowable, as well as the couple that they create together, which is also ultimately unknowable? Don't ignore the richness of your marriage, and of your life. It usually takes at least two or three years, but once you learn to enjoy the poetry, accept the differences, and "take me as I am," you'll enter the great phase of coupledom: Acceptance and Commitment. Where you once became enraged walking into a room and finding his stuff thrown everywhere, now you think, "my sweet guy is such a pig"—and chuckle. Where he once was thrown into turmoil when you wanted to go off to a sex party, now he thinks, "born a tramp, always a tramp"—and calls his friends to gossip about work, never giving it another moment's thought.

You've discovered some amazing things about life: Each of you is the way you are; no matter what attempts are made, you're never really going to change; that part of the world is basically beyond your control. You completely and utterly accept each other's flaws, and while of course there's sometimes still fighting and disagreements, the basics are solid to the core and you find yourselves always forgiving each other. Each of you thinks of the other, "He's doing the best he can . . . and that's really great." The aura of fear of imminent dissolution has vanished; you are more trusting, open, direct, and comfortable than you've ever been before. There's a danger of taking each other for granted and forgetting the need for delight, but overall this is the moment you've been waiting for, this is the moment that all men desire.

> A chicken and a pig were talking about the meaning of commitment one day. The chicken said proudly, "I give eggs every single morning—*I'm* committed."
>
> "Giving eggs isn't commitment, it's participation," countered the pig. "Giving *ham* is commitment."

Lifers

Men who've been together for twenty years or more are often markedly different from all other couples. They know their spouses intimately and have entirely dropped the fantasy that they can change their lover's habits and personality. They take him completely as he is, with a form of unconditional love. The differences between them, first thought of as exciting and adorable but then seen as irritating to one's very soul, are now seen once again as adorable.

You finish each other's sentences, complete each other's anecdotes, and do just what the other would choose to do since you already know just what that would be. You're living in a humming synchrony. Jealousy is practically nonexistent, and you no longer see possessions as his and mine, but as ours. You are so completely intermingled that life without each other is unimaginable, so there's utter stability. One man said it this way: "When I'm with him, it's like wearing a favorite old pair of jeans: there may be holes, patches, or frayed ends, but it's comfortable and cherished."

Sometimes this same stability, though, can lead to feelings of being trapped, taken for granted, or just ignored. I don't know, for example, if I ever want to be thought of as someone's tattered pair of jeans. For some lifers you're no longer the special someone in his eyes . . . you're just *there*.

Taken-for-granted-and-trapped men, if the situation gets too severe, may make an attempt to meet new men, feeling "It's my last chance." Aging can hit us hard (especially if we were head-turners when young), since it's so easy to feel we're being ignored by the hordes of youngsters in public gay life. At the same time, many lifer couples report that, confronted by a crisis (such as terminal illness or career troubles), they've found themselves falling madly in love with each other all over again. Instead of doing many things all by themselves as the five-year pairs would, they're back to doing as much as possible together. Overall, lifers report that they've arrived at what we've all been hoping for: great comfort, great delight, and unconditional love for each other. One longtimer had this to say:

When I think about what's great in our being together, it doesn't sound like much. Things like, we trim each other's nose and ear hairs. We scratch each other's back when it itches where you can't reach. We watch to see if the other forgets his wallet, his glasses, his keys. But it's so great having that; it makes life so much better, so much more *livable.*

There's a passion you have when you first fall for someone, and then there's the passion *we* have. We think, "This is it for the rest of our lives. This is *It.*" And you know, having that settled and decided is *really* something.

The New Family

Until the end of the Dark Ages (the fifties), Americans spent most of their time with their extended family. When hets get married and start raising children, it's still very common for them to be so emotionally engaged in their family unit that they withdraw from their other friends. While some gay couples do this as well, for the most part today's gay men and lesbians have developed their own extended families based on friendships instead of blood ties. Spending significant holidays with people you love and care about (instead of those who make it into an obligation) can be some of the happiest moments and memories of your life together. Here's how one man described it:

> I guess as we grow up, we make certain realizations about life, love, and family. This Thanksgiving I realized that families are not always something you are born into, they are also something you can develop and create.
>
> Every year my lover and I do a traditional Thanksgiving feast for all our friends. In fact we do most of the "family holidays" with our friends. I cooked a huge meal (always making far more than I need, just like Mama taught me). People showed up throughout the day. We listened to music, talked, laughed; my lover was running around pouring drinks and being very clever and charming as he always is.
>
> During dessert and coffee someone pulled out old video-

tapes of our past, not just of me and my lover but of *all* of us together over the years. As we watched these videos, laughing hysterically, remembering our common pasts, remembering, the parties, the dinners, the holidays, I was being hit with wave after wave of feelings of belonging, of loving and being loved. It was then that I realized, *"Shit!* This is not just a group of good friends, this is a family . . . this is *my family."*

Chapter 11

♂ # When It Falls Apart

When it is dark enough, you can see the stars.
—Ralph Waldo Emerson

The only relationship that lasts forever is the one where you die first. Your love will one day end, whether from crash and burn or death do us part. Loss is probably the most difficult of all emotions; the pain can go on and on, with some men grieving for years. How you go through grief and get on with your life is one of the biggest tests you will ever face as a man.

Why are we such a bunch of Splitsvilles? Gay men regularly get lambasted for having short-term, unstable relationships, but the same complaint about couples being flighty, unstable, and quick to break up is leveled by many foreigners against *all* Americans. They think we don't take our vows seriously, that we're not willing to stick it out, that our emotions just switch on and off like machines. Another interpretation, however, is growing with American sociologists; many of them feel that our high divorce rate has one simple explanation: We so ardently pursue our personal happiness that we aren't willing to put up with a bad situation and resign ourselves to lives of difficulty and suffering just to remain married. Perhaps gay men feel this way all the more strongly.

If your coupledom ends from crash and burn, it will practically never be simultaneous: One of you will decide to get out while the other's still committed to making things work. The exiter secretly mulls over the situation, comes to a decision, grieves over the loss, and breaks. The exitee must then mull, decide, grieve, and break as well, going through exactly the same process but at least one step behind. This lack of mental and emotional sync is what's so painful for both sides, with plenty of going-nowhere conversations such as:

"It's over."

"How can you say that?"

You might as well be on opposite ends of the world.

No one believes it, but it really is true: Making the exit is just as painful as getting dumped, which is why most guys do it badly. For months and months you've probably tried talking yourself into staying around, being confused and uncertain, hoping but not really believing that maybe things would work out. You're wracked with guilt, knowing that you're going to put someone you still care for in great pain; you're deeply sad, knowing that what was once a wonderful couple is now ending; and you're on edge, keeping this big secret and trying to figure out just how you're going to accomplish this nasty business. Meanwhile Mr. Soon-to-Be-Ex is planning your second honeymoon together in Paris.

With all this conflicting emotion going on, it's no wonder that most men turn into pussies, trying to get out of doing what they know is right. They'll try to provoke their lover into being the one who really does the calling-off through outrageous misbehavior; they'll turn small matters into big arguments, almost trying to set up some foreshadowing; some even just vanish into thin air.

You can do it wrong, or you can try to be a man for a change:

How to Dump

- **If you find yourself having a terrible time doing this right and knowing what to say, write out your thoughts ahead of time, maybe as a letter to him.**
- **Arrange to meet for lunch or drinks at a meaningless, neutral location.** It shouldn't be a place where you've gone many times before, and your setup shouldn't imply a date. In fact let him know something's up by saying, "I need to talk to you about something important."
- **Get to the point as soon as possible, but put the responsibility on yourself, not on him.** Say that the relationship isn't working for you, that you wouldn't be true to him or yourself if you kept things going, that there's nothing he can really do to fix it, that it's not what you really want out of life. Take all the blame on yourself and remember, if you think this is hard for you, it's probably *killing* him.
- **If you've met someone new, don't mention it, and do not start blaming him or listing his various shortcomings—that'll only make him think that if he changes, he'll get you back.**
- **Again with the empathy bit.** Try to be a decent, responsible adult, and keep him going through it as much as you can. If he starts to crash, give him some backup and compliments while keeping to the idea that it's not him, it's the two of you as a couple that's the problem.
- **If you want to remain friends, by all means say so, but also mention you're willing to wait for him to be ready to get together again.** Let him have time to mourn, recover

from the pain of losing you, and build back his self-esteem; he won't be able to immediately switch tracks.

♂

"How could this happen? How could he do this to me? What did I do wrong? What's the matter with me? What's the matter with him?" When you get dumped, your world turns upside down. The feelings you thought someone had for you turn out to have gone someplace else; the security and contentment you got from being loved are yanked out from under your feet; a key part of your life has vanished. You no longer have his body in your arms; you no longer have the feeling of contentment just being in the same room with him; you no longer have that man who knows you better than anyone else; you no longer have that special source of energy and inspiration. To top it all off, your PEA and endorphins are dropping like sprayed flies.

People (unfortunately, in your case) change. What they feel changes, what they need changes, what they want changes. Sometimes this is mild and subtle and sometimes it's dramatic and traumatic. Every time a couple ends, both sides tend to think it's the dumpee's fault, but in truth it's usually nobody's fault—only life marching on, as always.

Feeling abandoned and unloved is probably the worst emotion one can ever have. You'll stir your brain with questions and torments, blaming him, blaming yourself, completely unable to comprehend why things had to be this way. You are going to be deeply depressed, completely furious, utterly baffled, and trying to think of anything you can that might make things right again. At a certain point you may start tricking like a mad woman, trying to prove to yourself that you're still a hot guy. You may also think, "I guess I never really knew how fucked up (or unable to love; or stupid; or evil) he really was."

Sometimes he'll say, "It's over," and you'll say, "No way!" Many men can never let go; no matter what evidence is there, they make themselves believe, "He's still in love with me, I know it!" Often the man who can't let go starts idolizing his missing guy in a way he never did when they were together and the lover was physically present; all the lover's problems, shortcomings, and liabilities are forgotten and only the memories of what made him Mr. Dreamdate remain. You'll amaze your friends with your constant talk of what a fine pair you are and how great it'll be when he finally wakes up and comes back to you . . . when they know full well that it ended long ago.

In every case one guy thought it was time to give up before the other thought so; one thought things weren't enough while the other felt they were. It's too bad that we dumpees can't enjoy our sudden-exit relationships for the time that they lasted; what we're really upset about is that they ended before we were ready.

How to Get Dumped

▶ **You know something's up, so try to find out what it is; don't passively accept suspicious explanations.** When trouble brews, the techniques you learned earlier of moving in and backing off are crucial now, since he may not really know his own feelings and whether or not this is a temporary disenchantment or a permanent break. Try to get informed, but if he's not forthcoming, back off.

▶ **Once you hear "It's over," try to find out why, but don't drown in regret and blame.** If you're working on yourself, you will find the guy who'll work for you; it just didn't happen this time around. Thinking you could have done something differently is thinking you could have been a different person and, at least for now, you're not.

▶ **Take some time to grieve (see below).** You will probably go into shock and denial. If being apart from him is filling you with longings and fantasies, see him and get a dose of reality. Make a list of all his good and bad points; remember the good things you'll keep forever as a result of having known him and the negative qualities you're just as happy to do without. Talk things over with your friends, especially the ones who seem to know about this kind of stuff.

▶ **At some point try to realize that it had nothing to do with you personally, it just wasn't a match that worked.** The problems were "between" the two of you, not because of either one of you. You deserve to have a lover if you want one, and after some time spent getting your head back on, get out there and get to work.

▶ **When you can, really consider trying to be friends again.** Friends who are exes can have a wonderful, special bond. There'll always be a small sex charge going on, and you did at one time know each other like twins. See if you can't work it out.

Love in the Age of AIDS

If your lover is diagnosed as HIV-positive, you may think you know what this means, but really you don't. He will get a hideous illness and probably die sooner than expected, but that's all the two of you know. He may not get very sick for a decade to come; he may become only mildly ill, and that may last for many, many years; or he may become immediately stricken and die quickly. No one can say for sure.

Who's ready to think about the end of his life when he was expecting to be around for another fifty years or so? Death therapist Elisabeth Kübler-Ross has identified some emotional reactions that people have when confronted by a terminal disease (but contrary to popular thought, they don't necessarily occur in this order): denial (shock, numbness, sorrow, disbelief); bargaining ("If I exercise, go on a diet, take Chinese herbs, I won't die"); anger ("Life is so unfair!"); depression; acceptance. You the spouse will also go through these phases as well, and will have to bear the brunt of his wildly swinging moods and overwhelming emotions. Don't try to talk him out of his feelings with logic; he deserves to feel all of it. And don't try talking yourself out of your own feelings of grief and guilt by turning into Mr. Super Caregiver; there are plenty of cases of widowers dying of broken hearts. The two of you will also have great conflicts when you're out-of-phase in your grief, ideas, and attitudes; he may become accepting and facing the facts while you're still the one immobilized with depression.

Americans aren't particularly comfortable with tragedy; since you don't have much experience in this area, you will probably have no idea what to say or what to do. Many of his and your friends will withdraw because they're similarly uncomfortable and at loss for how to react; when my lover (in 1987) was diagnosed and ghastly ill, it took his own mother eight months to show up for a visit. Don't worry about being awkward; just be there.

While AIDS has brought out the best in the gay community, it has also brought out the worst in certain people. The number of men who've abandoned their ill and grieving friends and lovers is astounding. If you can't tolerate standing strong, make immediate plans so that he won't be deserted at a later, more crucial stage. Being a coward is something that will shame you for the rest of your life, but if you really aren't going to go through with the hand you've been dealt, at least try to exit with some compassion.

If you are a functioning human being and you are going to stand by him, however your romantic and sex life changes, make sure he understands this; it will be the most important commitment you've ever made. Let him tell you how he feels, tell him how you feel, and don't forget to hug, touch, and caress—something that will let him know you're there.

Many men respond to their lover's diagnosis by trying to become supermen. They shut down their own fears about infection and death, their own grief at losing their man, and their own questions about what will happen next, throwing themselves into a frenzy of studying alternative treatments, experimental testing, nutrition, medical developments, as well as making arrangements for food, transportation, shopping, medical care, and friends and family communications —on top of their own job of course. They also start treating their lover as though he were a retarded invalid or a fragile piece of china, taking over his life entirely, making decisions for him without consulting him first, avoiding any mention of "what might upset him."

Don't do it. No one, not even your lover, expects you to be able to do it all, and burning yourself out (which will happen soon enough anyway) is not the answer. Get as much help from AIDS organizations, social services, and government agencies as you can, keep up with your friends and your own social life, get counseling if you want it, and remain your lover's boyfriend instead of trying to be his everything. He still needs you as a spouse, which you won't be capable of being if you're trying to completely run his life; he also feels he's become a burden to you, and killing yourself will only make him feel worse. No one with intact faculties wants to be treated like a pathetic invalid. Don't try the saint route either: shutting down your emotions will only make him feel more alone with his feelings.

Men with AIDS frequently feel isolated. Their friends and lover are walking around on eggshells, always trying to be "up" and encouraging and never allowing day-to-day life, with its frustrations and troubles, into the room. While he's alive, let him take part in life; tell him everything, good and bad. When the two of you fight over something regarding his treatment, and you will, always remember: It's his life. At some point many men with AIDS develop an immense inner strength, almost a saintliness, with a new philosophic attitude about those they're leaving behind.

Going through all this means you also get to discover how today's Hippocratic oath has gone awry. Doctors and hospitals will refuse to call it quits until every avenue is explored, whatever the cost or effect on the patient (depending, of course, on your insurance coverage). One look at a group of emaciated, lifeless men attached to lung machines will make you a disciple of Dr. Kevorkian; as one of my AIDS widower friends put it, "Death isn't so bad; it's dying that's the horror." After going through all this myself, I tried to find the Yiddish for what I thought would become a popular new blessing, "May you be hit by a speeding bus," but unfortunately there's no good translation available.

Practically everyone reports that after his lover dies, his head is filled with "if onlys": "If only we'd spent more time together," "If only I'd told him more often how much I loved him," "If only we'd done *x, y,* or *z.*" The answer? To fight your sense of hopelessness and grief while he's still alive and do these things *now.* If he's always wanted to go somewhere; if you've always wanted to say something; if the two of you have always wanted some part of your life together to be different, now is the time. Listen to Casey Kasem: "Let your dreams come true and make your wishes manifest."

There has been much talk, especially from New Age doctors and therapists, that one's attitude can have a great effect on how an illness progresses; they believe that if you have AIDS and you have the will to fight it, you can live longer and better. If your lover's encouraged by this news and it inspires him, let your own cynicism lie quiet. If you believe this with all your heart but your lover doesn't jump into the fray, forgo your disappointment. How he reacts to the devastating personal trauma of AIDS is how he reacts; there's little you can do about it, so keep it to yourself. Who knows how much "fighting spirit" you'd have under the same circumstances?

A huge percentage of couples were having troubles and were near breakup when the diagnosis hit; they were just about to call it quits, and then . . . So now you're in the position where you still care for him but you're not really lovers anymore; you want to meet someone new, but you don't want to abandon him. Men find themselves in a hideous double bind on this issue, especially if they do indeed meet someone new who holds out promise that the soon-to-be-ex can't offer. They often feel that since he's dying, they can't leave or develop a new relationship; if they meet someone and start feeling hope and even happiness, the lover's illness makes them feel guilty.

The answer is to honestly discuss the situation with your ex and come to an understanding. Don't present it as "this is the way things are"; make sure to make it clear that you will be there to help him during his time of need. Then explain that you need to start dating again and even, if it's the case, that you've met someone who's pretty interesting. Reiterate that this isn't an abandonment and that you care about him deeply. If you make it clear that you're going to be there for him, that this relationship is solid and he can depend on you to help, he may be able to feel good about letting you go forward with your life; if you and your new guy get more and more serious, at some point you should all get together. Try as much as possible to "normalize" the relationships instead of letting everything remaining vague, confusing, and ill defined. Be as straightforward with everyone involved as possible, and this convoluted *ménage* can work itself out.

Widowhood and Grief

> *One often learns more from ten days of agony than from ten years of contentment.*
>
> —MERLE SHAIN

When you suffer a loss, whether from a breakup or from a death, sooner or later you will have to grieve. Trying to put your feelings of depression and loss out of your mind will probably only result in getting an emotional sock in the gut later on. Grief is learning to understand and accept that someone you love is gone for good and that there's nothing you can do about it. The emptiness and ache that you feel (including the feeling that part of yourself is missing) can take a very long time to fix—on average, four years. No matter how your man left you, you're going to go through this, and the ways to ease that terrible ache are the same for divorce as they are for death.

If your lover died from AIDS, you probably started grieving when you learned he was diagnosed. In the later stages of his illness, which may have included dementia and never-ending medical intervention, you constantly thought, "When is this nightmare going to end?" You then felt guilty, and since this had been going on for so long, you also felt that you'd already done all the grieving you needed to do.

Surprise! After his death you will be overwhelmed by a

mass of conflicting feelings, and you'll realize that the grieving has only now just begun. You'll probably have a sense of
relief that it's over, but that relief will make you feel hideously guilty once again; that you are alive and he isn't only
adds to the guilt. You're in withdrawal from your couple
endorphins, and the regular, day-to-day pattern of the life
that you shared together is wrenched away.

Especially if you were working like a dog on his behalf,
you'll feel an immense emptiness now that he's gone. You're
left wondering, "What do I do now?" You're drowning in
moods, with emotional swings careening like a roller coaster,
alternately feeling sad, guilty, regretful, and paralyzed. Out of
the corner of your eyes and ears, you see and hear him
everywhere.

You wiped yourself out doing everything possible to take
care of him, and now he's dead; who's going to take care of
you? Your powerful emotions will make you feel completely
cut off from the rest of the world, and after the dramatic
struggle of AIDS, normal, day-to-day life may appear completely stupid and meaningless.

This is what happened to me when my lover died in 1987.
Other people's small talk and whining about petty issues
became intolerable, and I withdrew from the world. I'd go
into the office as late as I could get away with, take care of
only the most crucial problems, and leave as soon as possible.
If anyone called, trying to go out or get together, I'd make
excuses; if anyone put on too much pressure, I'd cut him off.
Instead, I'd spend hours and hours absorbed in the minutiae
of an electronic music studio, avoiding other human beings.
This is pretty much how I ended up living, off and on, for
almost five years; sometimes a few days would be okay . . .
and then I'd crash all over again. . . .

During this period you may hear some friends philosophize about how we never "really" die. At first it may be one of the most irritating comments you've ever heard, but after a while you'll come to see that, from time to time, you were never as much "with him" before as you are now. You'll be flooded with memories of him and of the two of you together; you'll think of him constantly, like never before; you may even be more in love with him now than you ever were when he was alive, and it may be that he even has a far more important position in your life now that he's gone. Just as memories of past lovers and intimate friends keep them alive in your mind, so you'll now find that your relationship with him didn't end with his death; it will go on, in a whole new way.

As long as they're remembered, the dead live on, and relationships never end. When your assistant does something you don't like, suddenly you'll hear your dead mother's voice giving him a scolding—but it's you who's talking. You'll find yourself keeping your house spotless (just like your dead grandmother did), or saying, "I don't think so," which is what your dead lover said all the time. You'll have a problem and realize what he would have done to solve it; you'll go on a wonderful vacation and think how much he would've enjoyed it. We all have to be careful with our significant relationships because, however they end in the material world, they'll be with us for the rest of our lives.

At some point you may become obsessed with what he was like at the end of his life, and this paralyzing depression can become endless and seemingly insurmountable. One good technique is to remember all the good times you shared together, how much fun you had, all the things about each other that made you laugh. Would your lover prefer to be remembered as a man wasting away from illness or as a sexy, passionate, complete human being filled with life? Remember him whole.

Your grief may make your friends and relatives uncomfortable, but it is a natural, completely healthy process. Don't tell yourself to "be a man" and get over it and that you're weak to feel this way; the only reason you wouldn't grieve the loss of someone is if you didn't really care about him. But you did, and you will. It's time to be utterly selfish and self-centered: If you feel like going through photo albums, reading through your journal, looking at presents you've gotten, thinking about things you've shared together, and reliving memories of him, let yourself go. Think, "What would Maria Callas do?"

If you're the type who never cries, this is the time to get over it. A big sobfest, where you just let all your terrible feelings out and immerse yourself in how lonely and lost you feel and how much you miss him, will help in moving grief along. An all-out bawl can break the tension of feeling useless —that he's gone and if only you could have done something, but you couldn't—so drop the stick and cry your heart out. You'll feel much better afterward.

Depression and grief are paralyzing; most of the time you won't want to do anything at all. Go right ahead and do exactly that: Lie around in bed with some comfort kid's food (ice cream, pastries, chocolates) and some stupid, funny videos. Draw in your friends; they're the ones who'll come over with *I Love Lucy* and *Airplane* and won't hate you forever when you wake them up by calling and sobbing at two A.M. If the paralysis seems to go on and on, try to make yourself get out of the house, work, see friends, go to the movies— anything that can distract you from your pain for a few moments. Rent some porn and jack off to your heart's (etc.) content.

On days that you're overwhelmed by sadness, guilt, helplessness, or anger and you just can't shake it, the best idea is,

"Okay, today I'm pissed, out of it, a wreck. So it goes." Let yourself go through whatever you have to; learn to trust that your mind is correctly repairing itself. It's almost as if grief is a biological process and you mustn't get in the way; you can't fight your own body, after all.

One technique for when you feel you're smothering in bad emotions comes from Zen. The idea is that behavior shapes feeling. So if you need to feel loved, do something loving; if you need to feel happy, do something that makes someone else happy; if you want to feel peaceful, do something to soothe someone. It works like you wouldn't believe.

Another very helpful thing is to talk to your dead lover. If you think this is ridiculous, visit him at the cemetery or cremation site. Imagine you really can reach him and search inside yourself for the feelings and sensations that would be his response. You knew him so well; you'd know exactly what he'd be telling you now. Tell him *everything:* Explain what it's like with him gone, how lonely you are, how much you wish you'd said or done things differently, how angry you are that this had to happen. Go the full gamut and spill the beans; let your rage, hurt, isolation, and depression out like they've never been out before; let your feelings pour out of you until you've had enough. Talk again with him, anytime you want; you know in your heart exactly how he'd respond.

When recovery from grief starts, it's like a form of analysis. You go over the past relentlessly, searching like a private detective for the clues to what went wrong. "How could I have been different?" "Why did he treat me like this?" You are still deeply in love, and simultaneously hate his guts for what he's done to you. Everything was great for so long, how did it turn sour? Memories of things done and said, great and small, are compulsively remembered and dissected; the look in his eyes, the tone of his voice, even the color of his sweaters become fetishized.

What's the point of all this? What grief does is make us withdraw a bit from "living life to the fullest" and let us do some thinking, thinking that needs to be done. When a relationship ends, we're thrown into a great mystery: Why did something that started so well and seemed so promising turn out like this? Why is life so unfair? Grief allows our minds and hearts to uncover and explore this mystery, to see what happened, to create "sense" out of this moment in our lives. Mentally we come up with a story of what happened, a version of the events, both good and bad, that makes sense. When you can tell the story, when you can reduce the complicated, emotionally charged drama of your history as a couple into an anecdote, when you can get back your self-esteem and have new friends and interests and are back on the hunt once again, your grieving's over.

Time and acceptance are the only things that will heal this ache. You may not be ready to meet anyone else yet; you might even consider a few random acts of meaningless sex to get you back in circulation (and get your circulation back). If you're grieving and someone is hustling you to get over it, ignore him and take your own damn time. Sooner or later you'll get back on your feet (or back on your back). Many widows have a terrible time even imagining having sex or being close to someone new, as though they're being disloyal to their dead boyfriend. But think, if it was you who'd died, would you have wanted your surviving spouse to remain celibate and grieving forever? Of course not, and neither does he. He wants you to be happy, and the least you can do is respect that wish.

Love seems to promise that life's gaping wounds will close up and heal. It makes little

*difference that in the past, love has shown itself
to be painful and disturbing. There is something self-renewing in love. Like the goddesses
of Greece, it is able to renew its virginity in a
bath of forgetfulness.*

—THOMAS MOORE

Starting Over: *Laissez les Bon Temps Rouler!*

*Despite dashed dreams, with full memory of the
vicious quarrels, regardless of the inevitable realization that marriage can be irritating, dull
and painful, the vast majority of people who
divorce take another spouse. In America, 75%
of the women and 80% of the men who separate wed again. . . .*

   *We seem to have an eternal optimism about
our next mate.*

—HELEN FISHER

At some point your friends who've stood by you through
the end of your relationship may even know some humpy
single guys; when you're close enough in mood, let them set
you up. It is difficult getting back into the dating mode after
you've been with someone for a very long time; take it easy
and try some small steps first. Go out on the town with your
single gay friends. Say "hello" at the gym. Read some personals.

Many guys feel empty when they're not attached to someone, and if a relationship ends, they immediately throw
themselves into another one. These "rebounds" seldom
work out, as anyone knows, but the real issue is learning to

Finding True Love in a Man-Eat-Man World

enjoy the pleasures of being single (or at least stop being PEA-dependent). Some guys even report that after getting over their departed lover, they feel immensely happy and free, bursting with the energy of being out, about, and on their own.

Other men are so devastated by loss that they are terrified of trying to make it with someone new. They can only think, over and over, that the outcome will be just the same, so why even bother trying? They may meet a new guy who's absolutely perfect for them in every way, but instead of falling in love they are overwhelmed by "What if he dies? What if he leaves me?" They have been through agony, and if they fall in love again, there's always the possibility of going through that pain all over again. One guy had this to say:

My difficulty at this point is the conflicting feelings when I am with others even on a physical level. Sometimes I feel disloyal, torn, confused. I am seeing someone now, and we like each other very much. But I find that I hold back, am extremely cautious. It is taking a lot of work and self-awareness to pick my way through this minefield. It is just going to take a lot more time than I thought. The loss of a lover has its own signature, as does the loss of a child or a parent. In grief, care for yourself as you cared for your partner.

Coupledom means growing up together; singlehood means growing up yourself. Being alone gives you time to think, and time to measure your strengths and weaknesses. This is the time to again wonder, "Am I ready, willing, and able?" It's also a time to learn what you really want out of life and where you're going from here, a time to get back on those swings—and start reading this book all over again.

Love is our true destiny. We do not find the meaning of life by ourselves alone—we find it with another. We do not discover the secret of our lives merely by study and calculation in our own isolated meditations. The meaning of our life is a secret that has to be revealed to us in love, by the one we love.

—THOMAS MERTON

♂

Resources and Sources

Organizations

AASH (Agnostics, Atheists and Secular Humanists), 212-366-6481—for HIV-positives.

ACT-UP (AIDS Coalition to Unleash Power), 212-564-2437.

Actor's Fund of America, 212-221-7300, exts. 115 and 146—support group for PWA caregivers.

Alcoholics Anonymous World Services, 468 Park Avenue South, New York, NY 10016, 212-683-3900.

APICHA (Asian/Pacific Islander Coalition on HIV/AIDS), 212-349-3213.

Artists' Collective, 212-491-7228—for gay artists, collectors, and gallery owners.

Asians and Friends, 718-488-0630.

Resources and Sources

AVP (Anti-Violence Project), 212-807-0197—fights gay-bashers.

Axios Eastern and Orthodox Christians, 718-229-0217.

BiSocial, 212-459-4784—for bisexuals.

Body Positive, 212-721-1346—support group for HIV-positives.

BOSS (Business Owners' Support System), 212-228-8683.

Center Bridge, 212-620-7310—grief counseling for those who lost a loved one to AIDS.

CHP (Community Health Project), 212-675-3559—AIDS research information.

Clann an Uabhair, 212-603-9840—Scots social organization.

Congregation Beth Simchat Torah, 212-929-9498.

Couples National Network, Box 813212, Smyrna, GA 30081, 404-333-0937.

Couples Together, 212-662-3080.

Dignity, 212-818-1309 and 866-8047—for gay Catholics.

EDGE (Education in a Disabled Gay Environment), 212-929-7171.

Fire-FLAG (Fire Fighters Lesbian and Gay), 914-762-6261.

Foot Friends, 718-832-3952.

Front Runners, 212-724-9700—running club.

GALE (Gay and Lesbian Educators), 212-932-0178.

Gay and Lesbian Americans, 212-741-5497.

Gay and Lesbian Social Workers, 212-989-6083.

Gay Circles, 212-242-9165—men's movement.

Gay Fathers Forum, 212-721-4216.

Gaylaxians, P.O. Box 3031, Linden, NJ 07036—gay sci-fi enthusiasts.

Gay/Lesbian Scuba Club, 212-366-9079.

Gay Male S/M Activists, 212-727-9878.

Gay Pilots Association, 212-757-7627.

Gay Shamanism, 718-965-3712.

Gay Veterans Association, 212-787-0329.

Gejaro (Gay Esperanto Language Club), 212-254-7508.

Gentle Men, 212-529-0796—intimacy workshops.

GGALA (Greek Gay and Lesbian Association), 718-834-9648.

Girth and Mirth Club, 914-699-7735.

GLAAD (Gay and Lesbian Alliance Against Defamation), 212-807-7100—media activists, à la B'nai B'rith.

GLID (Gay and Lesbian Independent Democrats), 212-727-0008.

GMAD (Gay Men of African Descent), 212-420-0773.

GMHC (Gay Men's Health Crisis), 212-807-6664.

GOAL (Gay Officers Action League), 212-996-8808—gay cops.

God's Love We Deliver, 212-865-4900—free meals for homebound PWAs.

HEAL (Health Education AIDS Liaison), 212-674-4673—alternative AIDS treatments.

Holy Faery Database, c/o Harry Ugol and Michael Dreyer, 415-469-0625.

ILGA (International Lesbian and Gay Association), 212-620-7310.

ILGO (Irish Lesbian and Gay Organization), 212-967-7711, ext. 3078.

Israelis and Friends, 212-642-1086.

Just Couples, 212-475-1289.

Latino Gay Men, 718-834-8785.

Lesbian and Gay Teachers, 718-258-4102.

The Log Cabin Club, 212-886-1893—gay Republicans.

MAN (Males Au Naturel), 212-535-3914—nudists.

The Metropolitan Community Church, 212-629-7440.

Minority Task Force on AIDS, 212-563-8340.

Narcotics Anonymous World Service, P.O. Box 9999, Van Nuys, CA 91409, 818-780-3951.

National Attorney Directory of Lesbian and Gay Rights, Gay Legal Advocates and Defenders, P.O. Box 218, Boston, MA 02112 —for gay-friendly lawyers.

National Hemlock Society, P.O. Box 11830, Eugene, OR 97440 —the nation's leading right-to-die organization.

National Lesbian and Gay Journalists Association, 212-629-2045.

Network of Business and Professional Organizations, 212-517-0771.

New York Bankers Group, 212-807-9584, ext. 24.

OLGAD (Organization of Lesbian and Gay Architects and Designers), 212-475-7652.

OutWatch, 212-967-7711—antibasher street patrol.

Partners, P.O. Box 9685, Seattle, WA 98109—gay-couple newsletter (12 issues/$36).

Prime Timers, 212-929-1035—for over-forty.

Professionals in Film/Video, 212-387-2022.

PWAC (People with AIDS Coalition), 212-647-1415.

Queer Nation, 212-260-6156—social activists.

Quincunx, 313-662-7116—for gay astrologers.

SAGE (Senior Action in a Gay Environment), 212-741-2247.

Tel-a-Fairy, 415-626-3369.

Times Squares, 212-873-3962—square dancing.

TTY, 212-749-9438.

We Wah and Bar Chee Ampe, 212-598-0100—for Native Americans.

YELL (ACT-UP youth committee), 212-564-2437.

Sources

Diane Ackerman, *A Natural History of Love,* New York: Random House, 1994.

Anonymous, "The Gay and Lesbian Community Forum," America On-line, 914-471-6728 (data).

Anonymous, "Nothin' More Than Feelings," *The MaleStop,* 212-721-4180 (data).

Angelo d'Arcangelo, *The Homosexual Handbook,* New York: Traveller's Companion Press, 1968.

Nicole Ariana, *How to Pick Up Men!,* Tenafly, N.J.: Eric Weber Press, 1972.

Dorothy Atcheson, "Why Can't We Live Together?," *Out*, July–August 1994.

Tess Ayers and Paul Brown, *The Essential Guide to Lesbian and Gay Weddings*, New York: HarperCollins, 1994.

Melody Beattie, *Codependent No More*, New York: Harper/Hazelden, 1987.

Melody Beattie, *Beyond Codependency*, New York: Harper/Hazelden, 1989.

Betty Berzon, *Permanent Partners*, New York: E. P. Dutton, 1988.

Bob of Chicago, "Thoughts on Corresponding with Prisoners," *Black and White Men Together* 17 (September–October 1980).

Nathaniel Branden, *The Psychology of Romantic Love*, New York: Bantam Books, 1981.

Michael S. Broder, *The Art of Staying Together*, New York: Hyperion, 1993.

Leo Buscaglia, *Love*, New York: Fawcett Crest/Ballantine, 1972.

Tracy Cabot, *How to Make a Man Fall in Love with You*, New York: St. Martin's Press, 1984.

Pat Califia, *Advocate Adviser*, Boston: Alyson Publications, 1991.

Steven Carter and Julia Sokol, *Men Who Can't Love*, New York: M. Evans & Co., 1987.

Jeff Cohen, Bob Smith, and Danny McWilliams, *Growing Up Gay*, New York: Hyperion, 1995.

Amy E. Dean. *Proud to Be: Daily Meditations for Lesbians and Gay Men*, New York: Bantam Books, 1994.

John P. De Cecco, editor, *Gay Relationships*, New York: Haworth Press, 1988.

John H. Driggs and Stephen E. Finn, *Intimacy Between Men*, New York: E. P. Dutton, 1990.

Barbara Ehrenreich, *The Hearts of Men: American Dreams and the Flight from Commitment,* New York: Anchor Books, 1983.

Warren Farrell, *Why Men Are the Way They Are,* New York: McGraw-Hill, 1986.

Helen Fisher, *Anatomy of Love,* New York: W. W. Norton, 1992.

John Gray, *Men Are from Mars, Women Are from Venus,* New York: HarperCollins, 1993.

Gregory J.P. Grodek, *1,001 Ways to Be Romantic,* Boston: The Casablanca Press, 1993.

Jane Gross, "After a Ruling, Hawaii Weighs Gay Marriages," *The New York Times,* April 25, 1994.

Joseph Harry, *Gay Couples,* New York: Praeger Press, 1984.

Jack Hart, *My Biggest O,* Boston: Alyson Publications, 1993.

Robert H. Hopcke, Karin Lofthus Carrington, and Scott Wirth, editors, *Same-Sex Love and the Path to Wholeness,* Boston: Shambhala Publications, 1993.

Morton Hunt, *The Natural History of Love,* New York: Anchor Books, 1994.

Rik Isensee, *Love Between Men: Enhancing Intimacy and Keeping Your Relationship Alive,* New York: Fireside, 1992.

Robert Johnson, *We: The Psychology of Romantic Love,* New York: Harper Perennial, 1987.

R. N. Lawrence, *Date Talk,* New York: Scholastic Book Services, 1967.

Janet Lever, "Sexual Revelations: The 1994 Advocate Survey of Sexuality and Relationships: The Men," *The Advocate,* August 23, 1994.

David P. McWhirter and Andrew M. Mattison, *The Male Couple,* Englewood Cliffs, N.J.: Prentice-Hall, 1984.

William Masters, Virginia Johnson, and Robert Kolodny, *Heterosexuality,* New York: HarperCollins, 1994.

John Money, *Lovemaps,* New York: Irvington Publishers, 1986.

Resources and Sources

Thomas Moore, *Care of the Soul,* New York: HarperCollins, 1992.

Thomas Moore, *Soul Mates,* New York: HarperCollins, 1994.

Judith Newman, "How to Avoid Date Disaster," *The New York Times,* February 9, 1994.

Susan Page, *If I'm So Wonderful, Why Am I Still Single?,* New York: Viking Press, 1988.

Deborah Schupack, " 'Starter' Marriages: So Early, So Brief," *The New York Times,* July 7, 1994.

Dr. Charles Silverstein, *Man to Man—Gay Couples in America,* New York: William Morrow & Co., 1981.

Dr. Charles Silverstein and Felice Picano, *The New Joy of Gay Sex,* New York: HarperCollins, 1992.

Dorothy Tennov, *Love and Limerance: The Experience of Being in Love,* New York: Stein & Day, 1979.

Tina Tessina, *Gay Relationships,* New York: Jeremy P. Tarcher/Putnam, 1989.

John Tierney, "Picky, Picky, Picky," *The New York Times Magazine,* February 2, 1995.

George Weinberg, *Society and the Healthy Homosexual,* Garden City, N.Y.: Anchor Press, 1972.

Andy Warhol, *America,* New York: Harper & Row, 1984.

John Welwood, *Journey of the Heart,* New York: HarperCollins, 1991.

Celeste West, *A Lesbian Love Advisor,* Pittsburgh: Cleis Press, 1989.

Marion Winik, "Modern Love," *American Way,* February 1, 1994.

Karen Wright, "The Sniff of Legend," *Discover,* April 1994.

Robert Wright, "Our Cheating Hearts," *Time Magazine Online,* Transmitted: 94-08-07 14:08:34 EDT.